Cougar
Attacks

Other Books by Kathy Etling

Hunting Superbucks
Bear Attacks

Cougar Attacks

Encounters of the Worst Kind

KATHY ETLING

THE LYONS PRESS

Guilford, Connecticut
An imprint of The Globe Pequot Press

The Lyons Press is an imprint of The Globe Pequot Press.

Printed in the United States

10 9 8 7 6 5 4 3 2 1

Library of Congress Cataloging-in-Publication Data
Etling, Kathy, 1945–
    Cougar attacks: encounters of the worst kind/Kathy Etling.
      p. cm.
    Includes bibliographical references (pp. 175–79).
    ISBN 1-58574-221-X (hc)
    1. Puma attacks. 2. Puma attacks—North America. I. Title.
    QL737.C23 E85 2001
    599.75'241566—dc21

Permissions Acknowledgements
E. Boyd Hildebrand as told to Ken Crandall, excerpt from "Cougar Nightmare" from *Outdoor Life* (July 1963). Copyright © 1963 by Times Mirror Magazines, Inc. Reprinted by permission.

J. Frank Dobie, excerpts from *The Ben Lilly Legend*. Copyright © 1950 by J. Frank Dobie. Reprinted with the permission of Little, Brown and Company (Inc.).

Sam Nickels, excerpts from *Outdoor Life's Anthology of Hunting Adventures*. Copyright by Times Mirror Magazines, Inc. Reprinted by permission.

D. H. Lawrence, "Mountain Lion" from *The Complete Poems of D. H. Lawrence,* edited by Vivian de Sola Pinto and F. Warren Roberts. Copyright © 1964, 1971 by Angelo Ravagli and C. M. Weekeley, Executors of the Estate of Frieda Lawrence Ravagli. All rights reserved. Reprinted with the permission of The Viking Press, Inc. with acknowledgment of Willliam Heinemann Ltd., publishers, Laurence Pollinger Ltd., author's agent, and the Estate of Frieda Lawrence Ravagli.

Tracey T. Storer and Lloyd P. Tevis, excerpts from *California Grizzly*. Copyright © 1955 by the Regents of the University of California, renewed 1983 by Ruth Storer and Lloyd Tevis, Jr. Reprinted with the permission of the University of California Press.

Doug Ward, "Meet a hero—man punches cougar in head, rescues cyclist" (excerpt) from *The Vancouver Sun* (February 10, 2001). Reprinted with the permission of the publishers.

Portions of the Appendices are from material and information created by Harold P. Danz appearing in the book *Cougar!* published by the Ohio University Press/Swallow Press, Athens, Ohio.

For Julie, Rick, and Shelby

Contents

Acknowledgments

The writing rut in which I seem to have found myself is this: Three of my last four books have had as their subject matter attacks upon humans by wild animals. Two of those books focused on North American bears and their attacks; this one delves into cougars and their attacks.

Whenever a writer deals with what is generally an unpleasant topic for the victim or victims, should they survive such an attack, it is difficult to obtain accurate accounts. A journalist not on the scene at the time of the attack, or one who doesn't arrive shortly thereafter, will often encounter resistance. Why? Because the victims don't want to relive the traumatic events they have been trying to forget about. Because of this, I have not tracked down each survivor or, in the case of a victim's death, the next of kin. Instead, I have in many cases used incident reports filed by enforcement officers, state, provincial, or national park personnel, wildlife biologists, predator-control specialists, or any other authority who investigated an attack. Telephone interviews were also conducted to supplement many of the reports.

To further my research, I also pored over the reams of information I downloaded from the Internet, discovered in magazine or newspaper archives—many of which bore dates back to the 1800s and a few even earlier—or garnered from cable TV shows, or simply found in various books published from the time this continent was "discovered" more than 500 years ago. The labor of love that has resulted is a book that I hope will inform and enlighten its readers, giving them both a better understanding of why cougars will sometimes attack, as well as what one should do to lessen the chances of such an attack. Should a single person be saved from injury or death due to reading this book, then all the research and work I have invested will have been well worthwhile.

No book of this nature can ever be strictly an individual effort. Rather it is a collaborative work made more immediate and accurate by experts in the field, by people who know not only about cougars, their attacks, and the repercussions of such encounters, but also about cougar management, popular attitudes toward cougars, and the threats to people, pets, property, and the cougars themselves, throughout the history of this continent. Any book like this one will, by its very nature, be far-reaching in scope; my wish is that it won't be so far-reaching as to create confusion. Should it create in those who read it a desire to learn more about these fascinating and sometimes dangerous creatures, however, then it will have served another one of its purposes.

The list of those who helped me with my research material is extensive. Let me begin by thanking Jay Cassell, my editor at the Lyons Press, for his faith in assigning such a project to me.

I also would like to thank Harley G. Shaw, a cougar research biologist, as well as the author of *Soul Among Lions: The Cougar as Peaceful Adversary.* Harley spent many hours poring over my manuscript, and then offering cogent advice on how to improve what it was I was struggling to communicate. Harley, who retired from the Arizona Department of Game and Fish, was worried about possible fallout from any book that seemed to focus so intently and exclusively on the relatively few cougars that actually get into trouble with people, without providing more words and consideration for those many thousands of cougars that live out peaceful lives in close proximity to human beings. With Harley's help and significant guidance, I hope I have been somewhat able to put his mind at ease.

I would like to thank, as well, Dr. Lee Fitzhugh, cooperative-extension wildlife specialist with the University of California's Department of Wildlife, Fish, and Conservation Biology, at Davis. Lee helped me out with his unpublished attack data from the very first day, plus recommended other researchers I might contact. He also provided me with the titles of numerous reference books from which I was able to glean research material.

I would also like to thank Dr. Paul Beier of the University of Northern Arizona at Flagstaff. Even though Dr. Beier was out of the country when I began researching this book, it is upon his original published database of cougar attacks that I was able to build an extensive one of my own.

As for the others, they are legion: Tom Beck, Janet George, and Babs Brockway of the Colorado Division of Wildlife; Wardens Mike Quinn and Tom Flowers for all their help, recollections, and advice, as well as Gary Olson, Erik Wenum, Mike Quinn, and Bill Thomas of the Montana Department of Fish, Wildlife and Parks; Ron Goldhirsch and Amy Vanderbilt of Montana's Glacier National Park; Dave Moody of the Wyoming Game and Fish Department; Donny Martorello, Sean Carrell and Capt. John Broome of the Washington Department of Fish and Wildlife; Barb Haynes of Washington's Olympia National Park; Steven Torres, author of the excellent *Mountain Lion Alert,* as well as Terry Mansfield and Alexia Retallack of the California Department of Fish and Game; Dr. Maurice Hornocker, the Hailey, Idaho "dean" of cougar researchers, who kindly referred me to invaluable sources of information like Dr. Ken Logan and the aforementioned Dr. Lee Fitzhugh; Dave Hamilton of the Missouri Department of Conservation, who many years ago stimulated my imagination about large predators; Rich Beausoleil of the New Mexico Department of Game and Fish for all the time spent accumulating information for my research efforts; Raymond Skiles of Big Bend National Park in Texas; John Phelps of the Arizona Department of Fish and Wildlife; San Stiver and Larry Gilbertson of the Nevada Department of Conservation; Dale Elliot, a retired game warden with the Nevada Department of Conservation; and last, but not least, Matt Austin and Brenda Guiltner of the Wildlife Branch, Ministry of Environment, Land and Parks.

I would like to thank, as well, Neil Williams of Williams Books in Vancouver, British Columbia, for helping me to obtain the next-to-impossible: a copy of *Island Gold: A History of Cougar Hunting on Vancouver Island.* The book was invaluable in piecing together a complete history of cougar attacks upon humans on this island up to the 1990s.

To Harold P. Danz I offer my sincere gratitude for graciously allowing me to emulate his tidy and concise presentation of pertinent information.

Thanks are due to many researchers, newspaper editors, reporters, rare-book dealers, librarians, and state historians whose names alone would gobble up many more paragraphs of type. Thank you to the staff of Amazon.com for their amazing efforts to obtain for me as many of the out-of-print books on my "wish list" as possible. They succeeded far more often than not. And a sincere thank you is also due Barbara Brown, a researcher with the *Vancouver Sun* and *Province Infoline,* Pacific Press, Ltd., Vancouver, B.C., Canada, who tirelessly searched back issues of these two newspapers for information relating to cougar attacks in Canada.

To all of you: I could not have completed this book without your help and support. I thank you from the bottom of my heart.

—*Kathy Etling, November 2000*

Prologue

David Herbert Lawrence, born in 1885 in Nottingham, England, wrote *Sons and Lovers* (1913), *The Rainbow* (1915), *Women in Love* (1920), and *Lady Chatterley's Lover* (1928). He also composed this poem, first published in 1928, as an elegy to the mountain lion, which he perceived as disappearing from the North American landscape. Although the mountain lion of the early twenty-first century is hardly disappearing, here is Lawrence's eloquent poem about these magnificent carnivores:

> Climbing through the January snow, into the Lobo Canyon
> Dark grow the spruce trees, blue is the balsam, water sounds still unfrozen,
>   and the trail is still evident.
> Men!
> Two men!
> Men! The only animal in the world to fear!
> They hesitate.
> We hesitate.
> They have a gun.
> We have no gun.
>
> Two Mexicans, strangers, emerging out of the dark and snow and inwardness
>   of the Lobo valley.
> What are they doing here on this vanishing trail?
>
> What is he carrying?
> Something yellow.
> A deer?
>
> *Qué tiene amigo?*—
> *León*—
>
> He smiles, foolishly, as if he were caught doing wrong.
> And we smile, foolishly, as if we didn't know.
> He is quite gentle and dark-faced.

It is a mountain lion,
A long, slim cat, yellow like a lioness.
Dead.
He trapped her this morning, he says, smiling foolishly.

Lift up her face,
Her round, bright face, bright as frost.
Her round, fine-fashioned head, with two dead ears:
And stripes on the brilliant frost of her face, sharp fine dark rays,
Dark, keen, fine rays in the brilliant frost of her face.
Beautiful dead eyes.

Hermoso es!
They go out toward the open;
We go on into the Gloom of Lobo.

And above the trees I found her lair,
A hole in the blood-orange brilliant rocks that stick up, a little cave.
And bones and twigs, and a perilous ascent.
So, she will never leap up that way again, with the yellow flash of a mountain
    lion's long shoot!
And her bright striped frost-face will never watch any more, out of the
    shadow of the cave in the blood-orange rock,
Above the trees of the Lobo dark valley-mouth!

Instead, I look out.
And out to the dim of the desert, like a dream, never real;
To the snow of the Sangre de Cristo mountains, the ice of the mountains of
    Picoris,
And near across at the opposite steep of snow, green trees motionless standing
    in snow, like a Christmas toy.

And I think in this empty world there was room for me and a mountain lion.
And I think in the world beyond, how easily we might spare a million or two
    of humans
And never miss them.
Yet what a gap in the world, the missing white-frost face of
        that
        slim
        yellow
        mountain lion!

Foreword

Kathy Etling has tackled a difficult subject. The difficulty lies not in telling the story of puma attacks on humans but rather in maintaining a balanced image of the puma that results from the telling. Very few pumas attack humans, but the stories about the attacks leave deep impressions. For people who know little about pumas, attack stories may create their only impression of the species. Such impressions will certainly sway any political leanings they have toward puma management. There lies, therefore, in the telling of these stories, a danger of distorting the public view of the animal, ultimately to its disadvantage. Kathy's job here, then, is to walk the fine line of documenting human attacks, an important truth, but an infinitesimally small part of puma behavior, without overwhelming all other public knowledge. I don't envy her the undertaking.

In working with pumas over the past thirty years and, necessarily, with people interested in pumas, I've realized that how someone views the puma is usually influenced by their personal agenda. Early on, working with puma hunters, I realized that many of them wanted the puma to be a stock killer, to damage deer numbers, and, perhaps, to be a threat to humans. Such characteristics of the species justified their own behavior in chasing down pumas and killing them. Only a few hunters openly admitted that they simply enjoyed the sport and did not try to justify it with some more heroic purpose. Such thinking is common in all of us. We hunt deer to protect deer range; we shoot prairie dogs to reduce range damage or to keep horses from breaking legs. Seemingly, we have a hard time doing something just because we want to do it.

At the other extreme from hunters, of course, are those who would protect the pumas, and other wildlife, from all human interaction or exploitation. They, perhaps, are less inclined to justify their interactions or, in this case, lack of interactions with the puma. Protecting something seems to have a pure merit that can't be challenged. They are more likely to justify the behavior of the puma itself in some greater scheme of things—preventing overpopulations of deer; maintaining the balance of nature. I personally believe that such efforts arise from a more primal biological force that is akin to territoriality. Efforts to protect wildlands and wildlife are ultimately an effort at attaining land owner-ship—of imposing trespass restrictions without assuming the tax and protec-tion burdens that accompany private property. As human populations increase, such efforts will increase and will take many forms of justification. Saving pumas will only be one.

Between these extremes lies the bulk of humans, most of whom in the United States now live in urban environments and have no personal puma agenda. Their image of the species, if they have one, is formed by what they hear and see through the media. Only a few of them will ever go so far as to read a book about pumas.

So, we might assume that the audience of this book will be made up first of those who seek confirmation regarding the threat of pumas to humans, a smaller audience who idolize the puma, and a smattering of other readers who are simply curious about the subject. Unless written with care, this book will not modify any image held by the first of these; it may make the second category uneasy; it may influence drastically that held by the third.

But what is the true image of the puma, and who holds the truth about threats to humans? As a scientist, I like to believe that objective research will lead us closer to the truth, but we obviously will never carry out con-trolled studies of puma attacks on humans. It is one part of puma behavior that we simply cannot design field studies to address. We can only look, again and again, at the small sample of incidents for clues that explain their cause.

On the whole, research on pumas in the western United States has told us that pumas cover relatively large land areas, and that they kill and eat deer plus a variety of other prey including, in places, livestock. Based upon the experience of puma biologists and, for that matter, puma hunters for genera-tions before them, pumas aren't a major threat to humans. Over the past 100 years, involving thousands of direct interactions with the animal, virtually no puma hunters or puma biologists have been attacked. In my own research, I went into thickets, caves, and climbed trees with innumerable pumas, without any particular thought to my safety. Only on a couple of occasions did I realize in retrospect that an attack might have happened. Admittedly, all of my field-work occurred before the recent outbreak of human attacks. I assumed, based on information available then, that the animals would not attack and, fortu-nately, I was right (although in one case, probably barely so and only because a dog intervened). With knowledge of the attacks that have occurred over the past 20 years, I might not now be so brave.

Which is to say that, perhaps, even my image of the puma has changed, even though I know that the total number of attacks is insignificant relative to the larger sum of puma behavior. The underlying question here is whether or not the species itself has changed, or have circumstances surrounding the species brought about the increased frequency of attack? I will not usurp Kathy's book to provide my ideas on this question, but the extent to which she addresses it is, to me, extremely important—more so than the individual case histories. Can we say why puma attacks on humans have increased over the past 25 years in the western U.S. and Canada? When you read the accounts of the victims and the reflections of agency personnel, you will hear wide speculation and assignment of blame. How valid are the explanations being offered? And what, if anything, can really be done about the problem? Is it even a big enough problem to be addressed? I, and probably every other puma biologist or puma hunter, have opinions on the subject. We don't all agree. But an assessment of those differing opinions may, in the long run, be Kathy's greatest contribution in writing this book.

—*Harley G. Shaw, October 2000*

Cougar
Attacks

Introduction

When Jay Cassell of The Lyons Press approached me to do this book, I admit that I was somewhat reluctant to approach the task. Not only was the topic of cougar attacks one in which I was seriously uninformed, I realized in my very gut the inflammatory nature of the subject. Massed together on one side of the issue are the preservationists, the people who believe that animals, like the cougar, should be *forgiven every transgression*—no matter how bold—against people and their property. On the other side are those who believe the world is not safe so long as a single cougar remains living wild. Separating these two battle lines is the greatest majority of the people: those who are neither totally for nor totally against this animal known as the cougar or mountain lion or puma. It is for those people that this book has been written.

Like the preservationists, I believe that cougars are capable of behaving only the way genetics and their life experiences have programmed them to behave, whether dragging down a mule deer or threatening a hiker. And while I support the regulated hunting of mountain lions, whether with or without hounds, I am against eliminating this magnificent predator that inhabits our increasingly threatened expanses of wilderness. Since I have researched this material and cobbled it together into the manuscript that has become this book, I have come to regard the puma with something akin to awe. Here is an animal that can kill—and kill quickly—and that lives in close proximity to people on many different fronts, and yet only rarely does it get into altercations with people.

You will read the words upon these pages and I know you will be stunned by the numbers and severity of the various accounts of attacks and near attacks by cougars upon people. Space did not allow, in a book that was *supposed* to be about cougar attacks, for much mitigating information. I would, however, like to remind readers that they are thousands of times more likely to be killed on the highway traveling to cougar habitat, and hundreds of times more likely to be stung to death by wasps, hornets, or bees, die from the bite of a venomous snake, be struck by lightning, die from an allergic reaction to pre-

1

scription drugs, or even be attacked by a so-called "tame" cougar, than to be attacked by a wild cougar. Were I to have written a book on any of these preceding dangers, it would have been far thicker and much scarier than this one is.

This is probably the time and the place to examine the origins of some of these attacks. Attacks compiled in both of the "old-time" chapters may indeed be factual accountings, but the chance remains that they could also be relegated to the status of "lore" or "legend." My good friend, Harley Shaw, has anticipated potential criticism of including as factual the accounts of attacks and near attacks that may well have been passed down to the present day as nothing more substantial than hearsay. Harley suggested that I should insert footnotes indicating where each accounting was originally found, as well as attempt to provide some kind of believability factor for each. I have addressed this issue in the Appendix, which lists every attack recorded in North America. Suffice it to say that many of these tales, particularly old-time accountings, may simply be that: tales or tangled yarns that were spun around a campfire. Some tiny kernel of truth may exist in each. In some, truth may be altogether absent. Recall the many urban legends that have entertained you recently, such as the alligators living in the New York sewer system, whether gathered off the Web or orally related by coworker, relative, or friend, that quickly unravel when your newspaper or network anchor sets to work to get to the truth. Then apply this to a time when only a small percentage of people were able to write, and writing supplies themselves were in short supply, particularly along the frontier where so many of these incidents took place. It's not difficult to imagine a traveler, in search of his supper, hunkering down the campfire and racking his brain for a grisly story with which to pay back his host and hostess for their hospitality. A tale of grisly horror, such as that generated by a "painter," or panther, that stalks a human being, preferably a comely young woman, would suit such a moment nicely. Some of the old-time attacks, particularly those related in the chapter devoted to "Old-Time Nonfatal Attacks," neatly fit into such a mold. Truth or legend? It is hard to say with certainty, since much confirming detail either has never existed, or has been lost amid the swirling mists of time. Accounts recorded by respected figures such as Theodore Roosevelt more than likely took place in much the way he suggested they did. Those related by lesser men may not have. Even those incidents that pop up from time to time in the writings of such stalwart citizens as John James Audubon may not have been entirely true. Audubon, after all, is known to have embellished on more than one occasion. What it comes down to is this: Not all old-time or unattributed accounts are true; in fact, each should be digested with a grain of salt.

Let me conclude simply by noting that Stephen King, the best-selling novelist, has become the huge literary success that he is by capitalizing on the fact that people love to be scared. Because that is so, volumes written about bear attacks and books by the late Peter Hathaway Capstick, the African writer, fly off the shelves of outdoors booksellers. It is my great hope that in the reader's desire to be scared while at the same time enjoying a good read, that he or she also will be able to grasp the larger picture coalescing just beyond these written lines: It's not the cougar or human life that is truly in danger here, but an ancient way of life. As our wildlands continue to disappear at an alarming rate, as more people seek to "get away from it all" by packing up and moving into what was formerly remote and marginal habitat suitable only for cougars and their prey, of course attacks upon people by cougars are bound to increase. It is my firm belief that this in itself is not the problem but merely a symptom of a greater problem, and that is the loss of the wilderness and the great unsolved mysteries she once contained.

A wise person once said that "familiarity breeds contempt." That is true whether you are a cougar, which too often sees strange, two-legged "prey" hiking nonchalantly through its range, or whether you are a person who, perhaps once too often, reads about another human—maybe even an acquaintance—who has been approached, threatened, or mauled by a cougar. In reading the stories related in these pages, never forget that a cougar is an animal, first and foremost, and that we humans are pushing this animal into untenable corners. Some of these stories reveal what happens when the cougar becomes too familiar with the only predator possessing the power to determine its position in the future, whether it and its kind will even survive to exist in that future. Should it not, all of humanity would lose both something primeval of itself, as well as a creature wild, dangerously beautiful, yes, but of inestimable value.

—Kathy Etling, October 2000

1

Anatomy of an Attack

Were some expert to figure out conclusively what triggers a cougar attack upon people and be able to apply that to each instance of attack on record, it would be an incredible breakthrough in the field of animal behavior. As it is, however, biologists and behaviorists can only offer theories as to why one animal will attack on one occasion, then flee the next time under similar or identical circumstances.

John Lesowski, writing in the July 1967 edition of *Outdoor Life,* offered an interesting perspective on the centuries-old question of why cougars attack people. Lesowski wrote:

> It's my belief that cougar litters born in times of rabbit abundance learn to hunt rabbits, but not deer. If a rabbit die-off occurs, these young cats get pretty hungry before they find out how to go on a venison diet. They are the ones that come into dooryards and kill dogs and goats. I've known them to actually starve to death in a deer area.

Other experts believe that on Vancouver Island, which has a dearth of small prey animals, cougars there rely on deer when deer populations are high. When deer numbers plummet, however, mountain lions are forced to search for alternate sources of protein. Far too often they venture into towns and backyards looking for dogs, cats, or other domesticated animals. Such forays bring these hungry cats much closer to the human residents of the island than most of them prefer.

A similar observation may be made that when cougars—particularly young, displaced ones—move into areas where they not only are close to people but can actually observe them as they go about their daily routines, the animals may become "habituated." In fact, experts are now beginning to believe that it is the habituated cougar that presents the biggest risk to people. If it has not been shot at, run off by dogs, or beaten on with sticks, if it is rewarded with a tasty mouthful of cat or dog as it skulks near towns or suburbs, then that cougar may become emboldened toward people. The next step could easily be an attack.

Dr. Paul Beier, a respected scientist and cougar researcher with Northern Arizona University in Flagstaff, ventures his opinion: "It makes you speculate that it has something to do with urbanization," he said in an interview. "I suspect these lions are getting a chance to habituate because people now are hiking and jogging without dogs, and cougars learn they have nothing to fear from these two-legged creatures."

Kerry Murphy, a biologist with the Wildlife Research Institute of the University of Idaho, was quoted in *The Missoulian* as having said, "We haven't seen [urbanization] before. We don't know where it's going, or what trends may be developing."

"In California, cougar-human conflicts are still rare enough that it's impossible to make generalizations about where or when another will occur," said Steven Torres, cougar biologist with the California Department of Fish and Game.

"We feel that the increase in attacks upon humans is part of the problem with the rampant development now taking place in the state," Torres continued. "Most of these things [attacks and conflicts] are warning flags reminding us of the *real* problems, which are habitat loss and degradation and fragmentation.

"Killing lions—even the eradication programs which existed so many places for so many years—won't get rid of the animals. Humans tried their best to eliminate lions, but lions continued to persist even through the most intensive programs of persecution and eradication. The real threat to the future of mountain lions isn't hunting, it's the tremendous land conversion that's taking place all over the West."

Someone who wants to "get away from it all" moves into an idyllic foothill setting—just far enough from the madding crowd to be attractive, but not far enough to be out of cell phone reach or more than three hours from a good airport—buys a house and encourages wildlife, particularly warm, fuzzy animals like deer and raccoons, to feed close to their property. Of course, they've brought along Fido and the cat, but they continue to feed their pets outside like they have in the past. They cannot understand it when they see large pug marks outside their homes when they wake up each morning. They don't know why their dogs and cats are being eaten. They think a cougar can understand that a child is not a chipmunk. They are mistaken.

People who move into lion country should consider what they are doing. Sure, you can attempt to keep yourself and your loved ones safe, but you have to know what you're up against: a true predator, a 100-percent meat-eater that kills things that move—like you and your kids—and consumes them. A cougar that kills a person is not *loco,* as people once believed. A cougar that kills people may, in fact, have been displaced by more dominant cougars from a choice area, where food is abundant and the living is easy. Its only recourse, it may feel, is to hang out around dwellings where it may begin its stint as a human-killer, perhaps, by killing easy prey like pets, sheep, or foals. To advance from snatching a dog racing around the property to grabbing a child racing around the property represents a small step to a cougar, an animal that doesn't understand anything about our species' supposed superiority, and won't, either, until hit by a bullet.

Most cougars are shy and secretive. They would rather run away than confront a person. Such is the nature of the beast. The cougar that lets itself be seen is the cougar that will fail as a hunter. What isn't known is how many times a mountain lion is actually lying in the rocks above a housing development, watching the families below go about their daily business while mulling over in its cat's brain whether attacking one of those tempting morsels would be wise. Just because there aren't more attacks doesn't mean these cats haven't considered same. Thank our species' lucky stars that we are, in general, the polar opposite of both prey animals and mountain lions. We are loud, not particularly sneaky, we smell—to another animal—to high heaven, we travel in groups, and we often ride in or on machinery, which further discourages predators. In short, lions probably consider us a fairly obnoxious source of food, to be considered only under times of extreme duress.

Such extremes may occur when a younger lion is having a hard time making its living, a human gets too close to a cougar kitten or approaches a lion's hard-won kill, particularly if that lion is down on its luck or when the lion is injured. A single broken toe or claw can slow a mountain lion down enough to cause it to key in on low-risk, easy-prey items. Or maybe an opportunity just happens to present itself, and the lion simply cannot resist.

Another factor may also be at work. Could mountain lions be starting to consider humans as just another meal ticket?

"It's a possibility," concedes University of California wildlife specialist Lee Fitzhugh. "When that new animal—humans reacts in a manner that the lion recognizes as natural prey behavior—running, quick movements, excited chatter—the potential for an attack is increased."

The one thing that researchers do know is that, "Young mountain lions (two to three years old) are quite highly represented in accounts of human attack incidents, [especially] when transient or dispersing into new areas," according to Steve Torres writing in his excellent book, *Mountain Lion Alert* (1997).

As more and more people venture into mountain lion territory, the animals are losing—and will continue to lose—their fear of humans. And it is people who will have to adjust, most mountain lion experts predict. Unfortunately for both pumas and the wilderness as Harley Shaw has stated, "Greed and land prices will seal the fate of the puma, not human concern for another species."

A myth that continues to make the rounds, promulgated in many cases by puma apologists, is that attacking lions are always the older and weaker animals in a population, the animals that have to attack puny prey, such as people, in order to survive. Not so, say many experts. Mountain lions are opportunists. Young, old, strong, weak: Present them with an opportunity too good to pass up, and at some point one of them may not.

Why? Because all predacious animals "have got to adapt to changing environmental conditions, a changing prey base," said Tom Hobbs of the Colorado Division of Wildlife. "They've got to do that to survive. This year, there's a lot of mice around. We've got to eat mice; next year, it's what?"

In any event, the lion that attacks or kills a human, under *any* circumstances, is not evil. A lion cannot be evil, just as a lion cannot be good. A lion, like any animal, is a neutral moral agent, incapable of doing either good or evil because it is unable to understand the abstract concepts of good and evil. A lion is a lion; an animal. A lion has been designed to kill. When it happens to kill the "wrong" prey, that doesn't make the lion bad. That cannot make the lion bad. A lion that kills a human is simply being a lion.

Not that the lion should be allowed to exist after such a transgression. If a lion steps over the invisible line of acceptable lion behavior, of course, it should be removed, whether or not it kills its human prey. We humans are the ones who have drawn the line in the sand. We are the ones who make the rules. And this rule is inviolate: Lion, thou shalt not prey on humans. Too bad the lion is unable to understand that until the slug tears into its heart. Being a lion—an animal—it will still be unable to understand this, even at the moment of its death.

When one stops and thinks about it, death by lion is not such a bad death *if* it happens instantaneously. The mechanics of such a death are fascinating, especially when explained by an expert in cougar behavior like Erik

Wenum, Montana's wildlife conflict specialist. Wenum responds to an average of twenty problem cougar calls each month of the year. Such calls are usually made by people who live along the interface between Montana's expanding population centers and the vanishing wilderness. "A mountain lion has evolved with the prey animals it takes," Wenum said. "That's why the distance between a deer's cervical vertebrae and the distance between a mountain lion's canines are so very similar. When a mountain lion springs upon an animal's—or even a human's—back, its canines force the vertebrae apart. That motion stretches and snaps the spinal cord. And when the spinal cord snaps, you're dead. Structurally, the neck still looks intact because the neck—the vertebrae—have stretched. The spinal cord does not. Death is fast.

"Just look at the lion's skull. It's very broad around the massiter, which allows for many points of attachment," Wenum continued.

"The lion has sharp claws," said Wenum. "Its dew-claws—which are actually fifth claws that are unseen in the rounded, four-toed track—jut off the legs at odd angles to provide a better grip on prey. Using the dew-claws actually allows the lion to tighten its grip due to leverage, because the dew-claw digs in sideways."

Another notorious mountain lion tactic is to relax its grip as soon as its prey panics. Momentum loads into the cat's muscular body. When the prey stops, turns, bucks, or dodges, the cat's claws slip out of the prey as the lion's body slides forcefully forward to, perhaps, snap the prey's neck.

A mountain lion may also try to strangle its victims by clamping down on its throat. If it succeeds, death will follow swiftly since the throat region is where windpipe, carotid artery, and jugular vein are all located. Should these be compromised, death is almost inevitable.

Mountain lions are particularly adept at killing deer. This is what they do best, along with preying on small animals. Cougars are not particularly well suited to killing people. Humans walk upright, their heads are more bulbous than those of deer and other animals, plus the length and angle of the neck is all wrong for a cat to get a good, killing grip. That is why so many cougar victims live to tell the story of their attacks. According to one analysis reported upon by Reuters News Service, the current incident rate of cougar attacks has increased 4.7 times that recorded before 1970. To avoid possible trouble, learn all you can about cougars and how they attack and precautions to take before heading into cougar country. Then make an informed choice before venturing out.

As wildlife biologist for the Montana Department of Fish, Wildlife and Parks, Gary Olson, said, "Lions are funny animals. You never know what they're going to do. The big risks you face when you're dealing with them are these: They eat meat—YOU're meat—and they mean business. Luckily, if you can see them, you'll probably be okay. It's when you can't see them and when an animal means business that you're really in trouble."

"People may think it's fun to feed deer and elk, but lions follow the deer population," added Geoff Tishbein of the Colorado Division of Wildlife. "Feed deer or elk and sooner or later you'll have lions showing up. In fact, whenever you're in an area where there are deer, mountain lions are usually nearby."

The only way to deal with a lion that has attacked or killed a human is to kill the animal. "Removing the offending animal is necessary," said Lee Fitzhugh, "as that particular lion is more likely to identify people as prey in the future. But removing the offending animal does not change the predisposing factors, which will continue to exist. People should be aware of the danger that . . . exists. . . ." Nature abhors a vacuum, in puma country or anywhere else. A new puma will soon move into the biological "vacuum." Whether this new individual will begin to attack or threaten humans, no one can predict.

In conclusion, Tom Beck, large carnivore specialist with the Colorado Division of Wildlife, had this to say: "There are basically two opposing views to wildlife that have been put forth in our culture. One is of a blood-curdling bear or lion that man has to destroy so that he might preserve civilization. The other is that everything in the wild is this beautiful, balanced, controlled system we call 'nature.'

"Neither is true. Nature is not neat. It's messy. And people must learn to understand the dynamics of nature. Things are never static. There is always change."

2

The Biology of a Cougar

*P*uma concolor, or "cat of one color," was known for many years before the present day as *Felis concolor*. In fact, nearly every book that's ever been written on the big cats until now has referred to them as *Felis concolor*, a scientific binomial that has only in the last year been modified. Properly so, too, since the more accurate *Puma concolor* actually retained historical precedence over the use of *Felis concolor*. Different names, whether scientific binomial or simply popular regional colloquialism—are nothing new for this fascinating animal. Throughout its history, humans on the North and South American continents have called it puma, cougar, painter, catamount, *león* (in Spanish America), or mountain lion. It is the panther, or "painter," of legend and myth, silent, secretive, deadly, and cunning. "The Lord of stealthy murder," in President Theodore Roosevelt's own words. Deer tiger, Indian devil, Mexican lion, and Ghost Cat: All have been used to describe this creature. And, if that weren't confusing enough, the Native Americans had their own names: *Tuhu,* or "deity and guardian of the tribe" in the language of the Hopi, "Walking Silently Among the Rocks" in Navajo, and, perhaps most impressive and expressive, *Ko-licto,* or "Cat of God," by the nation of the Chickasaw.

Reverence for the cougar may have begun with some of the Native peoples, but it ended abruptly when Europeans set foot upon these continents, North and South. Mountain men judged puma flesh as better tasting than beaver tail or even buffalo tongue. According to Gilbert Acosta, writing in the May, 1963, issue of *Outdoor Life,* it tasted "like veal, only better." Even today, *aficionados* of the meat swear it remains the best tasting of all wild game.

Puma concolor is found only in the western hemisphere, where it currently ranges from northern British Columbia to Patagonia in southern Argentina. At one time, the cougar had the largest geographic range of any land mammal in the western hemisphere, illustrating how adaptive the big cats are. Cougars originally roamed from the Yukon south to British Columbia and eastward to New Brunswick. In the United States, pumas once ranged almost everywhere in the Lower 48, incredible as that may seem today. Bounties and habitat loss due to encroaching settlement either pushed the puma out of much of its traditional range, or made remnant animals so retiring and secretive that, until recently, no one even knew they existed. Pumas today inhabit much of British Columbia, the southwestern portion of Alberta, and all states from Nebraska and the Dakotas westward. A small population of panthers may also be found in Florida, clinging to survival in and around the Everglades.

Cougars are also returning to inhabit their former haunts. They are now fairly common in South Dakota and western Nebraska. Sightings in places as disparate as Pennsylvania, New Brunswick, Missouri, Illinois, and Tennessee are not only thrilling when reported by knowledgeable outdoors folk or re-corded on videotape—as the occasional cougar has been—they also are indis-putable. Whether former pet or questing migrant, this largest of the purring cats has been reappearing in places it had been thought to have abandoned forever.

Mountain lions survive quite well in many different habitats. They can be found in deserts as well as humid coastal-range forests. Elevation is no hin-drance. The big cats do well at sea level but equally well at altitudes in excess of 10,000 feet. In California, cougars are uncommon in the southeastern Mojave and Sonoran deserts, as well as in the open Central Valley. They are most abun-dant where there is a resident breeding population, plentiful numbers of deer, and adequate ambush cover. All else being equal, though, density of deer re-mains the best indicator of a habitat's suitability to sustain a population of lions. In those regions where deer migrate between summer and winter ranges, cougars commonly follow where the herds may lead them.

Although *Puma concolor*'s primary quarry is deer, the animals also prey on wild sheep, elk, rabbits, beaver, raccoons, grouse, opossum, wild turkeys, wild hogs, porcupines, and the occasional calf or sheep.

Mountain lions come in a variety of colors. Their coats can be gray-brown, reddish-brown, or a pale tawny shade similar to that of a golden palomino. Generally, underparts are white in color. Young kittens are spotted, with ringed tails. This distinctive spotted coloration is gradually lost as young cougars mature. Several attack victims in different parts of the continent have attributed their attacks to supposedly "mature" cougars that have been de-scribed as retaining "distinct spots upon the pelt." Chances are those "mature" cougars were, in reality, young animals. Biologists also believe that the black "panther" of legend and lore weren't panthers or pumas at all, but the melanis-tic phase of the larger-bodied jaguar.

As an animal ages, a grayness sometimes develops around the mountain lion's head and neck. The cougar's teeth are another good indicator of age. They become badly worn and are often cracked and broken in a very old tom.

Adults have black-tipped ears and tails. Generally, an animal's coloration blends in well with its natural surroundings, an adaptation for effectively stalking prey developed over eons. Older cats have large, round, yellowish or amber eyes. Kittens have blue eyes.

Historically, mountain lions have proved to be difficult study subjects. Secretive, solitary, and wary, even biologists who know where and how to look go years without actually seeing one in the wild. Since the general public in most areas of the country rarely, if ever, catches even a glimpse of one of these animals, the general assumption is that cougars are rare. They are not. Cougars are alive and well and increasing, or at least maintaining, population numbers in all portions of their range. The only notable exception may be the Florida subspecies, popularly referred to as "the Florida panther." According to cougar researcher Harley Shaw, rampant agricultural development coupled with continued housing construction will probably soon eliminate all but some manner of an artificially sustained population of these cats.

What is known about these creatures has been discovered mainly through the use of radiotelemetry. Study cats are chased, tranquilized, weighed, measured, and collared. They are then released back into the wild with their battery-powered collars programmed to send back signals to researchers armed with powerful receivers.

The heaviest cougar on record was a mighty animal weighing 276 pounds. A government hunter, J. R. Patterson, killed it in March 1917, near Hillside, Arizona. It measured eight feet, seven and three-quarter inches from the tip of its nose to the end of its tail as reported by Edward Thompson Seton in *Lives of Game Animals* (1925). Yet skepticism remains rife within the research community that such a huge cat ever existed—its weight was arrived at *after* it had been field dressed.

Although it weighed in at nearly 60 pounds less than Patterson's, a cougar killed by Teddy Roosevelt is more solidly documented. Shot in 1901 near Meeker, Colorado, it weighed 217 pounds and measured eight feet in overall length. The skull of that kill was listed as Number One in the Boone and Crockett Club's *Records of North American Big Game* as recently as 1964. Another big cat was taken on January 15, 1927, in Sagauache County, Colorado—the largest cougar taken by any government hunter in that state. No weight was recorded, but the front foot pad measured six and three-quarters inches wide. (The average cougar's foot pad is only three and one-half inches wide.)

These chunkers—if the weights and measurements are accurate—can be properly termed exceptions, not the rule, although the borealis effect does hold true for cougars as for other animal species. The borealis effect means that animals inhabiting more northern climes tend to be larger, heavier, and often darker in color than those from more temperate regions. It's a matter of adapting to an environment: larger, darker animals in the North will retain more heat and stay warmer than small animals with lighter pelts in the South. A survival advantage is thus bestowed upon both darker, heavier animals and also smaller, lighter-colored ones. Of course, the exception has to be that huge 276-pound cat from Arizona. As a rule, however, the cougars of British Columbia—which, on average, weigh between 110 and 200 pounds—are larger than those from California, where an adult male weighs somewhere between 100 and 160 pounds. A typical mature California female will weigh somewhere between 65 and 100 pounds. Contrast that with the typical British Columbia female lion, which weighs between 90 and 120 pounds. The largest cougars of all are most often found in the interior of British Columbia and in the Kootenays.

The average male California lion measures about seven feet in length, from the tip of its nose to the tip of its tail. The female will average about six feet in length. The animal's long, thick tail makes up almost one half, or 40 percent, of its total length. For a seven-foot long animal, that means its tail is 34 inches long, or almost three feet of its entire length.

The mountain lion is the second-largest cat inhabiting the western hemisphere. The species is divided up into numerous subspecies, which also accounts for some of the observable differences between various populations of lions. The largest cat in the western hemisphere is the colorful jaguar, another animal making its own stealthy comeback, especially along the U.S. border with Mexico. In contrast, a mountain lion can be identified by its long tail, plain coloration, and small head relative to the size of its body.

Puma concolor is one of the largest of the North American carnivores, and can, at times, be one of the fiercest. It is exceeded in size only by the black bear, brown bear, polar bear, and jaguar. Unlike black and brown bears, however, the mountain lion is a "pure," or "true," carnivore. In this it is similar to the polar bear, although even polar bears will occasionally dine on sedges or fresh spring grasses upon emerging from hibernation.

A cougar is pure power. Skeleton, muscle, tendon, and internal organs come packaged in a sleek, silky pelt, with little body fat. The puma is extraordinarily patient and sneaky. It exhibits great stealth when executing a stalk. But when it launches itself at a target, it can become a rocketing bullet of sinew, bone, and muscle that slams sharply into its prey and often knocks it off its feet. An average-size cougar is capable of killing even a 600-pound moose or elk, given the right circumstances, and doing it in a few seconds.

In its ability to find and kill prey, a mountain lion can be termed a "specialist." In its diet, it can also be called a specialist. But in its choice of habitats, a cougar is a generalist because it thrives in such a wide variety of terrains and climates.

Mountain lions are often said to roam a territory. That term is not exactly correct, but then it's not exactly wrong, either. The proper terminology—the one preferred by scientists—is "home range." A home range is simply the area a particular lion must roam in order to fulfill all of its needs: prey animals, no matter what the season; cover; denning spots; water; freedom from harassment; and, if a member of a breeding population, procreation. Home ranges vary in size depending on the suitability of the habitat and the density of prey. In Idaho studies, a female lion's home range varied from five to 20 square miles. A south Texas female required about 34 square miles of roaming room, while a male ranged over 82 square miles. A female caring for kittens uses a somewhat larger home range than does a female without young. In Colorado, a male lion will often travel as far as 25 miles in a single night and use, on average, a territory of about 300 square miles. When dispersing from one area to another, young male mountain lions have been known to cover as many as 400 miles in the quest for unoccupied [by other male lions], yet suitable habitats.

During the late spring and summer, cougars from one to two years of age become independent of their mothers, and begin their search for a new home range. It is during this time that the young adult males, in particular, are most likely to run afoul of humans. Females are tolerant of other females sharing a portion of their ranges, but males are not so tolerant. Adult males kill other males during conflicts for territory, food, or a female in heat. Some males will not abide sharing their turf even with females. One notable example studied by Idaho's Maurice Hornocker was Attila, a big male so bellicose that he attacked and killed three females that made the mistake of establishing home ranges near his. Males have also been known to stalk and kill a female's kittens if the female is unable or unwilling to defend them. Male cougars show no bias toward their own kittens, either, and are as likely to kill and eat their own offspring as that of another male. This behavior is probably associated with a cougar's biological need to maintain its territory. Researchers speculate that it may be one of the mechanisms which helps to control cougar numbers.

"Older male lions keep a population's social order in balance," said Gary Olson, wildlife biologist for the Montana Department of Fish, Wildlife and Parks. "We've seen lots of predation by males on any kittens they come across. The male doesn't know if they're his or not. He'll eat them all if the female can't protect them." Since hunters sometimes target the largest, most dominant male cougars in a population, there is concern that they are being replaced by subadults with no idea how to maintain social order. This factor may be contributing to a breakdown of lion social order in parts of the animal's range, and that may be one reason why attacks and conflicts are seemingly on the rise. More studies must be undertaken before any conclusive proof can be found, particularly in lieu of the fact that if large males truly maintained social order, then California—with its "hands-off" approach—should be a bastion of orderly mountain lion society, with plenty of mature males to keep the oft-threatening juveniles on their best behavior. This, of course, does not seem to be the case.

Research has revealed that a state's larger metapopulation is actually composed of many small populations of lions. Subpopulations are linked to one another by the young lions that disperse from their places of birth and settle as adults amid other subpopulations, thus adding to genetic diversity. As transient cougars travel through occupied ranges, they tend to avoid the resident cougars.

Any occupied range will be clearly marked by the resident cougar, through the use of visual and olfactory signals readily recognized by other cats. Perhaps the most common signals are scratch piles, where cats scratch up leaves and forest or desert litter into small heaps at regular locations, then urinate or defecate on the debris. All cougars make these marks, but males mark more frequently than females, and marks become more numerous when populations are high. Scientists believe that information such as the sex, breeding condition, and social status of individuals is transmitted through these scrapes to others in the lion society.

Cougars have four toes with three distinct lobes at the base of the pad. Since the claws are retractable, they usually do not leave imprints. An adult cougar's front pad mark will measure three and a half inches wide by three inches long or more; its hind pad, three inches by three inches. When lions are in a rush, which is common, they place their hind paw in the imprint made by the front paw.

Cougars are generally solitary animals. If tracks indicate two or more cougars traveling together, it is probably either a breeding pair or a female with large young. Three or more sets of tracks in a group probably indicate a female with kittens, the only true social unit to be found in mountain lion society.

A mountain lion's voice is striking, an unforgettable sound that has been described as piercing, nerve-wracking, demonic, terror-striking, or as a trilling wail. Lions may also emit a distinctive chuckle, as well as make many typical house cat vocalizations, including mews, hisses, spits, purrs, and growls. Kittens and adult males will also make whistle-like sounds. Kittens whistle to attract their mother.

Female lions most often begin to reproduce or breed when they are between two and three years old. Courtship begins when a roaring (described by those with listening experience as "more of a yowling") female in heat (prepared and receptive to breeding) makes frequent vocalizations and visits scrape sites to leave scent, or pheromones, highly attractive to males. Once a male locates the female, he will stay with her for up to ten days, during which the pair mates repeatedly. Males are polygamous, and will breed with many females.

Mountain lions will breed at any time during the year, so kittens may be born during any month following a three-month (96-day) gestation period. Many births occur during July through November. One to four kittens or cubs comprise the average litter. One Utah female gave birth to six kittens, but this is highly unusual. The female raises the kittens alone.

Females like to give birth in a rocky crevice or den. Favored locations will often be protected by roots or windfalls. Kittens are born with their eyes closed. They will not open them until anywhere from 10 to 14 days after birth. Newborn kittens nurse for at least five to six weeks.

Cougars are predators at the top of the food chain. Their actions are often unpredictable. We have little understanding about what might trigger attack, partly because the animals are such opportunists. Studies seem to indicate that cougars make use of prey animals depending upon the frequency with which these prey animals may be found in the cougar's environment, which only makes sense. One British Columbia study, however, seemed to point to the cougar as favoring large-antlered mule deer bucks disproportionately over other deer. Some cougar biologists, however, attribute such a notion to unreliable data.

The kill of larger ungulates is usually made following a careful stalk. Mountain lions must kill within two or three jumps—20 to 50 feet—after their stalk. If prey escapes, a cougar will seldom follow. The actual kill follows a sudden rearing up from the ground and onto the shoulders and neck or back of the prey. The most effective kills are accomplished when the cougar holds the head with a forepaw and bites down through the back of the neck near the base of the skull. Death follows quickly. The cougar will then drag the carcass to a secluded spot to begin feeding. It often consumes the most nutritious internal organs first, then eats muscle tissue later. After consuming its fill, the cougar will cover its kill with dirt, sticks, and leaves, returning frequently to eat until the carcass is consumed or the meat spoils. When a cat is traveling, however, it may eat once and not return. One article, written by an old-timer in British Columbia who worked as a predator control agent, related the story of a mountain lion he had tracked and eventually killed that made a habit of preying upon mule deer, but would eat only the deer's liver before moving on to make its next kill. Coyotes, vultures, and other scavengers all benefit from predators such as mountain lions. Such creatures often subsist during lean times on abandoned lion prey carcasses.

Cougars tend to kill both older deer and very young deer simply because the lions are opportunistic predators. Taking the old, with their failing senses, or the young, with little life experience, makes good survival sense. Food shortages, starvation, and disease will also affect these animals to a greater degree then the rest of the population, weakening them sooner and making them easier prey. Cougars do not target only the old or the young or the weak, however. Cougars usually kill many deer in prime condition annually. It all boils down to opportunity, not any so-called biological imperative, no matter what the nature channels might broadcast on television.

Predation can be a good thing. An in-balance predator-prey relationship can, in a wholly natural system—few of which remain these days—accurately reflect the health of the environment. Animal prey populations can increase so rapidly that the land's capacity to support them becomes overwhelmed. Predation helps to control such booms.

Conversely, during "bust" times, starvation may be an important factor in mountain lion mortality. Observations of so-called thin and weakened cougars seem to increase when cougar populations are high and prey populations are decreasing or low, particularly when combined with periods of extreme cold and deep snow. This may be true, since hunting becomes more difficult for lions at such times. If kills are made infrequently, cougars that have trouble making a living may start haunting areas near human habitation. Kittens born during such winters will also suffer increased mortalities.

John Lesowski, a cougar hunter as well as a British Columbia conservation officer, once kept a record of the stomach contents of the cats that he'd killed during a seven-year period in the Cariboo district of the province. During that time, he killed 39 cougars during the fall and winter. Surprisingly, rabbits represented 26 percent of the big cats' diet, deer made up 23 percent, then came carrion at 13 percent, and moose, domestic sheep, and porcupines, each accounting for 8 percent. In two cases, cougars had fed upon other cougars.

A cougar will occasionally take not just what it can eat, but anything it can catch. Stanley P. Young and Edward A. Goldman, in their book, *The Puma: Mysterious American Cat,* published in 1964, reported one such incident that took place in Glade Park, Colorado, more than 75 years ago. A cougar slipped into a herd of bedded ewes and during a single night killed 192 of them.

Cougars will sometimes carry rabies, but are far more likely to carry plague bacteria. Statewide, according to a story published in the *Los Angeles Times,* of June 1, 1990, 23 of 36 pumas tested positive for plague-bacteria antibodies. Two of three Orange County lions showed a positive result.

Orange County vector ecologist Rudy Geck said the lions could have picked up the bacteria by eating rodents, ground squirrels, or other common plague carriers. Cougar researcher Paul Beier correctly stated that there would be "lots more to worry about" than plague were people to come into close contact with the animals. There is no evidence that any cougar has transmitted plague to a human, although a few years ago a Wyoming taxidermist died of plague he'd contracted from a bobcat he'd skinned while not wearing protective gloves.

A mountain lion's natural life spans about 12 years in the wild and up to 25 years in captivity. It has few natural enemies: bears, wolves, other lions, and sometimes coyotes. Lions are also at risk from accidents, disease, traffic, and people.

Call it what you may—mountain lion, puma, panther, or catamount—this "Cat of God" engenders deep feelings in almost anyone who has ever considered the animals for any length of time. Love it or hate it, the mountain lion is and always has been an intrinsic fiber woven through the tapestry of the American landscape. As it stands poised to make its comeback, millions of people are discovering that the puma is a no-longer-vanishing player in this vast ecological system comprising so many fragmented and radically different parts. The big cats perform a major service by regulating prey populations in areas where hunters are either unable or unwilling to travel. What's more, mountain lions also provide a legitimate form of outdoor recreation for countless outdoors people, both hunter and nonhunter alike. The only absolute we can be sure of when dealing with and discussing these Cats of God is this: As long as people share their turf with mountain lions, controversies will continue.

3

Old-Time Nonfatal Attacks

Zebulon Montgomery Pike, while one day exploring up the Mississippi, reached the northwest edge of what is now Cass County, Iowa. The date was January 31, 1806, when Pike wrote the following entry:

Passed one very large meadow or Prairie, the course W. The Mississippi only 15 yards wide. Encamped about one mile above the Transverse of the Meado: Saw a very Large Animal, which from the leaps he made I should suppose to be a Panther; but if so, he was twice as large as those on the Lower Mississippi. He shewed some disposition to approach me. I squated down (miller being in the rear) in order to entice him to it, but could not.

Pike's journal entry notwithstanding, the first nonfatal cougar attack to be duly recorded took place in the early 1830s near Hudson Creek close to Jasper, Arkansas. It is difficult to determine whether or not this particular attack was solely the result of imprudent human behavior. Here is the way the story is related in the pages of *A Reminiscent History of the Ozark Region* (1894), so you be the judge. The narrative begins describing the victim, Mr. Samuel Hudson:

Mr. Hudson was an expert marksman and delighted in hunting, thus assisting materially in clearing the country of the wild animals once so numerous. His greatest day hunting was when he killed four bears and five deer. After he had first settled in the country he had an experience with a panther which he did not soon forget. He and his eldest son, then but a young lad, went into the woods about two miles from the house to cut down a bee tree. Mr. Hudson had just begun work when, happening to glance up the ravine, he saw an immense panther gliding along. He waited until the animal was within a few yards of him and then thinking he could kill it with a rock, threw three or four times but missed it. Each time the panther would jump and snap at the stones, but as yet he had not observed Mr. Hudson. The latter made a slight noise to attract its attention and was successful. It stood still for an instant gazing at him, seemed about ready to spring, and Mr. Hudson grasped his ax ready to meet it. Slowly the panther approached, its long tail waving from side to side, and after crouching for a moment launched itself through the air and on Mr. Hudson, seizing the latter's head in its jaws. Mr. Hudson dealt it a desperate blow but the ax slipped from his hands and did not touch the animal. He pushed the panther from his head and a desperate struggle took place. He had a knife in his pocket, but could not reach it but fortunately he had brought a butcher knife, a thing he had never done before, this the boy handed him. It was his last chance and he plunged it time after time into the side of the animal before it loosened its hold and fell dead. Mr. Hudson's arms and body were severely lacerated and he came near bleeding to death. The panther was one of the largest of its kind ever killed in the section, measuring nine feet from nose to end of tail.

Since the panther did not seem to connect Hudson's presence with the rocks that had been pitched in its general direction, we are left to assume that the cat was in such a temper that it might have attacked Hudson even if he hadn't tossed stones its way.

During August 1833, when John Townsend was camped in southeast portion of what is now Washington State, he wrote, "[the panther] has seldom the temerity to attack a man, unless sorely pressed by hunger, or infuriated by wounds."

Ben Lilly, the man still remembered as a legendary killer of both bears and cougars, greatly admired Nathan Bedford Forrest, a noted Confederate general of the American Civil War. Forrest, like Lilly, was a killer of panthers. In 1834, when Forrest was 13, the family settled in Mississippi, 10 miles from their nearest neighbor. In *The Ben Lilly Legend* (1950), author J. Frank Dobie tells the following tale, which has all the earmarks usually ascribed to "lore":

> . . . There were no roads, only horse trails. One morning Mrs. Forrest [Nathan's mother] and her sister Fannie Beck, who lived with the family, rode to the neighbor's for a visit. When they started back late in the afternoon, their hostess presented Mrs. Forrest with a hatching of young chickens in a basket. A mile or so before they reached home the sun went down and the woods grew dusky.
>
> Presently the silence was broken by the scream of a panther, unseen but only a few yards away in the dense woods. The excited horses broke into a run, Fannie Beck's in the lead. Fannie shouted back to her sister to drop the chickens and let the beast have them, but Miriam Forrest was not going to let

any varmint have her chickens. On they raced, necessarily holding the horses back somewhat on the narrow, twisting, log-impeded trail. An occasional scream told that the panther was following. They reached the stream of deep, slick banks just beyond which their cabin was located. Here they were compelled to slow down.

As they were descending, the panther leaped, its front claws tearing into Mrs. Forrest's side and neck, its hind claws into her horse's back and haunches. The plunging of the horse loosened the panther's hold and threw it into the water, but its claws had ripped Mrs. Forrest's clothes from her back and the flesh from her shoulders. The screams from the women brought 13-year-old Bedford and the other children from the cabin. When their mother descended from the saddle, she still held the basket of little chickens.

As soon as she was found to be only flesh-wounded and was made comfortable, young Forrest took his flintlock rifle down from the deerhorn rack above the fireplace and started towards the door.

"Son, where are you going at this time of night?" his mother asked.

"I am going to call the dogs and trail that panther and kill him if he stays on the earth."

She could not dissuade him. The trail would be cold by morning, he said. Away he went. The hounds soon picked up the scent, and until about midnight Bedford kept with them through briars, swamp and canebrake. But the dogs were getting ahead of him and he feared they would run beyond his hearing. He cut a small grapevine, tied one end of it around the neck of an old hound to lead him. At times the other dogs were out of hearing, but the old hound followed true. Finally he heard them barking "treed." He had to wait for daylight to locate the panther up in the big white oak under which the dogs bayed. It was stretched out on a limb, lashing its long tail and softly snarling. He primed the pan of his flintlock afresh, aimed, and sent a bullet through the critter's heart. He got home with the scalp about nine o'clock.

According to *De Vane's Early Florida History:*

In 1858 a settler was splitting and squaring logs for the puncheon floor of his cabin, along Oak Creek in the prairie east of Sarasota. His daughter, age twelve, was washing dishes on a table in the yard while her younger brother played beneath it. A panther came from the woods and caught the boy by the foot. The daughter grabbed the boy and pulled him away from the panther, which then turned on her. The fracas brought the mother, father, and two dogs running, whereupon the panther let go of the girl and ran into the crawl space beneath the puncheon floor. The man grabbed the adz he had been using that morning, raised a puncheon which had not been nailed fast, and smote the cat, the only panther ever known to be killed before or since with a foot adz.

Lord Southesk, a British traveler to the western Canadian wilderness, in 1875 set down in his journal the following thoughts:

> Marking out a small party of hunters or travelers, it [the cougar] will follow them for days, and watch their camp at night, till at last it discovers one of their number resting a little separate from his companions. Then, when all is dark and silent, the insidious cougar glides in, and the sleeper knows but a short awakening when its fangs are buried in his throat.

Lord Southesk was merely reporting upon what had, in all probability, been related to him. In truth, the attack of an unmoving object is usually not the cougar's *modus operandi,* even if the object smells like potential food. Cougars key in to movement in general, flight in particular. A wail, cry, scream, or other sound of distress may also attract a cougar's attention. In only two instances reported upon by Dr. Paul Beier were the victims attacked while in either a sleeping bag or inside a tent.

Far more common than Lord Southesk's opinion were those of journalists like Francis Parkman who, in 1892, wrote that "the mountain lion shrinks from the face of man."

Theodore Roosevelt, he who wrote of several instances of fatal lion attacks upon humans, also wrote these words:

> The cougar is as large, as powerful, and as formidably armed as the [Old World] panther, and quite as well able to attack man; yet the instances of its having done so are exceedingly rare. But it is foolish to deny that such attacks on human beings never occur . . . it cannot be too often repeated that we must never lose sight of the individual variation in character and conduct among wild beasts.

Panthers or cougars supposedly look upon pregnant women as a real delicacy. According to Charles Fergus, writing in *Swamp Screamer* (1998):

> In the late 1890s in north-central Florida near the Oklawaha River, a young woman, heavy with child, was walking back to her cabin after visiting her parents, who lived nearby. Close behind her she heard a panther scream. Believing that the cat was following her, and reasoning that it might stop and inspect any article she left along the trail, the woman began shedding her clothes. Each time she dropped a garment she would hear the panther snarl as it ripped the

item to shreds. By the time she got home, she was naked. The panther circled the cabin until the woman's husband arrived, then faded into the woods.

Lore or actual occurrence? No one today can state with certainty, but the elements are present for a real humdinger of a tale: suspense, and a comely young woman deprived willingly of her clothing.

An unknown man, who had spent time both as a cowboy and an Indian scout, related the following tale, which took place in the late 1800s, near the old man's boyhood home in Texas, within the pages of *Outdoor Life's Anthology of Hunting Adventures* (1946). He told the tale to Sam H. Nickels, who relates it here, to illustrate how deadly a mountain lion can be when "savage from hunger":

One night, two men and a little girl sat in the front room of a cabin which stood on a low bluff a short distance from the banks of the Brazos River. There was a big fire blazing in the rock-and-mud fireplace, and one of the men had opened the door for a moment. They were seated near the fire smoking and talking, and had their backs toward the door. The little girl was seated upon the floor between their chairs, playing with a rag doll. The womenfolk were in a little lean-to kitchen at the back of the house where they were busy washing the supper dishes.

Suddenly without warning, there came a spitting snarl, and a big mountain lion leaped from the open doorway on the little girl. Unable to stop on the board floor, it grabbed her in its paws and rolled with her into the fireplace. The child's father pulled his six-shooter as he jumped from his chair, and he jammed the weapon against the brute's head and fired with his right hand, while he jerked the little tot from its clutches with his left.

Luckily, the lion had turned over and landed beneath the child as they went into the fire. Except for her terrible fright, she was unhurt.

The men dragged the dead lion to the door and threw it out into the snow. Next morning, they back-tracked it and found where it had crossed the river on the ice about 300 yards above the cabin. Seeing the light from the open door, it had come straight to the house. Its tracks showed that it had walked clear around the cabin a couple of times, stopping each time at the door. Finally it had crept inside. An examination of the slain brute showed that it had been starving . . .

"Yes, son," the old man said, as my wife called us to dinner, "lions is dangerous. With your newfangled, fast-shootin' guns an' a pack of trained dogs to keep 'em treed while you kill 'em, they don't often have a chance to do much damage. But you go out an' jump a wounded or hungry lion when it's just you an' him, an' you're mighty liable to git hurt. My advice is never to trust 'em."

Theodore Roosevelt, writing in *The Wilderness Hunter* (1893), wrote of a mountain lion altercation that occurred in Montana:

I knew two men in Missoula who were once attacked by cougars in a very curious manner. It was January, and they were walking home through the snow after a hunt, each carrying on his back the saddle, haunches, and hide of a deer he had slain. Just at dusk, as they were passing through a narrow ravine, the man in front heard his partner utter a sudden loud call for help. Turning, he was dumbfounded to see the man lying on his face in the snow with a cougar which had evidently just knocked him down standing over him, grasping the deer meat; while another cougar was galloping up to assist. Swinging his rifle round he shot the first one in the brain, and it dropped motionless, whereat the second halted, wheeled, and bounded into the woods. His companion was not in the least hurt or even frightened, though greatly amazed. The cougars were not full grown, but young of the year.

A brief notation in the book *Island Gold: A History of Cougar Hunting on Vancouver Island* (1990) is the only reference I could find for the first re-corded mauling to take place on that island. Author Del Hall writes, "27 June 1902, Mr. A. Daly, Mauled, West Coast, Van. Isl."

Hall had to have had a basis for this statement, but with no footnotes or explanation, I was unable to further substantiate any details about this attack.

To the best of my knowledge, which was aided by the writers and re-searchers on the topic of cougars and their attacks upon humans who preceded me, thirty-one known non-fatal attacks occurred upon in the United States and Canada from the time the first attack was recorded in the early 1800s until 1902.

4

Old-Time Fatal Attacks

N o reference exists that thoroughly details every attack upon humans by members of *Puma concolor*. Should such a database exist, it would almost certainly consist of more entries than those few that modern authors have been able to find and verify. How many settlers were attacked while traveling across the plains, far from their homes? How many cowboys driving herds along the various trails, or cavalrymen riding along the frontier, or Native Americans on hunting parties, really came to grief at a puma's fangs or claws, or quaked in boots or moccasins at mere proximity to the beast? Since many attacks are broken off by the puma before any physical contact is actually made with a human, the hardy early Americans may not have judged such near-events as being worthy of their reportage.

This continued to be the case well into the nineteenth century. We know various people were attacked by mountain lions—several were even killed—but many details have been lost in the mists shrouding much of this continent's early history. Whether the story originally was orally related or written down, most such accounts suffer from both a dearth of facts and descriptions. Modern investigators are provided with the bare basics and little more. It is left to our imaginations to flesh in the rest, and here we may find ourselves in trouble. What may have come down to us as fact may actually have been hearsay, or just a good yarn spun around a campfire.

What we do know is this: Of Native Americans and mountain men, the settlers and the cowboys, the cavalrymen and railroaders, none of these groups of people ever regarded *Puma concolor* with quite the same degree of fear and dread in which they beheld *Ursus arctos horribilis*, or the grizzly bear.

Perhaps that is to be expected. The grizzly bear was a fierce denizen of both plains and mountain when Christopher Columbus first landed in this brave New World. The grizzly feared no person, least of all the Native American with his arrows, spears, and atlatls. The grizzly, which had evolved with larger bear species such as the cave bear and the short-faced bear, had learned that to survive it must stand and fight. And stand and fight it did, to defend its kill, its cubs, and even its space.

The puma, however, was—and is to this day—more a creature of stealth than of bravado, an animal that prefers to slip about unnoticed and to blend in wholly with its surroundings so as to keep the element of surprise in its favor. The cat that is too bold is the cat that will fail as a hunter. A cougar is fast, but if it does not capture its prey in a few bounds, it usually will break off the chase. Compared to a grizzly—an animal fleeter than a quarter horse for several hundred yards—the cougar is the epitome of a quitter. It fails to make the kill more often than not.

Native American peoples were divided in the ways in which they regarded the mountain lion. The animal was either totem or near pariah. The Hopi, for instance, called the puma *tuhu,* and considered him to be strong and fearless, the greatest of hunters. It is thought that many of the Southwestern tribes obtained meat from scavenging kills made by the mountain lion, a bit of history that contributes to the high regard in which the Hopi hold *tuhu,* even to this day. Few lions have ever inhabited Hopi land, a dry, arid region with little of the succulent forage that attracts deer. Deer may be scarce in the land of the Hopi, but mountain lions are far scarcer. To learn that the Hopi revere the lion, perhaps, is not so surprising then, since, historically, these people probably had little contact with the animals.

Yet one of the stories related by members of the Hopi tribe casts the mountain lion in an entirely different light. The legend of the Kachina Clan, or *Ungwish-wungwa,* tells of a young boy who is sent out into the darkness to discover the source of strange sounds that are heard near the camp. The People painted him with reddish clay, and gave him a prayer plume before being sent on his way. He had not traveled far before he met the old Spider Woman, who gave him two charms: the root of a plant, and a feather. The feather would precede him on his journey to show him the way, while the root was to serve as his "medicine" in order to pass four dangerous places guarded by terrible beings. The first dangerous place he came to was guarded by a "great mountain lion." The boy chewed on the root and spat on the lion before the crouched figure could pounce on him. The next place was guarded by a bear, while the third and fourth places were protected by snakes. The boy, who was on a quest for the truth, found his way with the help of power bestowed upon him by Spider Woman, a supernatural being in the Hopi culture. Amulets—the root and the feather—protected the boy from harm from animal beings which, unlike other Hopi interpretations, are malevolent, including the mountain lion.

At Bandelier National Monument in New Mexico, there is a site dubbed "the Shrine of the Lions" by National Park Service personnel. Although visitation to this site is now discouraged to all except Native Americans, the forms of what may be two cougars, reverently carved from volcanic rock perhaps more than 600 years ago, are still visible. In the Cochiti pueblo located to the west of Bandelier, the Lions of Cochiti, which were created from two large boulders, are similarly revered. The age of the Lions of Cochiti is thought to be about the same as that of the Shrine of the Lions. Both sites are thought to have been the work of Native Americans from the Keresan pueblos, and both depict two large lions ready to pounce upon their prey. Were they formed or created to imbue upon the People the stealth and cunning of the puma, with which they might defeat their enemies? We cannot know with certainty. Like so much of the Native American spirit world, this knowledge is forever lost. We do know, however, that modern Native Americans still visit these sites to carry on the traditions of their elders.

Other tribes such as the Zuni carried small hunting fetishes carved from bone, shell, minerals, or various semiprecious stones. These Zuni fetishes represent the six Zuni hunter gods who rule the game animals of the American Southwest. Zuni hunters would carry such carvings to ensure the success of their hunt. Their choice of talisman depended on their intended quarry. The mountain lion fetish, for example, was preferred for hunting buffalo, elk, and deer.

The leaders of some Pueblo hunting societies were called Cougar Men. These hunters also carried small lion fetishes with them. A Cougar Man would scream like a lion to intimidate deer and, once a kill had been accomplished, he would smear blood from the carcass on the mouth of his fetish. A fetish properly respected would confer upon the hunter great hunting skill. Likewise, the lion it represented could then intercede for human interests to other animal spirits.

Another tribe of the Southwest, the Apaches, fashioned cougar skins into maternity belts, probably because they had observed the female lion giving birth with such ease.

Tribes like the Seminole of the Southeastern United States, on the other hand, hunted cougars. They ate their meat. They used their skins for clothing and rituals, and their bones, claws, and teeth were carved into amulets or worn as decorations. Pacific Northwest tribes did not like the cougar and also hunted the cats (although they did not eat them). Native Americans of the Southwest hunted mountain lions, too. Elliot Coues, a surgeon attached to a column of cavalry journeying to Fort Whipple, near present-day Prescott, Arizona, noted in 1864:

> That the Indians pursue it [the cougar] successfully with only their bows and
> arrows I know to be a fact, as I have found skins in their possession cut in various places with the sharp stone points of their arrowheads.

At the time of Columbus's voyage, Native Americans on this continent and South America consisted of many different tribes, each with its own cultural traditions and rituals. Some beliefs and rituals were commonly held, but there were dichotomies as well. And yet overall, Native Americans viewed the lion with the respect that befitted such a powerful and cunning being.

In 1500 Amerigo Vespucci reported seeing "*leones*" on Nicaraguan beaches. In 1502 Christopher Columbus saw them on the Honduran shoreline. Bernal Díaz del Castillo, who accompanied Cortez to Mexico in 1519, reported that the cougars displayed in Montezuma's zoo were fed a diet of "deer, chickens, little dogs, . . . and also . . . the bodies of the Indians they sacrifice." This may have appalled the Spaniards, but no true carnivore in its right mind would turn down a meal of meat, no matter what its origins. That fact rang true again in 1539, when Hernando de Soto wrote of his expedition through Florida. De Soto noted that the Florida Indians guarded their mortuaries after dark to keep "panthers" from eating the dead.

When the white man arrived in the Americas he brought with him a long-standing grudge against predators. "In soul [the panther] is mean and thievish, and in a word, a beast of low cunning," Aristotle wrote. Edward Topsell, an early Elizabethan zoologist, or what passed for one in those days, wrote, "it is a fraudulent though beautiful beast . . . wanton, effeminate, outrageous, treacherous, deceitful, fearful and yet bold." These puma traits, Topsell believed, bore a close resemblance to those of Woman. Topsell would hardly have been a popular guy today.

The Jamestown settlers knew of cougars, as did all the rest of the people who gradually filled up the easternmost portions of what are now the United States. As recently as the late 1700s, William Bartram, while traveling through the Southeast, wrote this about resident "panthers": "They are very large, strong, and fierce, and are too numerous, and are very mischievous." Reports like Bartram's formed the foundation of a platform dedicated to vilifying, bountying, and then hunting to near extinction in eastern regions the animals known as panthers, lions, or cougars. Despite assertions by early naturalists such as John James Audubon and John Bachman to the contrary—that the cougar is a man-shy predator, rarely willing to stalk our species—the persecutions continued unabated. Audubon and Bachman further declared in their *Viviparous Quadrupeds of North America* (1845–48) that the cat prowls "with a silent, cautious step, and with great patience makes its noiseless way through the tangled thickets." But the die had been cast and mountain lion numbers dwindled to almost nothing, aided by the establishment of bounties and warrants or statutes like the one in South Carolina, which bade each Native American inhabitant to kill each year a cougar or a wolf, a bear, or two bobcats, or else suffer a public flogging. With the wilderness so quickly being brought to heel, with the land being overtaken at such an incredible rate, men in search of adventure turned their heads toward the West.

Meriwether Lewis and William Clark were charged by Thomas Jefferson to explore and to locate the Northwest Passage to the Pacific. At the same time, the two men were also directed to make or maintain peace with Native peoples of the interior continent, as well as to gather information about any plants, birds, rivers, topography, and animals they might encounter during their westward journey. Among the extensive journal entries detailing their discoveries on their search for the Northwest Passage is this one about the mountain lion:

> The tiger-cat inhabits the borders of the plains and the woody country in the neighborhood of the Pacific. This animal is of a size larger than the wildcat of our country, and much the same in form, agility, and ferocity . . . The skin of this animal is in great demand amongst the natives, for of this they form their robes, and it requires four to make up the complement.
>
> The panther is found indifferently, either in the great plains of the Columbia, the western side of the Rocky mountains, or on the coast of the Pacific. He is the same animal so well known on the Atlantic coast, and most commonly found on the frontiers or unsettled parts of our country. He is very seldom found, and when found, so wary it is difficult to reach him with a musket.

One of the rare instances of mountain lion–human conflict to ever be recorded in any of the trapper's journals appears in the memoirs of mountain man James Ohio Pattie. His *Personal Narrative* (1831) describes an occasion when he awakened in the middle of the night to find himself staring into the eyes of a giant panther, crouched on a log six feet away. Said Pattie, "I raised my gun gently to my face, and shot it in the head." Whether the panther had any intention of pouncing on Pattie is left to conjecture, but the panther fared no better than did most of the grizzly bears who crossed paths with the intrepid breed known as the mountain man.

Trapper Osborne Russell, another of that breed who roamed the West for years, must never have experienced so significant a panther encounter as did Pattie. About the most that this mountain man could summon up to record about lions was:

> This animal is rarely seen in the plains but confines itself to the more woody and mountainous districts . . . it is very destructive on Sheep and other animals that live on high mountains but will run at the sight of a man and has a great antipathy to fire.

Ernest Thompson Seton was one of the very first writers to openly admire the cougar. In *Lives of Game Animals,* he discussed at length the cougar's secretive nature, finding it altogether admirable and not deplorable as did so many of his peers:

> From many hunting incidents that shed light or color on this freebooters life, I select the following from my scrapbooks and journals: On the night of Sept 14, 1899, I was camped with my wife on the High Sierra in California near Barker's Creek, not far from Mount Tallac. It does not rain there at that season, so we had no tent, but each night rolled up in our blankets and slept on the ground about half a yard apart. During that night there was a great alarm from the Horses. They broke loose and stampeded. Next morning we learned the cause. A Cougar had come into camp, had prowled around us as we slept, so said the tracks, but had gone off without attempting to harm any of us.

Seton later wrote of yet another encounter that well illustrates the big cat's stealth:

> In mid-September, 1902, while camped in the Bitterroots of Idaho, I found in the dust the tracks of a band of Mule Blacktail moving all one way. I followed for a time and found the track of a large Cougar joining on. After a quarter of a mile, I came on the fresh-killed body of a female Deer and in the woods near by were her two fawns running about. But they were big enough to take care of themselves and made off.
>
> Later, one of our party saw the Cougar but it calmly glided away keeping a tree trunk between itself and the rifleman.

Through the efforts of writers like Seton and those who adopted, if not Seton's style, then his overt affection for even the largest and most dangerous predators, the public's perceptions of mountain lions gradually underwent a transformation. Although pumas continued to be killed, trapped, and poisoned in what truly could be termed a systematic attempt at eradication, a groundswell of emotion was beginning to coalesce. This, despite either an increasing number of attacks, or much better efforts to record them. Although pumas are classified as "true," or "pure," carnivores, members of the species bear more than a passing resemblance to the much beloved house cat. That stroke of evolutionary luck has helped—through subsequent years and despite an increasing number of conflicts with humans—to endear pumas to a large number of the human inhabitants of this continent. As Seton wrote, "Our cougar is in all physical respects a cat, simply a cat multiplied by twenty."

Still, during the two centuries preceding the one that has only recently gotten under way, human attitudes toward these predators often verged upon the murderous. The only good panther, or "painter," or tiger-cat or catamount was a dead one, at least to many an early American or Canadian's mind. Enough factually reported incidents, at least for the eras in which they occurred, and word-of-mouth reports kept trickling in from various regions to keep the anti-panther fires fueled.

The first known cougar victim was Philip Tanner, 58, whose tombstone stands in a quiet cemetery in Lewisville, Chester County, Pennsylvania, at the time known as "Betty's Patch." This quiet community lies close to the Pennsylvania-Maryland border. Tanner, a millwright, owned a mill on Pigeon Creek and lived nearby. The man was attacked by a cougar and killed at the edge of some timber, perhaps while inspecting an impending timber harvest. Tanner's epitaph reads: "Here lye the body of Philip Tanner who departed this life May 6, 1751 – age 58 years." The study of the art which graces early tombstones like Tanner's is a discipline unto itself, but even here Tanner's tombstone stands out: A chiseled cougar crouches upon its face for all eternity in the aspect of ambush, reminding all who pass near that the man whose remains lie in the soil beneath the headstone died a victim of this animal's fangs and claws. The attack took place about a half mile from Tanner's final resting place.

There next came a scattering of attacks in the South in the early 1800s. Benjamin Vernon Lilly, bounty hunter extraordinaire, saw himself as a man with a mission: to eradicate every bear or lion that crossed his path, and even many of those that didn't. He recorded many of the tales he'd heard during the years he spent in pursuit of predators in a handwritten manuscript that was reproduced in the J. Frank Dobie book *The Ben Lilly Legend*. From this manuscript, we learn of several of the earliest panther attacks upon humans.

According to the Lilly manuscript, in the early 1800s:

a squad of Negro men were clearing swamp land north of Vicksburg. They noticed a panther slipping around in the woods and warned two white men, brothers who lived in a cabin nearby. Not long afterwards while one of them [brothers] was chopping wood about a hundred yards away from the cabin, he heard the other one scream. He had left him [the other brother] covered up in bed, shaking with a chill. He rushed to the cabin and as he went through the door [he too] was leaped upon by a panther. He had his ax but could not use it effectively. The panther escaped; it had killed the sick brother and the second one was so badly wounded that he died.

No record is made of the men's names, nor their ages. One was in a weakened condition because he was ill, possibly with yellow fever, although that is pure conjecture. Had the panther been close enough to see the sick brother it surely would have detected the man's weakness. A cougar does not ponder its actions; it is made to hunt and to kill. This one did. Unfortunately, the other brother, hearing the screaming, rushed in and suffered an identical fate.

In northeastern Louisiana's West Carroll Parish, near the Bayou Macon River, another anonymous adult male met a fate similar to that of the two Mississippians. Ben Lilly's reminiscences of this incident were related to him by a Judge Henegan, also of West Carroll Parish, in 1882. Lilly wrote that the attack took place many years before and involved an Indian and a white man who decided to go deer hunting after dinner. Lilly takes up the narrative:

It was winter time and snow was on the ground, making sign-reading easy. They [white man and Indian] stayed together for a while but saw no deer and so separated. The white man got back home about dark. When morning came and the Indian had still not showed up, he [the white man] got help and went to hunt him [the Indian]. After trailing him about a mile from the place where the two had separated the day before, the trailers saw where the Indian had struck the tracks of a big buck deer and followed them. The trailers went on for about half a mile and found the Indian dead on the ground. Tracks made it plain that a large panther had leaped from a leaning oak tree under which he [the Indian] was passing, knocked him face down, apparently killing him instantly, and then rolled him over and sucked blood from his throat.

Before killing the Indian, the panther had killed the buck about sixty steps away and had sucked blood from his throat. Perhaps it scented the trailing Indian. Anyhow, tracks showed that it backtrailed the buck and waited at the leaning oak only a short time for the Indian's arrival. In making both killings the panther's tendency to jump upon a moving object seems to have been stronger than the desire to eat.

Yet another unknown adult male was killed either in southeastern Georgia or the northern part of Florida, also in the early 1800s. Again, the culprit was surely what is known today as the Florida panther. Accounts of so many brutal—and fatal—attacks could not have done much to enhance the big cats' image or reputation. Theodore Roosevelt, President of the United States and the father of the modern conservation movement, reviled panthers as "a beast of stealth and rapine," and as "ferocious and bloodthirsty as they are cowardly." He is often quoted as calling mountain lions "the big horse-killing cat, the destroyer of the deer, the lord of stealthy murder . . . with a heart both craven and cruel." In 1885, Roosevelt wrote: "When the continent was first settled, and for long afterward the cougar was quite as dangerous an antagonist as the African or Indian leopard, and would even attack men unprovoked." Roosevelt may have had a valid reason to write so vividly about the beast. His account continues:

> Early in the present century one of my ancestral relatives, a Georgian, moved down to the wild and almost unknown country bordering on Florida. His plantation was surrounded by jungles in which all kinds of beasts swarmed. One of his negroes had a sweetheart on another plantation, and in visiting her, instead of going by the road he took a short cut through the swamps, heedless of the wild beasts, and armed only with a long knife, for he was a man of colossal strength, and of fierce determined temper. One night he started to return late, expecting to reach the plantation in time for his daily task on the morrow. But he never reached home, and it was thought he had run away. However, when a search was made for him his body was found in the path through the swamp, all gashed and torn, and but a few steps from him the body of a cougar, stabbed and cut in many places. Certainly that must have been a grim fight, in the gloomy, lonely recesses of the swamp, with no one to watch the midnight death struggle between the powerful, naked man and the ferocious brute that was his almost unseen assailant.

Roosevelt told another tale of a black man being attacked and killed by a cougar. This one was cited several times in Roosevelt's writings, in *The Wilderness Hunter* (1893), *Hunting the Grisly and Other Sketches* (1900), and in *Outdoor Pastimes of the American Hunter* (1908). General Wade Hampton, a famous Civil War general and well-known Southern hunter, had related to Roosevelt the following story about a black man "who was one of a gang engaged in building a railroad through low and wet ground was waylaid and killed by a cougar late one night as he was walking alone through the swamp."

The West had not yet been thoroughly infiltrated by frontiersmen and settlers, so reports of attack by "panthers" were received only from the eastern and southern states until the late 1860s. Sometime before 1827, a man hunting with dogs and another companion was attacked and killed in the Catskill mountains south of Albany, New York. Here is the account as it is recorded by Georges Cuvier and Edward Griffith in *The Animal Kingdom Arranged in Conformity with its Organization* (1827):

> Two hunters went out in quest of game on the Katskill Mountains, in the province of New York, on the road from New York to Albany, each armed with a gun, and accompanied by his dog. It was agreed between them that they should go in contrary directions round the base of a hill, which formed one of the points in these mountains; and that, if either discharged his piece the other should cross the hill as expeditiously as possible, to join his companion in pursuit of the game shot at. Shortly after separating one heard the other fire, and, agreeably to their compact, hastened to his comrade. After searching for him for some time without effect he found his Dog dead and dreadfully torn. Apprised by this discovery that the animal shot at was large and ferocious, he became anxious for the fate of his friend, and assiduously continued the search for him; when his eyes were suddenly directed, by the deep growl of a Puma, to the large branch of a tree, where he saw the animal crouching on the body of the Man, and directing his eyes toward him, apparently hesitating whether to descend and make a fresh attack on the survivor, or to relinquish its prey and take to flight. Conscious that much depended on celerity the hunter discharged his piece, and wounded the animal mortally, when it and the body of the Man fell together from the tree. The surviving Dog then flew at the prostrate beast, but a single blow from its paw laid the Dog dead by its side. In this state of things, finding that his comrade was dead, and that there was still danger in approaching the wounded animal, the Man prudently retired, and with all haste brought several persons to the spot, where the unfortunate hunter, the Cougar, and both the dogs, were all lying dead together.

This incident was related to Major Smith by Mr. Scudder, the proprietor of the Museum at New York, where the animal was preserved after its death as testament to the story.

Cuvier and Griffin also recorded a Jaunuary 1830 attack "upon an unfortunate woman in Pennsylvania." According to Cuvier and Griffin, "the ferocious brute seized upon her as she was passing along the road and killed her in an instant." Ernest Thompson Seton later added that he felt this report appeared to be factual.

In 1844, a Dr. Reinwald, who lived on a farm, was making his way through the snow to visit a patient in Lycoming county, Pennsylvania. His nephew's wife, Mrs. William Reinwald, is reported to have said in P.A. Parson's article, "All Over the Map," which appeared in the August 1947, edition of *Outdoor Life,* that "the doctor's body was found lying in the snow with the back of his neck bitten through; medical instruments scattered about, large cougar tracks all around."

Our focus now shifts to the West, where Capt. John G. Bourke, assigned to the Third Cavalry, U.S.A., was serving along the frontier shortly before Gen. George Crook arrived to take over the government's campaign against the Apache. Bourke wrote of a cougar attack that took place in the area between Florence and Tucson, Arizona—near then Camp Grant, Arizona—in the late 1870s:

> Before we start out in pursuit of the attacking Apaches, let me relate the story told all over southern Arizona about the spot where this Gatchell-Curtis train had been surprised. It was known as the scene of the ambuscade of the Miller-Tappan detail, and frontier tale-tellers used to while away the sultry hours immediately after the setting of the sun in relating how the soldiers under Carroll had been ambushed and scattered by the onslaught of the Apaches, their commander Lieutenant Carroll, killed at the first fire. One of the survivors became separated from his comrades in their headlong flight into Camp Grant. What became of him was never fully known, but he had been seen to fall wounded in the head or face, and the soldiers and Mexicans seemed to be of but one opinion as to the direction in which he had strayed; so there was no difficulty in getting a band of expert trailers to go out with the troops from the camp, and after burying the dead, make search for the missing man. His foot-prints were plainly discernible for quite a distance in the hard sand and gravel, until they led to a spring or "water-hole," where one could plainly read the "sign" that the wounded man had stopped, knelt down, drunk, washed his wound, torn off a small piece of his blouse, perhaps as a bandage, and written his name on a rock in his own blood.
>
> So far, so good; the Mexicans who had been in the searching party did not object to telling that much, but anything beyond was told by a shrug of the shoulders and a "*quién sabe?*"

One day it happened that José María was in a communicative mood, and I induced him to relate what he knew. His story amounted to just this: After leaving the "water-hole," the wounded man had wandered aimlessly in different directions, and soon began to stagger from bush to bush; his strength was nearly gone, and with frequency he had taken a seat on the hard gravel under such shade as the mesquites afforded.

After a while other tracks came in on the trail alongside those of the man—they were the tracks of an enormous mountain lion! The beast had run up and down the trail for a short distance, and then bounded on in the direction taken by the wanderer. The last few bounds measured twenty-two feet, and then there were signs of a struggle, and of *something* having been dragged off through the chaparral and over the rocks, and that was all.

Searchers discovered it was easy to follow the victim's footprints across the sandy soil. They tracked the man to the waterhole where he had been able to quench his thirst before being attacked by the puma.

J. Marvin Hunter, who researched and compiled a *Pioneer History of Bandera County* (1922), recalled how:

> In 1876 a negro named Henry Ramsey lived near Indian Creek, several miles from Bandera, and one night he heard a disturbance out in his front yard. When he opened the door to investigate the trouble a large panther sprang into the room and attacked him. The only weapon the negro could secure quickly was a large butcher knife and with this he killed the panther, but not before the ferocious beast had bitten and lacerated his arms and body and torn his clothes into shreds. Old Doctor Peacock attended the wounded man but in a few days symptoms of hydrophobia appeared and the negro died in horrible agony.

A particularly gruesome account was reported by the *Battle Mountain Messenger,* on October 27, 1880. The account relates how an unknown young Nevada man had been killed some time during the past week by a "California lion." His body was "almost wholly devoured, only the flesh on his feet and head remaining."

March 30, 1882: The place is near Kalama, Washington. A five-year-old boy named Gussie Graves was playing near his home when he was pounced upon by a cougar. The boy's screams alerted neighbors who rushed to the scene. They were able to wrest the boy away from the cat, but it was too late. Young Gussie had been injured so severely that he soon died.

Whereas early attack victims had been mainly adult males, a shift to smaller prey was now taking place. Both Gussie Graves and the next person to die by cougar were young boys. The name of the next victim, an eight-year-old, was once more lost or forgotten during the intervening years. What we do know, however, is that the youngster was busy cutting wood near the Bruneau River in southwestern Idaho when a cougar ambushed him from where it had been hiding in the surrounding brush. The boy's father, who was working nearby, raced to get his rifle, but to no avail. Although his shot killed the lion, the boy was already dead. Amazingly, the cougar still had the boy in its jaws when the father shot it.

Ben Lilly was told of the following attack, which took place sometime before 1888, by a trapper friend, saying the attack was "no hearsay matter with him [the trapper]." Here is Lilly's account:

Late one evening a boy fourteen years old was chopping wood near his home in the woods [possibly near Hickory Grove, Mississippi, since that was where Lilly's old trapper lived]. His brother eleven years old was carrying the wood in. Just as the younger boy was leaning over to pick up a stick, a panther leaped upon him, knocking him to the ground. The older boy rushed upon the animal with his ax, trying to hit him, but the panther caught him [the older brother]. A young man who was in the stable feeding a horse heard the noise, ran out, picked up a billet of wood used to rive boards, and with it hit the panther in the head, killing it. That night both boys died from their wounds, and they were buried in the same grave.

In the late 1880s Sam H. Nickels was reported by Claude T. Barnes as relating the following fatal lion attack. A Mexican woman and her young daughter had gone to a spring to get water. The girl started gathering acorns when a cougar suddenly rushed out, pounced upon her, and carried her off. The woman fetched searchers with dogs to the scene, but all they recovered was one of the girl's small arms, along with tattered remnants of her clothing. They followed the cougar for some distance, but lost the track near the present town of Capitan, New Mexico.

On June 19, 1890, in California's Quartz Valley, seven-year-old Arthur Dangle was playing amid some oak trees close to his house when two cougars attacked. Here is the account of that attack as written about by a neighbor of the Dangles, Mr. Charles B. Howard:

. . . we went to the Dangle place, where we learned that Arthur had been playing about 100-yards from the house and about 50 yards from the barn, at 4 o'clock in the afternoon. His mother, having occasion to call for him and getting no response, the father crossed the road, above the barn into some small oaks, which bordered the foothill, to see if he could find the boy, and there a short distance up the gulch, in plain sight, two lions had little Arthur, who was 7 years of age. They had already killed him. The father, Joseph Dangle, made all possible haste to the house to give the alarm and secure a gun, but the mother in her desperation drove the lions off from the body of the boy, the animals then taking to the woods. It was about dark when some neighbors and I reached the Dangle home. I immediately sent for Charles Weeks, who lived about five miles away, and who had charge of a dog belonging to an Indian chief, and which dog I had been negotiating with the Indian to purchase, and later on got the dog and owned him until he died. It was a well-known fact that he never let a lion get away. We held a consultation and concluded to wait until just daybreak before we let the dog go. As there were two lions, we wanted to make sure of getting them both. Accordingly, at the first streak of day, in fact, before I could see the sights of my rifle, we turned old "Kelsey," the best lion dog on earth, loose and he immediately took up the trail. Those of us who could keep up did so. We didn't have over a quarter of a mile to go. I was standing immediately under an oak tree when the dog "Kelsey" stopped beside me; looking up into the oak, I could just make out the form of the big lion. I could almost have touched him with the end of my gun, his hind feet on one limb, his front feet on a limb just below, looking down at us. Lafe Lewis, standing beside me, said, "Charlie, shoot him," and I did so, killing him. Immediately the other lion sprang again up into a pine tree and clung there, and was promptly shot by George Allen, Charlie Weeks and myself, and the hunt was over.

The following account was discovered in *Outdoor Life's Anthology of Hunting Adventures*. The narrator relates a gruesome tale that had been told to him by a man who had been a cowboy and Indian scout in New Mexico during pioneer days. The narrator tells about how he had mistaken a [mountain] lion's scream for that of a woman, [when the old man] "he looked at me for a moment, then shook his head." The old man's story continues:

"You maybe got off lucky, son," he said. "On account of it smellin' that fresh-killed deer you had hangin' in the yard, it might've jumped you. Just wasn't hungry enough, maybe, or it might be you didn't meet the right lion. I've knowed of 'em doin' such things."

He went on to tell of an experience he had when he was a young man. He and a companion had camped for several weeks in [New Mexico's] Gallinas Mountains. When they finally ran short of fresh meat, they decided to go out and kill a deer.

Early one morning, they started away on foot into the higher hills behind their camp. Each carried one of those heavy, old-fashioned .50 caliber Sharps buffalo guns, and they walked for nearly a mile without seeing any sign of deer.

Finally they decided to separate and each hunt in a different direction. At the next fork of the canyon, one of them turned away to the right and the other kept straight on.

The old man said he had been hunting not longer than fifteen or twenty minutes when he hear the boom of his partner's old Sharps. He stopped and listened. When he failed to hear any more shots, he felt sure that his companion had killed a buck. As one deer was all they wanted, he threw his rifle across his shoulder and turned back to help carry the meat into camp.

He made his way down to the main canyon. There he picked up his companion's tracks and hurried after him. He had just rounded the next bend and was headed toward a thicket of junipers and young pines when he saw his partner lying on his face in the trail in front of him. A few steps away lay a mountain lion. Both were dead, but the lion's body was still twitching when he got to it.

The young fellow's shirt had been almost torn off by the lion's claws and teeth. The side of his throat had been ripped open, and his broken rifle lay near him. He had shot the lion through the body, but it lived long enough to kill him before he could reload the old single-shot Sharps.

The aforementioned scenario could have played out in two different ways. One: the hunter was attacked first and forced to fight back, which meant shooting the cat in mid-battle; or two: the hunter first shot the cat, which then retaliated by attacking the hunter. To the deceased, it would have been a moot point, for in each scenario the result was the same: his death. The old man who related the tale didn't impart enough additional information to shed conclusive light on the topic, although from the way in which the story begins, it seems extremely probable that this lion had been lying in wait for its victim and surprised him, thus favoring the first scenario.

Ben Lilly, who relates the next cougar attack, was convinced of the panther's penchant for the taste of human flesh. Here is what he said on the topic:

The cat family seems to have a natural taste for human flesh. While sitting up with a corpse in a house in the country, I have seen cats beg and mew in the same way they do when near a person who is dressing a chicken or a rabbit or fresh fish. House cats have been known to eat on the face of a dead person. They eat the same food that a dog eats, but a dog will give up his life guarding the body of any human being dear to him.

A few pages later in J. Frank Dobie's *The Ben Lilly Legend,* Lilly adds to this by stating:

I could relate many instances in which a panther ate the body of a grown man, leaving only the larger bones as evidence. In some cases, the panther dragged or carried the person away still screaming and trying to fight back. Generally, as I have heard the stories, the panther started to eat on the body as soon as the person was dead.

The locale: southeast Texas. The year: unknown, although it was prior to 1906. The witness: an elderly man who had once made his living as a tanner. This old man told Ben Lilly of "at least a half dozen instances of panthers killing early settlers around his old home in southeast Texas." This particular attack involved a settler, his wife, and two small babies. The family had just moved into their cabin and the husband was clearing additional land to farm. The wife was burning trash and cleaning up the yard, which had a fence around it. When:

she heard one of the babies crying, [S]he went in and quieted it and brought the other one [baby] outside and set it down on the ground. She went on raking up trash and burning it. Then the baby on the ground began to cry. She quieted it and resumed her work.

Her back was to the baby when she heard it give a terrible squall. She looked in time to see a panther bound over the fence carrying the baby into the dense thicket beyond. She ran after the panther, but it disappeared. At this instant the baby in the house set up a squalling. She rushed to it, gathered it in her arms and, carrying it, ran towards the yard fence to follow the panther. The baby in her arms was still squalling. Now the panther leaped back and came towards her. She made for the house and got inside just in time to slam the door in the face of the panther. She barred it with a large slab of wood hewn for that purpose.

When the man came, he found his wife holding the bar to the door and screaming. He did not own a gun, and he ran to the neighbor's to borrow one. When he returned, the panther was reared up with his front paws on the door. He was afraid to shoot lest the bullet go through the door and kill his wife. The panther ran off into the thicket. The man now got word to the neighbors. By next morning all the men in the settlement were gathered with all their dogs. Among the men was one by the name of Paine who had a pack of hounds. They hunted every day steady for two weeks. If I remember right it was eleven panthers they killed. They never found even a scrap of the dress worn by the baby that the panther carried off.

On July 6, 1909, another attack occurred in California. Miss Isola Kennedy, age 22, had taken three young boys to a nearby creek where they could go wading. The boys ventured out into the water where a cougar leaped onto the back of one Earl Wilson, age 10. Miss Kennedy charged into the fray armed only with her hatpin while the two remaining boys went for help. The hatpin served her well, for she managed to get the cat off of young Wilson and hold it at bay until help arrived. The cougar was shot, and all would have been well had the animal not been suffering from rabies. Earl Wilson, although not seriously injured, died soon afterwards. Records of the day indicate that the youngster died of tetanus, but since Miss Kennedy died two months later, and people had claimed the cougar was rabid, it is fair to assume that rabies claimed both these victims.

5

Human-Instigated Attacks

Back in the 1840s, in the central coast region of California, three grizzly hunters working along a creek bordered by willows and grapevines came upon a waterfall that plunged into a green pool. A large tree had fallen across the pool, forming a natural bridge. This account of a grizzly bear's natural animosity toward the mountain lion was taken from Tracey I. Storer and Lloyd P. Tevis Jr.'s book, *California Grizzly* (1978):

> With the sounds of the torrent came . . . the growls of two wild beasts, alternate and furious.
>
> On the right hand, squatted on one end of the bridge [fallen tree trunk], was a small, male grizzly, and opposite to him, at the other end, a full-grown panther, who was tearing up the bark of the trunk, and gathering and relaxing herself as if for a spring. The alternate roaring of these infuriated beasts filled the valley with horrible echoes.
>
> We watched them a minute or more. The bear was wounded, a large flap of flesh torn over its left eye, and the blood dripping into the pool. My companion bade me shoot the tiger, while he [Colin Preston] took charge of the bear. We fired at the same instant; but, instead of falling, these two forest warriors rushed together at the centre of the bridge, the bear rising and opening to receive the tiger, who fixed her mighty jaws in the throat of her antagonist, and began kicking at his bowels with the force of an engine. At the instant both rolled over, plunged, and disappeared. We could see them struggling in the depths of the pool; bubbles of air rose to the surface, and the water became dark with gore. It may have been five minutes or more before they floated up dead, and their bodies rolled slowly down the stream (Anon., 1857).

Storer and Tevis found record of another natural fight between grizzly and mountain lion. This one originally was found in the *San Bernardino Argus* of 1873.

Some hunters were witness to a desperate fight in the San Jacinto mountains, the other day, between a mountain lion and a bear. The fight is described as terrific. The superior strength of the bear easily enabled him to throw his antagonist down, but the latter used his paws and jaws so fearfully that the bear could not keep him under. Both animals were covered with blood. They fought till both were exhausted, when the lion dragged himself off to the jungle, leaving the bruno in possession of the field.

Our human species, *Homo sapiens sapiens,* can count among its members a number of individuals who possess a combustible pair of traits: an idle mind and very little common sense. Many such people die before they become very old, proving the Darwin's notion of "survival of the fittest." Some, however, have grown old enough to write their memoirs, or to tell their tales to those who write accounts for them, which is how some of their bizarre behaviors are known to the present day.

Consider this story, found in the pages of *California Grizzly:*

... mountain lions sometimes were taken in the live traps built near Monterey to catch bears for the arena. Then a bear-and-lion fight would be arranged. Mr. Post saw such a contest at Castroville in 1865 when he was six years old and remembered it vividly. The lion, which seemed to have no fear, leaped onto the bear's back and while clinging there and facing forward scratched the grizzly's eyes and nose with its claws. The bear repeatedly rolled over onto the ground to rid himself of his adversary; but as soon as the bear was upright, the cat would leap onto his back again. This agility finally decided the struggle in favor of the lion.

Noah Smithwick wrote of an adventure with a "panther" in *The Evolution of a State; or, Recollections of Old Texas Days* (1900):

Another time a squad of us were out scouting on the head of Gilleland's creek. The country was mostly open, but here and there were motts of chaparral and prickly pears, forming a veritable stronghold for any animal that chose to avail himself of it. In passing one of these motts we saw a large panther run into it by a narrow pathway. We immediately circled his lair, and whenever a fellow caught sight of the game he blazed away, regardless of those on the further side.

One or more shots taking effect, the panther assumed the offensive. We had a green [untried] fellow along, Butler by name. Not being able to handle a rifle, we armed him with a musket. Anxious to distinguish himself he dismounted and started into the jungle on foot to "beard the lion in his den."

Just then the enraged beast came into view from my position, making straight for Butler, its hair turned the wrong way, its tail erect, and eyes like balls of fire.

"Look out, Butler, he's coming!" I shouted. Just then Butler caught sight of the panther.

"The Jesus!" he cried, "look at his eyes!" And dropping his musket he crashed through the brush and prickly pears, regaining the open just as the infuriated animal made a spring for him [Butler]. Fortunately the panther was so crippled that his spring was rendered ineffectual, and before he could collect himself for another I shot him dead. It took Butler some time to get rid of the cactus needles, and he never got rid of the joke while he remained in the service.

Theodore Roosevelt wrote this account in *The Wilderness Hunter* (1893):

In 1886 a cougar killed an Indian near Flathead Lake. Two Indians were hunting together on horseback when they came on the cougar. It fell at once to their shots, and they dismounted and ran towards it. Just as they reached it it came to, and seized one, killing him instantly with a couple of savage bites in the throat and chest; it then raced after the other, and, as he sprung on his horse, struck him across the buttocks, inflicting a deep but not dangerous scratch. I saw this survivor a year later. He evinced great reluctance to talk of the event, and insisted that the thing which had slain his companion was not really a cougar at all, but a devil.

Roosevelt's narration continued with this tale of near-tragedy, again brought about by human instigation:

A she-cougar does not often attempt to avenge the loss of her young, but sometimes she does. A remarkable instance of the kind happened to my friend, Professor John Bache McMaster, in 1875. He was camped near the head of Green River, Wyoming. One afternoon he found a couple of cougar kittens, and took them into camp; they were clumsy, playful, friendly little creatures. The next afternoon he remained in camp with the cook. Happening to look up he suddenly spied the mother cougar running noiselessly down on them, her eyes glaring and tail twitching. Snatching up his rifle, he killed her when she was barely twenty yards distant.

Vice President–elect Theodore Roosevelt went on a cougar hunt in Colorado in 1901. His hunting companions were Philip B. Stewart and Dr. Gerald Webb of Colorado Springs. The weather was frightful when they reached Meeker on January 11, after having driven forty miles from the railroad. It was eighteen below zero. John H. Goff met them in Meeker and the men left the next morning on horseback for Goff's ranch. Roosevelt himself stayed out for five weeks, during which he hunted north of the White River, close to Coyote Basin and Colorow Mountain.

No one has ever questioned Roosevelt's bravery. However, when his cougar hunting exploits are gauged against a typical modern-day mountain lion hunt, one is left questioning the man's sanity. Here Roosevelt relates in his own words one such adventure:

The next day, after two hours' ride, we came upon an old trail. It led among low hills, covered with piñon and cedar, and broken by washouts and gullies, in whose sharp sides of clay the water had made holes and caves. Suddenly the dogs began to show great excitement, and then one gave furious tongue at the mouth of a hole in some sunken and broken ground not thirty yards to our right. The whole pack rushed toward the challenge, the fighters leaped into the hole, and in another moment the row inside told us that they had found a cougar at home. We jumped off and ran down to see if we could be of assistance. To get into the hole was impossible, for two or three hounds had jumped down to join the fighters, and we could see nothing but their sterns. Then we saw Turk backing out with a dead kitten in his mouth. I had supposed that a cougar would defend her young to the last, but such was not the case in this instance. For some minutes she kept the dogs at bay, but then gradually gave ground, leaving her three kittens. Of course the dogs killed them instantly, much to our regret, as we would have given a good deal to have kept them alive. As soon as she had abandoned them, away she went completely through the low cave, leaped out at the other end, which was thirty yards off, scaled the bank, and galloped into the woods, the pack getting after her at once. She did not run more than a couple of hundred yards, and as we tore up on our horses we saw her standing in the lower branches of a piñon only six or eight feet from the ground. She was not snarling or grinning, and looked at us as quietly as if nothing had happened. As we leaped out of the saddles she jumped down from the tree and ran off through the pack. They were after her at once, however, and a few yards farther on she started up another tree. Either Tony or Baldy grabbed her by the tip of the tail, she lost her footing for a moment, and the whole pack seized her.

She was a powerful female of about average size, and made a tremendous fight. Savage enough she looked, her ears tight back against her head, her yellow eyes flashing, and her great teeth showing as she grinned. For a moment the dogs had her down, but biting and striking, she freed her head and fore quarters from the fighters, and faced us as we ran up, the hounds still having her from behind. This was another chance for the knife, and I cheered on the fighters. Again they seized her by the head, but though absolutely staunch dogs, their teeth had begun to suffer, and they were no longer always able to make their holds good. Just as I was about to strike her she knocked Turk loose with a blow, bit Baldy, and then, her head being free, turned on me. Fortunately, Tony caught her free paw on that side, while I jammed the gun-butt into her jaws with my left hand and struck home with the right, the knife driving straight to the heart. The deep fang marks she left in the stock, biting the corner of the shoulder clean off, gave an idea of the power of her jaws.

Another attack took place between Adams and Barriere lakes in south-central British Columbia. The date was December 22, 1929. The lion hunter was E. Boyd Hilderbrand, neighbor to Jimmie Fehlhaber, the 14-year-old orphan who had been living with Hilderbrand's neighbor at the time he was killed by a mountain lion. In Hilderbrand's own words, "This was one of the few authenticated cases [at the time] of a cougar making an unprovoked attack on a human. It gave me a lot of satisfaction to hunt these cats . . . I was one of the first to reach the grisly scene of [Fehlhaber's] death. What I saw left me with an unquenched hatred for cougars and started me on a lifelong onslaught on all members of the breed."

This night, Hilderbrand had retired early at about 7:00 P.M. He was awakened sometime later by the scream of a cougar. Hilderbrand's lion dog, Spot, took up the chase in the middle of the snowstorm that had the land in its grip. Hilderbrand, who was 37 years old at the time, gave chase. Within a span of several hours, and in the midst of the snowstorm, Hilderbrand killed three mature cougars. He then found his way back to his camp and went to bed, even though Spot was barking "treed" on a fourth cougar.

Spot returned to Hilderbrand's side sometime during the night. The next morning, the man was unsure that he would be able to locate his three dead cougars until he started out. He immediately cut the pug marks of the fourth cougar. Simply by following those tracks, he was able to locate each of the three cougars he'd shot the preceding night. The fourth cougar almost seemed to be paying its respects to each of its buddies.

Hilderbrand continued to track the fourth cat. He heard a row, followed, and determined that he'd been listening to the cougar kill a big five-point mule deer buck. Soon afterwards, he heard Spot bark treed. When he followed, he saw the cougar standing on a leaning windfall, some fifteen feet above the ground and about sixty yards distant. Hilderbrand shot at the cat, but the hair puffed on the cat's ribs, a little too far back. The cat took off, but Spot treed it again within sixty yards.

Hilderbrand takes up the account:

Spot was doing her best to get a chunk of cougar between her teeth, and the cat was spitting vehemently, while taking vicious uppercuts in her direction. I walked up to within 15 feet and drew the handgun out of the holster, raising it at arm's length with the barrel almost straight up.

In that instant, fate decided to throw in the final chilling touch to my greatest cougar-hunting adventure. A huge mass of wet snow dropped from directly above me and landed squarely on the upended barrel. I should have known better than to take my eyes from the cat, but I never thought she might jump me. I reached down, broke off a small twig, and inserted it into the pistol barrel. I was working out the snow when a sudden movement caught my eye and caused me to looke up. The cougar had crouched and was already in the middle of an open-jawed, death-dealing spring.

She came sailing at me as if she'd been shot from a circus cannon—a heart-stopping vision of hate-filled eyes, white teeth and hook-rimmed paws. In one instinctive lunge, I threw myself down and to one side. The cat sailed by, practically combing my whiskers with a vicious hooking swipe as she passed. If she'd ever landed on bare ground I wouldn't be telling this story. But when she hit that deep, wet snow and tried to turn, she momentarily lost her footing. In the extra second it tok her to get her feet gathered, I had time to half roll and twist and face her charge.

There was no time to worry about snow in the barrel. I thrust the pistol in her face and felt, more than heard, the staccato hammering as I ran a full magazine of slugs into her oncoming head and body. She died in midstride, falling within inches of my outstretched leg.

It would be foolish to say I wasn't scared, but at a time like that the will to survive overcomes all fear. I was completely aware that I had come within a hairbreadth of vanishing in the Canadian wilds. Apparently, all the indignities I had inflicted upon this cougar were just too much. I had set my dog on her, killed her companions, taken a deer away from her, and then followed all this up by wounding her.

There are many more thrilling tales of men and women who have forced the cougar to react in what may have been, for that particular cat, an uncharacteristic way. But as long as there are men and women who dare to push the envelope, and as long as there are cougars in the wilderness, such conflicts will continue to occur.

6

British Columbia and Alberta Attacks

Many knowledgeable people consider British Columbia to be the cougar attack capital of North America. A study completed in 1991 revealed that 29 of the 50 confirmed attacks that had been recorded at that time had taken place in British Columbia. With more than 4,000 cougars now estimated to be inhabiting the province, it is a trend that continues to the present day. The province's highest mountain lion concentrations are found in the Kootenays, the southern interior, Vancouver Island, and the Cariboo region. Supposedly, a few years ago one bold lion even wandered inside the parking garage of the Empress Hotel in Victoria.

Cougars and bears present a very real danger to people in British Columbia. During the 29 years from 1969 to 1997, 133 people in the province died after encounters with animals. Sixty-six of these deaths were caused by domesticated animals, however, while a slight majority of 67 were attributed to wild animals, according to statistics released by the quarterly report of B.C.'s Vital Statistic's Agency.

Here are the details of British Columbia's recorded mountain lion attacks, as provided by several different sources, including the Wildlife Branch, British Columbia Ministry of the Environment, correspondence forwarded to me by various interested parties, newspaper accounts, and interviews. A few of these attacks have not been reported upon before:

In the early 1800s, a woman who had been riding near York, B.C., was thrown from her horse after the animal was startled by a cougar. The cougar followed the woman as she then retreated toward her home. During the walk, the cat became increasingly aggressive to the point of lunging at her with its claws and ripping her dress.

The woman's father later went hunting for the cougar and, with the help of his two dogs, killed the animal.

1915: A boy, 10, was attacked and injured while standing near his father's home near Bella Coola, B.C. J.R. Lowther reported that "this was the first instance of a human being attacked in the province." The citation, which was unavailable, was referred to in an internal B.C. Ministry of the Environment document as: Lowther, J.R. 1915. Unknown publisher. 132 pp.

1920: A cougar attacked a brother and sister near Duncan, B.C. No other details are known. This attack was referenced in Ministry of Environment, Lands and Parks, records of July 1972. Wildlife Branch Files.

October, 1942: Jack Carson, a trapper who lived on Horsefly Lake, was hauling in a load of winter supplies between the lake and Quesnel. Carson's cabin was located four miles north of Horsefly Lake. To get what he needed inside before the worst of the winter converged on the place, Carson had been making two trips each day.

Carson decided to lighten his load by discarding his rifle, a 6.5 mm. Mannlicher. He actually left it at the cabin on the day in question, but upon further reflection, went back in and brought it along.

The man had covered about half of the distance to the lake when he heard a sudden disturbance in the thick forest just ahead of him. With no big trees to hide behind, Carson stepped in back of a small lodgepole pine to see what kind of crittur might be racing towards him. At first, the man felt certain it was a moose, since it was deep in the rutting season. But as it drew near, the one thing Carson was able to discern was that it wasn't a moose. When the animal finally flashed into his line of sight, Carson had a brief moment in which the color of its coat registered in his brain: it was tawny, rather like a faded deer. With that small amount of information to go on, Carson now believed it was a deer charging at him at a dead run, but in the very next moment, he had to amend that thought as a big cougar leaped out of some nearby brush and rose towards his face!

Luckily, the small pine Carson was standing behind blocked the cougar's leap. The cat slammed into the tree and dropped down onto the ground directly in front of the stunned man. Carson aimed his rifle and squeezed the trigger. Nothing. Then he remembered. After cleaning and drying the gun back at his cabin, he'd forgotten to bolt a shell into its chamber. Now he might be about to pay for his forgetfulness with his life.

The cougar lay crouched at his feet for an instant, then bounded up onto a windfall fifteen feet away from the man. It crouched there, ready to leap, its long, thick tail twitching back and forth in constant, agitated motion.

Before the animal could gather itself, however, Jack Carson recovered his wits. He jacked a shell into his rifle's chamber, aimed at the big cat's head, and this time, the gun fired. The cougar's body went slack as she tumbled from the windfall.

Carson later estimated that a mere four or five total seconds had elapsed from the time he had first heard the commotion in the brush until the moment the cougar dropped dead from the windfall. It had seemed, it had almost *been* a lifetime.

When Carson skinned the cat, he noticed her udders were full of milk. The big female may have been defending her kittens, which may have been secreted nearby.

From a letter by G. A. West, supervisor, British Columbia Predator Control, February 11, 1960:

May 1951: A man was attacked when he stepped out of his cabin near the town of Boston Bar on the Fraser River Canyon. [The man's] dog drove the cougar off, but was killed doing it.

This attack was further elaborated upon in Harold Danz's *Cougar* (1999): The victim stepped out of his door to see a cougar on the porch. The cougar immediately attacked the man, knocking him down and mauling him. His dog came on the run, barking, and the cougar turned his attention to the dog, permitting the man to reach the safety of his home. After killing the dog, the cougar left.

Squamish, B.C. 1951: A man who had stopped to repair his bulldozer was rushed by a cougar. He ran a few steps, mounted his rig and was lightly clawed by the cat as he did so. This may be the same incident as the one mentioned below, which took place on 30 June 1957. The details are quite similar, plus one account indicated that the reporting party was unable to read the year properly and could not tell whether it was 1951 or 1957.

June 30, 1957: Chris Wyssen, 29, a Swiss immigrant who had lived in the area for about five years, was operating a bulldozer in a logging operation about eight miles north of Squamish. Wyssen, who was bulldozing out a road on property owned by A. C. Finter, was driving his rig down a logging road when he decided to stop for a moment to "grease" his 'dozer. When he was through, he turned around and "I saw a cougar slinking along behind," Wyssen later said. "I let out a yell and jumped back up on the bulldozer track. The cougar flashed up one of its forepaws, ripped my pants and scratched my leg."

Wyssen said he noticed four other cougars watching from a nearby log pile.

"I turned up the throttle on my 'dozer and roared the motor as loud as I could," he said, as he attempted to frighten the "pack" away, "but they didn't budge."

The bold cougar that had scratched Wyssen the man later estimated at about 120 pounds. After it lashed out at the man, it just lay down upon the ground close to the bulldozer and watched the man. Wyssen said this worried him enough that he decided to leave the area. In his excitement, though, he was unable to get the bulldozer into the proper gear. He ground gears and made a clattering racket for several moments before he was finally able to find the proper gear and drive off in the direction of his parked car.

The five cougars remained undaunted. They loped after the man on the machine until he was finally able to lose them.

When informed of the incident, a RCMP (Royal Canadian Mounted Police) officer wasted no time in arriving upon the scene. He was joined by Wyssen, Finter, and Finter's son, Donald, age 10. Two cougars were killed by Irwin Thorn, a local hunter, soon after the attack on Wyssen. Skate Hames, of Campbell River, and Al West, of the provincial game department in Vancouver, later arrived with six dogs to see if they might be able to locate and destroy the remaining cats. Although the men remained in the area for five days, they neither found nor killed any additional cougars.

A. C. Finter later stated that he believed that "the cougars had not eaten for a month." The two that had been shot right after the attack were about five feet long and weighed no more than thirty pounds each. Although five cougars initially were said to have been involved, a B.C. Predator Control report placed the blame on a female and her three half-grown kittens, all in very poor shape.

July 1958: According to the B.C. Wildlife Branch, two cougars attacked a group of children during the month. Two young girls were wounded in the attacks. The cougars were later killed. One animal was a three-year-old male, the other a three-year-old female. Both were in good condition. No other details are available. Biologists consider these incidents as two separate attacks due to the number of cougars involved.

June 15, 1963: The three children of Robert Moore, a millworker from Prince George, were just returning from a fishing trip when disaster struck. The children—Michael, 8, Diana, 7, and Bobbie, 6—were not far from the family's home ten miles north of Prince George when a cougar suddenly appeared from out of a clump of bushes growing close to the road.

The animal scarcely hesitated. It lunged at Bobbie, the youngest, clawed into the youngster's shoulders, and then sank its fangs into the back of the boy's head. The fangs narrowly missed severing an artery.

Michael and Diana, who had been walking a short distance ahead of Bobbie, heard their younger brother scream. Michael looked around and noticed a discarded spade lying along the roadside. He picked it up and charged at the cougar.

"While Mike beat at the cougar with the spade, Diana pelted it with the fish they had just caught," said Robert Moore.

"I think the combination of the spade, the fish, and the kids yelling persuaded the cougar that he had met his match."

The children's shouts were heard by Mrs. Moore, who summoned Mr. Moore to the scene. By the time the father arrived, however, the cougar already had fled.

Descriptions of the cougar pointed to a young animal, perhaps a yearling, that was just learning how to fend for itself.

March 5, 1965: Jim Baker, 43, owned a cattle ranch near Loon Lake, about 25 miles northwest of Ashcroft, B.C. On March 5, Baker had gone out into one of his pastures with John Simpkins, 15, who had decided to quit school to try his hand at ranching and cowboying. The two were building a barbed-wire fence.

Simpkins was standing about 60 feet downhill from Baker when the rancher caught sight of a cougar easing out from behind a clump of junipers just a few yards from Simpkins.

The rancher yelled, "Look out, a cougar!" but Simpkins only had time to turn his head. "I saw it in mid-air, right above me," he would say later, "then it landed on me with such force, its weight knocked me flat on my back." Measurements taken later determined that the cougar had cleared 16 feet in a single leap in its eagerness to reach the teenager. With this action, the cougar had treated the boy exactly as it would have a deer, according to statements provided to the press by John Lesowski, investigating officer for the British Columbia Department of Fish and Game.

Simpkins was in a desperate situation. The cat was on top of him, lunging with its fangs at his head and neck. Simpkin's first action was to simply throw up his hand to protect his face and throat. The cougar remained undeterred. It bit through the shielding hand and then lunged for the part of his head directly above Simpkins' eyes. The cat's razor-sharp canines ripped apart

Simpkins's forehead and scalp. Baker knew that if Simpkins didn't keep his chin firmly lowered, it would be all over in a moment. He shouted instructions to that effect and was gratified when Simpkins seemed to understand and respond. The boy's chin moved down. At the same time, Baker raced toward the two combatants.

When Baker reached the fight, he didn't hesitate. He jumped astride the cat and tried desperately to drag it off the boy. But the cat was determined. "It was holding on tight and wouldn't let go," Simpkins later said. The animal's jaws clamped down even tighter on young Simpkins. "Blood was streaming down my face into my eyes, but I saw Jim pull out his knife and sit on the cougar's back so it couldn't turn around at him." Baker had jerked out his pocketknife. Now he jabbed its blade deep into the cat's throat. Although he wasn't able to sever the cougar's jugular, the sudden stabbing pain must have been enough to convince the animal to break off its attack. It screamed and, perhaps in pain, ran to a nearby brushpile.

Running now on pure adrenaline, Baker snatched one of the hammers the two had been using to build fence. He headed toward the cat with one idea fixed in his mind—to kill this animal before it killed them. When he was only four feet away, however, the cougar bounded up into a tree and out of Baker's reach.

Baker now gave up on the cougar and ran back to help the badly bleeding boy. Simpkins had gone into shock, and Baker had all he could do to get the boy to the hospital alive. Between thirty and forty stitches would be needed to close the lacerations on his face, head, and arm, but he would survive. After ten days in the hospital, John Simpkins came home. He was one of the lucky ones—someone who had survived an attack by a predatory cougar.

The morning following the attack, Jim Baker returned to the attack scene with a neighbor. The cat had fled.

Another twenty-four hours would pass before John Lesowski and Frank Richter, another B.C. conservation officer, arrived on the scene. The two officers picked up the lion's track more than a mile away from the attack scene. Crusted snow made tracking impossible, and trailing nearly so.

Later that day, Richter spotted a small, gaunt cougar cross the road near the scene of the attack. The officers' dogs quickly treed it and the officers shot and killed the animal.

The cougar was a female, about three years of age. She measured over six feet in length, but weighed just 70 pounds instead of the 100 to 125 pounds a healthy three-year-old B.C. female lion should have weighed. An examination later determined that the animal was starving.

June 18, 1966: (This is apparently the same attack as one included in a Wildlife Branch summary as having taken place in October, 1966.) Ken Nash, 16, went out to round up his father's cows on the family ranch near Chilcotin when a cougar started to chase him. As the boy ran off, he lost his rubber boot. When the cougar broke off its pursuit to jump on the boot, the boy was able to make it back to the farm home.

When Ken's father later shot the animal, pieces of the boot were found in its stomach along with the remains of a small prey animal. A conservation officer who performed the necropsy on the cougar said that it was "abnormally lean."

June 15, 1970: Kootenay National Park, 1970: A cougar attacked Daphne Smith, a 50-year-old woman who had gone hiking in the park with a group known as The Rocky Mountain Ramblers Association. Sometime during the day, Smith got separated from her hiking group on the Kindersley Creek Trail about three miles from the park's highway, not far from Radium Hot Springs in eastern B.C. As Smith trekked down into a gully, she saw a cougar running directly at her from some trees.

"I stopped and stood my ground," Smith said. "She came up to within four feet of me and we stared at each other for about 60 seconds.

"Then she lunged at me. I dodged, and her claws caught me in the left arm, lacerating it most of the way around."

The cougar backed up, giving Smith time to slip her pack from her back and set it up as a shield. "I knew I was in a bad situation," she said. "I knew that you must never run from a wild animal, or show fear. I began talking to her the way you would if you were trying to soothe a dog or a cat."

Smith believed that the cat was trying to protect a litter of kittens, although no evidence was ever uncovered to support that supposition.

"As long as I kept talking and remained motionless, the cougar would make no move toward me. When I stopped speaking or tried to move out of the way, the cougar would twitch its tail and bare her fangs."

Smith pulled her raincoat out of her pack and used it to cover her arm so that the smell of blood wouldn't further excite the cougar. After a 30-minute stand-off, the cougar let the woman move slowly away. "The cougar sniffed at the blood I'd lost upon the ground, but she remained calm. She wouldn't leave. She just lay down [upon the ground] and continued to watch me."

Smith backed up slowly until she reached a large log. She couldn't get over it without a lot of motion that might incite another attack from the cat. She called out for help, trying not to scream, again because she was afraid of exciting the animal. The other hikers heard the woman's calls and one of them blew on a whistle, which succeeded in frightening the cougar away.

After giving Smith first aid in the field, the hikers then transported her to Invermere Hospital, where her lacerations were stitched.

Smith later stated that she had no fear of wild animals. She said that the fault was hers because she "should have had my whistle in my mouth and made a lot of noise as I walked. Then the cougar probably would not have come close at all.

"I wasn't conscious of the pain. I just wanted to get away from the cougar. I got her under control with my voice, but I was afraid that I wouldn't be able to hold her much longer."

December 21, 1970: Dennis Collie, 29, was returning from the wash-house at 10-Mile Camp, a logging operation near Harrison Lake in lower British Columbia. A mountain lion, lying in ambush, leaped onto Collie as he passed. "I thought it was one of the other guys roughhousing," Collie remarked afterward. "But then I felt the teeth and the claws."

The animal bit Collie's jaw and was clawing at his shoulders and back. Collie fought back, struggling with the mountain lion for about three minutes and finally succeeding in getting the animal on its back.

Camp owner Don Williams came running out with a .303 rifle but was afraid to shoot for fear of hitting Collie.

When Williams finally shot, Collie jumped up and started running away. Williams was able to kill the cat with a second shot.

Collie was taken to a hospital to be stitched back together. "I don't know how many stitches it took," he was reported to have said in the Dec. 23, 1970 edition of the *Vancouver Sun*. "I lost count."

The animal was a two-year-old female cougar of normal weight. Williams took its pelt and had it made into a beautiful cougar rug, which he then gave to Dennis Collie.

January 2, 1971: Young John Lawrence Wells, age 12, was playing by some railroad tracks about 200 yards from his home with his sisters, Bernadette, 10, and Valerie, 7. The children were on an embankment, playing in a culvert. The youngsters tried to convince their dog to go through, but the animal wouldn't budge. When Lawrence crawled out of the culvert, a cougar rushed up and seized him.

"The dog must have sensed something," said Nathalie Cenname, one of the family's neighbors.

The cat started dragging the boy away as the Lawrence's two sisters raced off for help. John Wells, the children's father and a local prospector, grabbed a rifle and responded immediately. Mrs. Wells also rushed to the scene. When the pair arrived at the culvert, they couldn't see anything. The husband and wife then crawled inside the culvert just in time to see the cougar drag their son's body away toward the underbrush.

The father fired his rifle at the animal. He aimed high, in hopes that his son was still alive. He shot three times, wounding the cougar. The animal then dropped the boy and fled. Unfortunately, young Wells was dead when his father reached him.

The Royal Canadian Mounted Police later trailed the cougar and found it lying in the brush about 50 yards from where Wells had shot it. One officer shot the cat twice more to be certain it was dead.

The Vancouver Sun (April 6, 1971) reported Lawrence's father as saying, "When it killed my son, it couldn't have weighed more than 90 pounds. It was starved." Dr. Paul Beier, the noted cougar researcher, indicated in his landmark 1991 study, "Cougar Attacks on Humans in the United States and Canada," that this cat was an old male, approximately 12 years old.

Late summer or early fall 1972: From a letter to Matt Austin from Ray Slavens, dated June 12, 1997:

> Matt, in reviewing this I noticed a Jan. 1971 [incident at] Lytton, 12-year-old. [See above.] This sounds similar to one that is missing in [the] 1972 [records]. I believe it was [in] Lillooet where a young boy was killed by a cougar in the garbage dump. The bowel of that cougar was tangled [up] with a sheet of plastic. I started in Burnaby in June 72 and left in July 73 and took part in the necropsy so I am sure it was late summer or early fall of 72. I do not believe that it was a large cat, a small male, as I remember.

As far as can be determined, this is the first time this particular fatality has been reported upon outside of British Columbia.

June 1, 1975: William Atsma of Abbotsford, B.C., his wife, and her four children were camped on the Pitt River across from Coquitlam in lower British Columbia. The family's camp was on a beach near Polder Landing.

On Sunday morning, the family decided to hike to the top of a nearby mountain so that they might overlook their campsite. Eight-year-old Kevin Jones and his 13-year-old sister, Marilyn, decided to run up ahead of the rest of their group. The boy had just started off along a row of bluffs when a large cougar grabbed him. Marilyn turned around and ran back, shouting, "There's a cougar up there. He's going to get Kevin."

At first Atsma didn't believe the girl. Then he heard Kevin screaming. Atsma grabbed an oar from their boat and quickly ran up the hill to the boy's aid.

When Atsma arrived upon the scene, the cat had already subdued Kevin and was in the process of dragging the boy's body into the brush. "I just stuck out the oar and started waving it at the cat," Atsma said. "I yelled as loud and as long as I could." The strategy worked. The 38-year-old construction worker was able to drive the cougar away from Kevin, but the cat now started circling Atsma.

"He was crouching, getting ready to pounce," Atsma said. "I pushed the oar at him again and shouted, 'Get away, get off!'"

Eventually, the cat retreated and slunk back into the brush.

At first Atsma was terrified that the cougar had killed his foster son. Then he noticed that the boy was still breathing shallowly. Picking him up, he raced back to the boat, paddled back to the car, then drove him to a hospital for treatment. The boy was seriously injured with face, neck, chest, and arm wounds.

Animal-control officer Jack Lay brought dogs to the scene. The dogs were able to pick up the cat's track and tree it. Lay then shot the cat. The animal was a large male cougar in very good condition. It weighed 130 pounds.

Lay later remarked that William Atsma had been "very brave and very lucky." He further added this: "If the cougar had been determined, there is no way a man swinging an oar would have scared it off. They're so quick. The cat would have been on him before he could even swing the oar."

February 19, 1979: A girl, age 9, was attacked by a cougar at Boston Bar. She did not have time to react before the cougar was on her. She did try to fight back. The attack was not fatal, but there is no record of the girl's injuries, either.

The cougar was later shot. It was a five-year-old female with a measured mass considered below normal for its age.

July 3, 1991: It was Wednesday, a brilliant, sunny day. Larraine Leach, 44, was expecting five preschoolers to arrive that day at her day-care center. Because the weather was so nice, Leach planned on taking the group for a nature walk to a nearby river. All the children arrived by 10:00 A.M., so Leach gathered them up, called to her German shepherd, Pal, and the small party set off on their walk. As the children walked downhill toward the river, they picked berries that were growing along the way. When Leach looked up from her berry picking, she was terrified to see that a cougar had pinned two-and-a-half-year-old Mikey Allen to the ground and was licking his face. Not exactly an attack, perhaps, but frightening just the same. Was the lion checking the boy to find out if he tasted 'edible'?

To make matters more tense, one of the girls was giggling and telling the cougar to "Stop licking Mikey's face!" At that point, the cat started mauling the boy.

Leach sprang into action, grabbing the cougar by its neck and shaking him vigorously. The cat now focused its attention on the daycare provider, hissing and spitting as it faced her. The cougar quickly cuffed the woman on the ear and head. Leach called to her dog, Pal, but the dog refused to respond.

When Leach backed away from the cat, Pal charged and chased the cougar to a nearby tree.

Mikey was taken to Lillooet District Hospital, where forty stitches were needed to close the wounds on his face and back. Another girl, Lisa O'Laney, was treated for minor injuries received when the cougar clawed her during the melee. Both children were released from the hospital the same day.

The cougar was shot eight days later by a neighbor.

May 16, 1993: A 16-year-old boy was walking his German shepherd near the bank of a creek close to Cherryville when a cougar attacked him. The boy's father and grandfather were walking some distance behind the teen-ager. When the cougar leaped, it landed on the boy's back, throwing him to the ground. The attack happened so quickly that the boy was unable to react ahead of time. Now he was in a desperate fight. He finally managed to throw the cat off of him, then climbed a nearby tree. The cat walked off on its own several minutes later.

Lumby RCMP Constable Henshel and Conservation Officer Rattee were summoned to the scene. They called in a cougar hunter who tracked, treed, and shot the cat 300 yards from the attack site. The one-and-a-half-year-old female cougar weighed 65 pounds and was judged in a letter by A. Envet to K. Atkinson, 17 May 1993, to have been "gaunt."

The victim was treated for minor scratches at a local hospital.

May 29, 1993: A remarkably similar attack took place in Cherryville less than two weeks later. A seven-year-old boy had been gold-panning with his father. The youngster had been standing off a short distance from his father when a cougar leaped out of the brush and onto the boy's back. As soon as the boy cried out, the cougar jumped off and ran for the cover. The boy was not hurt.

The father and son alerted the Gold Pan Resort owner, who got his firearm and hurried to the attack site. Now the cougar moved out of the bushes and began to stalk the resort owner. The man killed the cougar within ten yards of where it had attacked the youngster.

Again, the offending animal was a one-and-a-half-year-old cougar. The distinct possibility exists that it may have been a littermate to the cougar killed in the preceding case.

May 25, 1995: A railway worker was mauled on a Canadian Pacific railroad grade along the shoreline of Kootenay Lake. The man was taken by surprise, but was able to call for help on his company radio while warding off the cougar with his free hand. A fellow worker raced a half-mile down the track and succeeded in driving the cougar away with a track wrench.

The victim was transported to the Creston hospital, where he was treated for lacerations to his right arm and puncture wounds to the throat.

When conservation officers arrived at the site they were able to track down and kill the animal. Conflicting reports place the male cougar's weight at either 55 or 70 pounds.

July 7, 1996: Eight-year-old Lance Veinguessner was attacked near his family's cabin on Arrow Lake near Nakusp in southeastern British Columbia. The boy was in a group that included three other children and several adults when the attack took place. The cougar actually rushed into the middle of the group, grabbed Lance, then tried to drag him off by the throat. His father ran up and hit the animal, causing it to release him.

Lance was rushed to a Vancouver hospital. His wounds included severe damage to the trachea, vertebrae, and abdomen.

Conservation officers arrived at the scene within thirty minutes. They quickly tracked and killed the cougar, a two- or three-year-old malnourished male.

July 7, 1996: In a rare "two-fer"—two attacks on the same day—young Christine Frank, 5, was attacked while playing on a swing in front of her home in Lytton. Afterward, the cat fled into the brush. Christine was air-lifted to a hospital to be treated for unspecified injuries.

August 19, 1996: One of the most tragic cougar attacks of the past decade took place on this day near Princeton, British Columbia, a mining and ranching town 120 miles east of Vancouver. Cynthia "Cindy" Parolin, 35, had gone horseback riding through the Similkameen backcountry with her three children: David, 13, Melissa, 11, and Steven, 6. Parolin always packed a rifle when she went riding during hunting season. But this was summer, and no game was in season. The family rode along a gravel road in a fairly remote, heavily timbered area. The road doubled as a timber company haul road, used for transporting trees to sawmills, pulp mills, and processors. The family was headed to meet up with Cindy's husband, Les, and her other son, ten-year-old Billy, for a camping vacation.

The horses started to become nervous and fidgety; then, suddenly, a cougar charged out of the roadside brush and lunged at young Steve. The boy was mounted, but that didn't deter the puma. The animal leaped up around the horse's neck, grabbed onto the boy's shoe and pulled it off. The cougar frightened the boy's horse and the animal reared. Steven slid off, and when he did, the cougar attacked him, clamping its jaws around the boy's head.

Meanwhile, the mother, Cindy Parolin, screamed and jumped off her horse. Breaking off a branch from a dead tree, she charged the cougar and hit it full force in the ribs. The puma leaped off Steven and now turned its attention to the woman. A karate student, Cindy punched the cat. The two now fell to the ground, wrestling. While she was battling the animal, she yelled to her other two children to get Steven out of there and to find help.

Their horses were long gone, so David and Melissa picked up Steven and carried him the mile down the trail to where the family car was parked. David then went for help while Melissa stayed in the car with the injured boy.

Rescuers fetched by David to the attack scene, returned with the children about an hour later. It was now 7:30 P.M. "It must have been horrible," said Dawn Johnson, one of Cindy's friends, in *The Alberta Report*. "Cougars pounce and back off, pounce and back off. Cindy was of average height, five-foot-five, and of average weight, but she was fit. The animal must have spent the entire time wearing her down."

One rescuer, Jim Manion, could hear Parolin screaming. He hurried to the scene and found the cougar on top of her. The man threw rocks at the cougar, which moved off Parolin and began walking toward him. He aimed his shotgun and pulled the trigger, only to have the gun jam!

Manion now backed toward his pick-up. The cougar stopped, and Manion thought it was going to run away. Instead, it turned and came right for him. "By that time I had the gun working," Manion recalled. He fired from the hip. The charge hit the cat full-bore, and literally lifted the animal off of the ground, killing it instantly.

He rushed over to Mrs. Parolin. "Are my children safe?" she asked. When Manion replied, "Yes," RCMP Sergeant Tom Payne said she seemed to relax. Then she said, "I'm dying."

Manion picked up the woman and carried her to his pickup. She was pronounced dead on arrival at Princeton General Hospital. Her scalp, face, and torso had been so severely injured that she had lost too much blood to survive the trip to the hospital.

Steven Parolin, who suffered severe scalp lacerations, was also admitted to the hospital. Doctors closed his head wounds with 70 stitches.

The dead cougar was later found 150 yards from the attack site by Princeton senior conservation officer Jim Corbett and two colleagues. The animal was thin but, in the words of Orville Dyer, an investigating officer, "not emaciated." The small male cougar, described by Dyer as "bigger than a kitten but smaller than a fully grown adult," weighed 63 pounds.

Dawn Johnson later emphasized how much Cindy "loved the outdoors and respected its hazards." Johnson added that Cindy "was fiercely protective of her family. She wouldn't have thought twice about sacrificing herself to save any one of them."

Adding to the family's troubles were reporters who demanded to know "if she was such a smart woman, then why did she get down off her horse to fight the cougar?"

Remarks like that infuriated friends and relatives. Dawn Johnson was most outspoken in her defense of the dead woman. "If [Cindy] had gone on her camping vacation two weeks later it would have been the start of the early elk hunt, and she would have been packing a rifle." As it is, British Columbia's strict gun laws allow only prospectors and some forest workers to carry pistols, and a special $20 permit is required for rifles outside of hunting season. "Certainly if guns were carried, many of these attacks would be prevented," agreed B.C. conservation officer Corbett.

At Parolin's funeral service, 600 mourners gathered to hear the Rev. Chris Haugland state, "God was with [Cindy Parolin] every moment of her life, strengthening her to do what she had to do."

April 17, 1999: A young girl,* 8, was running with two other girls down a roadway at Kawkawa Lake Camp near Hope. The three girls were just 30 yards ahead of a large group of children and adults. The time was 12 o'clock.

---

*B.C. has strict privacy laws. Although the name of the child is known, the parents' request that it not be released will be honored.

Suddenly, from out of nowhere, a small female cougar raced up behind the victim, leaped on her, and knocked her down. The girl screamed as the cougar bit at her face and started chewing on her head. One woman with the group was able to rush up to assist the child, striking the cougar repeatedly with a tree limb she'd picked up. The cougar finally released the girl and backed off a short distance. The woman grabbed the girl and ran from the site.

The girl was rushed to Fraser Canyon Hospital and then transferred to Children's Hospital in Vancouver. She was suffering from severe facial lacerations, eye damage, and punctures in her chest. For some time it was feared that the child would lose an eye.

At 12:45 P.M., conservation officer Jim Corbett arrived. Corbett soon treed a cougar within 60 yards of the attack site, and officer Jim Strahl destroyed it. The cougar's age was estimated at between six and eight months. Its weight was between 35 and 40 pounds. According to Corbett, "It appears [the cat] hasn't eaten for some time."

Corbett said the woman's quick thinking saved the girl's life. "She ran to a child that wasn't her own and beat off the cougar," he said. "She thought only of protecting the child, not herself. She's a hero, no question about it."

January 24, 2000: In an ironic twist of fate, a man who supplies cougar hounds to the province's conservation officer service responded to a complaint of a cougar killing a dog. The dog's carcass had been recovered after being dragged into a ditch behind the backyard of a house near Bella Coola. Although shots had been fired at the cougar during the night, none of them had hit the animal.

The man, who had neither dogs nor firearm with him, searched the wooded area behind the house and immediately ran into a cougar crouched before him. He turned and slowly started toward his vehicle, where he'd left his gun. The cougar had other ideas, and attacked the man from behind, keying in on the victim's head and neck. The victim rolled to the ground, grasped the cougar's lower jaw, and attempted to pin the animal's forepaws underneath him as he yelled for help.

Another man heard the man yelling and responded. Reaching the scene, he fired four shots at the cat, killing it. The female cougar weighed about 80 pounds, which was estimated to be below her normal weight.

The victim was treated for serious lacerations to his head, neck, chest and hands.

January 2, 2001: Residents of Banff, Alberta will long remember this date as the day the cougars went mad. Three separate—and frightening—incidents occurred in and about a town where cougar incidents have been relatively rare historically.

The events began at 3:00 A.M. on Sulphur Mountain, about two miles southwest of Banff, when a cougar grabbed Sarah, an eight-year-old husky owned by John Peck, on the sidewalk in front of her master's house. The cat relinquished its hold on Sarah, only after Peck and his neighbor, Heinz Odenthal, rushed outside with flashlights. Peck and Odenthal searched the area and found the cougar close to the river. Much later Peck found the bruised and battered dog waiting for him at his place of business. He rushed her to a vet, where she was treated for extensive claw and puncture wounds. Sarah was well on her way to making a full recovery as this book was going to press.

That same morning, 6:45 A.M., Cheryl Hyde, an executive secretary for the town of Banff, was walking her pet schnauzer in the woods behind her house. Hyde didn't know that she and her dog had drawn perilously close to a cougar's partially-consumed elk kill until the cat confronted the pair. Startled, Hyde started screaming, then began to slowly back away, but the cougar advanced. Hyde reacted by kicking repeatedly at the animal. Luckily for Hyde, her screams had awakened her neighbor Gary Doyle. Doyle's first thought was that someone outside was attacking a woman. When he went outside to investigate the noise, he saw Hyde backing away from a relentlessly advancing cougar. Thinking quickly, Doyle flicked open his back gate. "The cougar was just two or three feet away from her and crouched low to the ground, as if ready to spring," he said. "I grabbed Cheryl, pulled her inside, and slammed the gate."

According to Hyde, Alberta game wardens later caught the cougar for relocation to a different area. "It was a large female," she said, "that weighed about 120 pounds." She also recalled that the cougar approached at times to within a mere foot of her. When she kicked at the animal, it did not swat or lunge, just merely kept advancing. "I'm lucky and I know it," Hyde stated. "The cougar was right there with me, until [Doyle] slammed the gate."

Officials also removed the elk carcass upon which the cougar had been feeding from the area. Wardens later hazed elk that had wandered close to a town farther into the backcountry. Some theorized that competition with wolves for the prey animals may have forced cougars to hunt close to town—and close to human beings. "This means cougars, which are normally wary, are rapidly losing their natural fear of people," said Ian Syme, Banff National Park's chief warden.

The Hyde encounter was a serious one, but resulted in no injuries to the woman, her rescuer, or her dog. When Hyde confides that she's "lucky," she is probably more aware of that fact than most other near-victims have been. Her awareness may stem in good part from her knowledge of the tragic incident that occurred later the same day.

It was noon in Banff National Park. Frances Frost, 30, a resident of nearby Canmore, had left her condominium to cross-country ski the Cascade Ski Trail. This scenic trail winds its way along the shoreline of Lake Minnewanka. Frost, who worked part time at a coffeehouse, often skied alone. On this day, though, she had company: a large cougar that stalked her, then leaped upon her back at about 1:00 P.M.

Soon afterward, another skier noticed Frost's body lying about 20 yards from Lake Minnewanka Road. He hurried off to report his discovery. When park wardens reached the scene, they found the cougar standing guard over Frost's body. They shot the healthy looking adult male, then evacuated the area and closed both the Lake Minnewanka Road and the nearby Cascade Fire Trail.

Back in Banff, Ed Frost, Frances's father, was watching a TV news report about the attack. Something clicked in his head, and he found himself dialing his daughter's phone number to leave a message. "Frances, I know it's not you," he said. Unfortunately, it was.

Frost, who was a lover of nature and wildlife, was cremated. Her ashes were returned to the wilderness she so loved.

7

Vancouver Island Attacks

Vancouver Island. The very name can send shivers up the spine of anyone acquainted with this picturesque island's ominous history of cougar attacks. Vancouver Island lies just off the western shore of British Columbia. Estimates vary as to the numbers of cougars inhabiting the island, but everyone agrees on one thing: There are plenty of mountain lions. Current population estimates place cougar numbers at somewhere between 700 and 800, the densest population of cougars found in North America.

Dan Lay, the former predator-control officer for the island, described the island's cats as "by far the most vicious cougars in all of [British Columbia]." Lay suggests that adult male cougars may be pushing juveniles out of occupied territories and into conflicts with humans. This is the pattern of adult male cougar behavior wherever the big cats can be found, so there must be other extenuating factors.

One of these factors might be the limited number of prey species found on the island. According to Paul Beier, absent prey species include porcupine, opossum, cottontail rabbits, coyotes, bobcats, badgers, and spotted and striped skunks, each of which, when present in abundance, could account for a substantial portion of the cougars' total diet. Beier further speculates that this "lack of small prey may be especially critical for a yearling animal less proficient at taking deer, and may contribute to the increased attacks on humans on Vancouver Island."

Where have Vancouver Island's attacks taken place? Mainly along or near the island's more remote and less-populated western shore, where cougars have less experience with humans as predators. Here is a summary of those attacks:

1914: A group of children were playing near Victoria on Vancouver Island. A cougar rushed at the children and injured two of them. The rest of the group managed to drive the animal away. No further information is known. This incident was related in a letter by G. A. West, supervisor, B.C. Predator Control, dated February 11, 1960.

September 23, 1916: Tony Farrar, age 8, and his cousin, Doreen Ashburnham, 11, decided to fetch their ponies at Doreen's parents' farm. The farm was located on the north shore of Cowichan Lake. Both children were carrying their ponies' bridles when a cougar surprised them. The cat leaped onto Tony, its claws digging deeply into the boy, while its jaws clamped around Tony's head. Doreen thought of lashing the cougar with her bridle, but was fearful she might hit Tony. Instead, the girl began beating on the cat with her fists and hands. The cougar loosened its hold and Tony was able to pull away.

The two cousins, in what could have been a fatal move, then ran for help. Tony's scalp was badly torn and his arms were ripped and lacerated. Doreen was also mauled, although not nearly so badly as Tony, whose wounds required 72 stitches.

Charles and Henry March, who lived on the other side of Cowichan Lake, were summoned. The two hunters used their dogs to chase down the cougar, which they then killed.

According to news accounts of the day, on July 26, 1917, Tony and Doreen were awarded the Albert Medal from the King of England for "Gallantry in saving life on land." The medal came to the pair after former U.S. President, Theodore Roosevelt, pleaded their case on the children's behalf. In 1974, the Albert Medals were exchanged for George Crosses. The medals are stored within the Canadian War Museum in Ottawa.

May 4, 1934: Holberg, a small town on northern Vancouver Island, has seen more than its fair share of cougar problems. On this particular day, Soren Gunder Jensen, a 56-year-old man known as "Sam," was walking along the Government Road at Holberg when he was suddenly attacked by a cougar. Jensen, who had been going out to cut some wood, was carrying an axe across his shoulder. When the animal struck him, it did so with such force that it knocked the axe out of Jensen's hand and onto the road. The animal then bit Jensen's upper left arm. Jensen's first impulse was to try to break the grip of the animal's jaws by using his free hand to force them apart. He was unable to do this, so he then began struggling to reach his axe. After several long, anxious moments, he was able to grab the axe handle. He aimed a blow at the mountain lion with the intention of sinking the axe bit between the animal's shoulders. Instead, he only hit the cat's shoulder a glancing blow. As soon as it was hit, the cougar released Jensen and bounded back across the road. The animal made no attempt to follow Jensen when the man began his retreat back toward his home.

When Jensen explained what had happened to him, one of his neighbors, Niels Hansen, took his dog and his rifle to look for the cougar. As soon as Hansen approached the place where Jensen had been mauled, the cougar appeared and began to chase Hansen's dog. Hansen shot and killed the cougar.

Sam Jensen spent three days in the Port Alice hospital. His wounds consisted of several puncture wounds on his arm, lacerations, and a clawed-over scalp. After he was discharged from the hospital, Jensen checked into a local hotel where a doctor treated him for another week before the man was finally allowed to return home.

B.C. Wildlife Branch files also refer to an incident on this same day at Quatsino Sound, V.I. Although there may have been two cougar attacks on this day, the details of the other one—"cougar clawed a man who was later hospitalized because of the wounds"—sound suspiciously like the attack upon Jensen.

April or May, 1935: Ole Johnson was employed as a bucker by Olsen & Becker, the logging company that worked the Indian Reserve near Quatsino on Vancouver Island. While Johnson was at work this day, he bent over to clear his saw of brush so that he might finish the cut on which he was working. As he bent over, however, he felt something big fall upon his back. Johnson's first thought was that a large limb had fallen out of another tree and had struck him on his back. When he turned his head, the cougar on his back clawed and tore his face badly, opening it up from the nose and mouth clear back to his ear. Johnson began yelling for help. His screams brought his fellow workers to the scene.

A report from the British Columbia Wildlife Branch becomes uncertain at this point. "Reports on this case are somewhat vague and conflicting; one is that a policeman from Port Alice shot this cougar the next day, and another is that Johnson killed the cougar himself with his axe." In "Crazy Cougars," a December 1955 Outdoor Life article written by Frank Dufresne, the author writes, "it took two other loggers armed with axes to get the [cougar] off Johnson's back. But it didn't run very far, because a rifle-toting policeman killed it next day at the scene." No one may ever know for sure the real ending to this dramatic attack.

1940s: A cougar attacked and killed a small boy on the western coast of Vancouver Island. This was reported in a round-up of attacks organized by B.C. large carnivore biologist Matt Austin. The data is in the Wildlife Branch files. Since the following attack is also related within this file, along with the proper dates, this particular attack may actually be unrelated and unreported until now.

On June 19, 1949, seven-year-old Peter Taylor was playing at Walter's Bay, a beach near Kyuquot, Vancouver Island, not far from where his parents were picnicking with some neighbors. Suddenly, a cougar rushed out of the brush and attacked the youngster. When the parents heard the commotion, they realized what was happening, and raced to the boy's aid. More rescuers, brandishing boat tools, arrived and were able to pull the boy away from the cat, which had dragged its prey into the thick brush. Peter was still alive, although mortally injured. His head and scalp had been mangled and torn and the skull had been punctured. The boy's face was also deeply slashed and gouged, and one hand was dangling by a thread. The boy's father later told an investigator that the boy's "head was nearly torn off." The boy died, in part because heavy fog prevented an Alberni Air Lines mercy flight carrying a doctor and blood plasma from landing any closer than Ucluelet, fifty miles from Kyuquot.

B.C. Game Department hunters Jim Dewar, Skate Hames, and Bud Frost were notified of the tragedy. The weather had grounded all planes on the day of the mauling, but the three boarded an airplane the next day for travel to Kyuquot. Upon landing, their lion hounds soon treed the cougar, which was promptly shot. Investigation revealed that the cougar had been feeding on two raccoon carcasses, both of which were discovered just fifteen feet from where Peter Taylor had been attacked.

Fifty-one years ago, attitudes had not changed in any significant sense toward mountain lions; yet an article that ran in the *Daily Colonist* suggested that the boy had wandered too close as the cougar was feeding on what the newspaper reported was a "deer," and so the animal was merely "defending what was his own." The June 21, 1949, edition of *The Province* indicated that a pathological examination of the "killer" cougar was being conducted to establish "if the animal was *loco*. Game officials believe cougars which attack human beings are mentally affected and are searching for proof of their theory."

The Vancouver Sun stated that the dead cougar weighed eighty pounds, a weight considered normal for its age.

From a letter by G.A. West, supervisor, B.C. Predator Control, February 11, 1960:

July 1951: A man was mauled near the settlement of Holberg on the north end of Vancouver Island in July of 1951. No further details are available.

January 26, 1951: Ed McLean, 62, a telephone lineman who worked at Kelsey Bay, on Vancouver Island's northeast coast, had returned to one of his company's line cabins late that afternoon. McLean was accompanied by his black dog, which was part spaniel. While McLean was busy cutting wood and preparing his dinner, he noticed a cougar prowling about the premises. The man disregarded the animal, as he'd seen it hanging around the cabin before. McLean had no gun because the deep snow had made travel difficult, especially since he was already toting equipment needed to repair a downed line.

When McLean went back inside, he made certain that his dog had come in with him, then closed the cabin door behind him. At 9:00 P.M., the man undressed down to his heavy wool underwear. He checked about the cabin one last time, then stopped in front of the cabin's door. Looking through the door's window, he noticed the cougar lurking just outside. The man immediately extinguished his gas lantern, thinking that the cougar might have been attracted by the light or the movement of his hand.

No sooner had he done so when the cougar leaped right through the window, breaking the glass and grasping McLean's right elbow in its mouth. While McLean's frightened spaniel scurried out of sight beneath the man's bed, the man was somehow able to get the cougar underneath him, pinning it beneath him. The cat's fangs groped up McLean's arm, and buried into his shoulder. As the lion continued the attack, McLean remembered the butcher knife he'd left laying on the table at the opposite end of the cabin. The man now pushed the animal across the rude wood floor ahead of him, still keeping it pinned hard beneath him, all the way to the knife. But when he reached for the knife, the cougar surged beneath him and sank its teeth into his right hand, nearly severing the man's thumb. McLean still managed to reach up and grab on the knife; his strength fading, McLean stabbed the throat of the desperate cougar. The cougar started clawing at the man's head and shoulders, but now McLean could feel his knife hitting bone. The cat was definitely growing weaker, and the man was certain that he had cut the animal's throat clear through to its jugular. "My arms were chewed up so badly I didn't have strength enough to get away from him until he grew weak from loss of blood," McLean recalled in an article published in the *Vancouver Sun*.

Finally, McLean was able to drag himself over to the door. When he called his cowering dog to his side, he was shocked to see the cougar whip around to follow. Pulling his dog outside, he quickly slammed the cabin door shut.

When McLean closed the door, he could hear the cougar inside the cabin, gasping for breath. He made his way down to the dock, got into his rowboat, and started out across the bay for another line cabin, about six miles down the shore. McLean had to row into a bitter west wind clad in nothing more than his woolen underwear. He was barefoot, hatless, and his arms, hands and face were badly lacerated. Luck was on his side, though. Had the wind and the tides not cooperated, the boat might easily have drifted out to sea. Instead, he was able to make it the other line cabin, even though he barely had enough strength to stagger weakly up the path and into the cabin after dragging his boat up onto the shore.

When McLean got inside the cabin, he tried telephoning for help, but was unable to locate anyone. McLean's mutilated hands were now so sore and frozen from rowing that he couldn't even light a match. He climbed into a sleeping bag that he kept at the cabin, and began the ordeal of hanging on to life until the next morning, when he might be able to reach someone.

At 9:00 A.M., McLean was finally able to contact his Kelsey Bay office. Fred Dingwall and Bill Fersch were immediately sent out to rescue him. When Dingwall and Fersch finally reached McLean, the lineman was in terrible shape. The stormy nighttime trip across windswept seas had drained him of all his energy. He was suffering from exposure, as well as from extreme loss of blood. His wounds had hemorrhaged so much that his sleeping bag and mattress were saturated with blood. McLean's wool underwear was so thoroughly soaked with dried blood that the garment had to be cut from his body.

McLean was transported to the Salmon River Logging Company office, where he received first aid. He was then driven to Lourdes Hospital in Campbell River, arriving there late in the afternoon of the day following the attack. Meanwhile, Dingwall and Fersch returned to the cabin where the attack had taken place. When the two looked through the hole where the glass had been—and through which the cougar had launched its attack—they saw the cougar lying on McLean's bed. [Some accounts state that the cougar was beneath McLean's bed.] The animal was not yet dead. When it heard the men outside, it raised up as though readying itself to do battle once more. Wisely staying outside, one of the men shot the cat where it lay.

The cougar was later found to be a starving young female, one and a half years of age, weighing just 56 pounds.

McLean remained in the Campbell River hospital for four days. He was treated for loss of blood, exposure, and a badly chewed right elbow, left forearm, and left thumb. His body was full of claw marks and his ear had been split. He was allowed to return to Kelsey Bay on February 15.

Sometime before 1952: According to the B.C. Wildlife Branch's report, Alfred Lovik, a large man (as the report refers to him), was riding his bicycle when he encountered a cougar on the Government Road at Holberg. The cougar attempted to grab Lovik, and the man dismounted and thrust his bicycle out between himself and the cougar. Every time Lovik tried to remount his bike, the animal would move in and try to attack. Lovik was forced to back away, holding the bicycle between himself and the cat, until he reached Holbert, a distance of close to two miles.

When Lovik finally reached civilization, he was in a state of nervous and physical exhaustion. The cougar finally retreated into the nearby woods.

The report concludes: "I have no dates on this case, but it is [likely] near the same time as the other two [Jensen and Johnson], [and] likely coincides with a loss in the population of deer."

The winter of 1951–52: Here is another attack, hitherto unreported. This attack report was uncovered in B.C. Wildlife Branch correspondence between A. Haims and W. Winston Mair, dated August 30, 1952:

There is another case this last winter of an Indian of Alert Bay being attacked [by a cougar] while tending his traps on the beach. His name is Heber Weber, [and is] reportedly a reliable man. The report as I have it is secondhand, but it seems he was [checking] a mink trap and the cougar, a small one, attacked him, seizing him by the boot. Weber was able to drag it to his row boat, where he reached his gun, a .22-caliber rifle, and shot it.

March 2, 1953: Two men—R. H. "Buck" Richmond, who managed the Alaska Pine and Cellulose plant at Port Alice, and Gerald Walters, a woodsman and guide who was working at the time as a millwright for Richmond—and their sons were fishing Victoria Lake, near the north end of Vancouver Island. After several hours of fishing, they went ashore and built a fire for their lunch.

Walters, 43, walked into the timber to gather more wood for the fire. Bending over to pick and choose from the dry twigs and branches lying scattered about the forest floor, he happened to glance up and see a cougar crouched low behind a downed log, ready to spring. It hissed, then launched itself directly at the man.

"A cougar's got me!" Walters screamed. Hesitating at first, Richmond finally heard enough to convince him that Walters was in trouble. He grabbed an ax and raced to the scene.

When he arrived, he found Walters and the cougar rolling about on the ground. Walters had one hand thrust down the cat's throat and the other on the cougar's loose throat skin, trying to pull the cat's fangs away from his face and throat. For her part, the cougar was biting and clawing the man's hand for all she was worth. Richmond stood there, helpless, as the combatants rolled over and over on the ground. There was no opportunity for him to use his hatchet. Then the tide of the battle turned, as the cat rolled atop Walters and pinned him to the ground. Richmond saw his chance and attacked, driving the ax blade all the way through the cougar's spine. Amazingly, even that wasn't enough to stop the animal. The cat was significantly weakened, however, and Walters was able to twist her head to one side. Three hard whacks with the back of Richmond's ax finally killed the animal.

The female lion measured five feet seven inches. It was very thin and, according to John Lesowski, the investigating officer for the British Columbia Fish and Game Branch, near starvation and crazed by hunger. According to Richmond, "The animal was apparently desperate for food."

Gerald Walters suffered severe lacerations on his right leg and bites to his right hand. Richmond said Walters's woodsmanship helped save his life. "He knew enough to grab the cougar by the neck to keep it from clawing him," Richmond said. Eyewitnesses to the struggle included Richmond's two sons, Terry, 11, and John, 10. Walters's woodsmanship helped, but the man probably owed his life to Buck Richmond's quick thinking.

June 10, 1953: The first time the cougar had been seen prowling around the logging camp near Big [Kaikash] Creek, not far from Beaver Harbor, was on Tuesday. But there was no gun in camp, so loggers chased the cat away by hurling stones at it. Later that evening, Peter Coon chased a cougar away from his home after the cat had scratched persistently at the door of the cabin. Presumably, this was the same cougar.

The next morning, the Coon family discovered a sweater that had been torn to bits just outside their home. Mr. Coon had had enough. He told his wife to remain inside while he found someone to help him hunt down the cat and destroy it.

Mr. Lawrence "Hilly" Lansdowne, the owner of the logging camp, had also had enough. He was worried enough to warn all women and children to stay indoors until a gun could be brought from Alert Bay. Mrs. Coon didn't want to stay alone when her husband left, however. She asked if he would accompany her to a neighbor's house, where she planned to stay until the cougar was killed. Her husband relented and the pair left their cabin. Mrs. Coon was following close behind her husband when the cougar attacked. The animal, which apparently had been lying in wait beneath the family's cabin, pounced on Mrs. Coon and quickly pinned her to the ground. Lansdowne first attempted to pull the cat from Mrs. Coon, then shouted to some of his men to throw rocks at the cat. The cougar became furious after several rocks had found their marks. It reared up on its hind legs, and when it did, Lansdowne was able to grab hold of it and throw it off his wife. He then picked up Mrs. Coon and carried her into the house.

The woman was taken to Alert Bay for medical treatment. Mrs. Coon suffered severe lacerations to her shoulders and arms. Her hands were also badly chewed, as she had fought to keep the animal's fangs away from her face and throat. One report says that the cougar's claws and teeth had peeled the flesh completely off a portion of the woman's ribs.

The cougar, which disappeared into a log pile stacked near the Coon residence, was later located and killed by Skate Hames, who was hunting with three of his hounds. Hames shot the cat as it rushed from the log pile to fight with his dogs.

Paul Beier's data reports no age for the female cougar. Hames, the government hunter who killed the cougar, stated only that it was "an emaciated female weighing approximately 60 or 70 pounds."

Ironically, records for that year of overabundant mountain lions indicate almost 300 bounty kills, and even that seemed to make no discernible dent in the population.

1957: Another poorly documented attack: A man was attacked near Victoria Lake on Vancouver Island. No other details are known except that the cougar responsible was killed. It was a female that weighed 110 pounds and was "considered healthy" according to Wildlife Branch Files that reference James Y. Nicol's article in *True West,* Vol. 5, No.3, Jan/Feb, 1958.

September 12, 1969: David Zimmerman, 13, was living at the Franklin River logging camp, about 20 miles south of Port Alberni on Vancouver Island. On this beautiful fall day, the boy was on his way to his play fort. As David walked along the road, a cougar hiding in some brush rushed out and attacked.

"I started to back up," David said later, "but it came forward, sprang and grabbed my leg. I started to scream and it moved back about ten feet. Then I took off my coat and started to wave it [at the cougar], and it backed off."

David Zimmerman made a run for it and managed to escape with nothing more serious than a scratched and lacerated leg. The wounds were described as "minor."

Residents of Franklin River later tracked down and killed the cougar. Afterwards, residents of the community expressed alarm. A few called for the reestablishment of a bounty on cougars.

May 28, 1972: The date may be questionable, as other cougar researchers have reported that this mauling took place in June 1972, but the details are not. Al Hurford, age 25, from Courtenay, B.C., was camping in Strathcona Park, near the Campbell River area of Vancouver Island, when he was attacked after dark by a cougar. Hurford was one of three fishermen at the lakeside camp that night.

The attack on Hurford is unusual because it is one of the few incidents where a mountain lion deliberately approached an individual, either asleep on the ground or in a tent or other building, with the intention of killing the person. This cat slashed Hurford's head, then tried to drag him out of his sleeping bag. Hurford awakened with a start and immediately started yelling. The cougar retreated. Hurford later received 30 stitches in his scalp and 40 stitches in his arm to close up his wounds.

The cougar was never located, although a hunter tracked it with dogs after the attack. All that came of that effort was that a 130-pound hound used by the hunter was thought to have been killed by the cat during the tracking effort.

June 1972: B.C.'s Wildlife Branch files state only that "a baby survived a mauling at a Ralph River campsite," and that the "cougar was not located." Since this campsite is in Strathcona Park on Vancouver Island, site of the above lion attack on Al Hurford, it was thought that the same animal might be responsible for both attacks. Dan Dwyer, B.C. Fish and Game, on July 31, 1997, suggested that this incident occurred in 1970, not 1972.

July 26, 1972: Robert Kelly, 8, was playing with his brother, Charles, at the Miller campsite at Beavertail Lake, near Campbell River. Their mother, Roberta Kelly, was about 50 feet away from the boys, swimming in the lake. Along with a friend, the West Vancouver family had gone to the island for a camping trip/vacation.

The boys eventually decided to go back toward their campsite. Charles struck out in the lead, with Robert following. Charles turned around to say something to Bobby, and that's when he saw the cat. Charles later said, "Did you ever see a cougar's eyes when it's staring at you? They look so huge!"

Charles yelled "Look out!" at Bobby, but the cat had already sprung out at the boy and slapped him down to the ground, "the way a house cat strikes at something," in Roberta Kelly's words. The cat then pounced upon the boy. Charles shouted to Robert to "Be quiet! Play dead!" but the cougar started carrying the younger boy into the bush.

The first Roberta Kelly became aware that something was happening was when she heard both her sons screaming. She ran out of the lake and down a wooded path; when she finally saw the cougar, it was on top of Bobby and was dragging him toward the bushes.

The mother came up screaming at the cougar. She came close enough to the cat and must have sounded angry enough so that the cat dropped the boy and ran back into the brush. The mother's timely—and heroic—actions undoubtedly saved Robert's life.

Little time elapsed between the time of the attack and when Mrs. Kelly appeared on the scene, yet the cougar still inflicted massive injuries upon the youngster. The boy suffered deep lacerations where he had been clawed, and his entire scalp had been pulled away from his skull. Some people think that Robert's wounds were so severe because he played dead. The advice for anyone who ventures into cougar country is that if attacked, fight back.

Robert was rushed in critical condition to the hospital in Campbell River for emergency treatment. He was given a number of blood transfusions, and had improved enough to be removed from the critical list by the following day. Although he had to undergo plastic surgeries, thankfully there was no brain damage.

The cougar disappeared back into the woods. The animal responsible for this attack was later estimated by George Taylor, head of the federal game branch in Campbell River, to have weighed more than 100 pounds.

That same day, just 14 miles north of Campbell River, Milt Adams of Browns Bay reported that he had been chased into his house by a cougar that had sneaked up on him from bushes near his home.

July 14, 1976: Gold River, on Vancouver Island, became the site of a tragic mauling on this day. Young Matilda May Samuel, 7, had gone berry-picking with a 15-year-old girl and a 17-year-old boy. Matilda was visiting relatives who lived on a nearby Indian reserve, located across the road from the Mucha-lat pulp mill where many of the local people worked. When the three decided to go berry-picking that afternoon, they chose a spot full of berry bushes growing between the river and a gravel road. Had they known that a cougar just a few hours previously had stalked a worker who had been riding his mo-torcycle to work at the mill, they undoubtedly would have changed their plans. As it was, the cougar not only had stalked the motorcyclist, but had given serious chase once the man drove away. Unfortunately, the man had not re-ported the incident.

As they picked berries, the two teen-agers became separated from the seven-year-old. When they heard a sudden thrashing noise coming from some-where behind them, they turned around to see the cougar already upon young Matilda. They shouted at it and the animal backed away, but only momentarily. Then it pounced on Matilda again. It probably killed the girl immediately, be-cause the animal started dragging her body into nearby shrubbery.

The teenagers ran for help. They were able to flag down a passing ve-hicle, but by the time help could be summoned to the scene, the child was dead. A patrol of mounties (RCMP) located the girl's body about two hours after the attack. The victim had succumbed to severe head and facial lacera-tions. The body was found about 30 feet from where the child had been attacked.

When questioned later, the teens said they had been too scared to do anything more than run for help.

The cougar was treed and killed a short distance from the scene of the attack. The animal was a two-year-old male that measured seven feet from the end of its nose to the tip of its tail. The cat reportedly had one-half inch of fat on its belly, which was judged adequate for a two-year-old cougar at that time of year, plus it had recently consumed deer meat.

The attack on Matilda May Samuel took place very close to where the attacking cougar had recently killed a deer. Necropsy results revealed that the cat had been feeding on the kill. The fact that the deer carcass was so close to the attack site could mean the cougar was merely protecting its kill.

According to Danz, the B.C. Ministry of the Environment reports that Matilda was 14, while Paul Beier's records indicate that she was 7. All other records agree with Beier.

August 9, 1979: Eva Walkus, 4, was playing on a swing with Ernie, the girl's six-year-old brother, at their home on the Tsulquate Indian reserve near Port

Hardy on Vancouver Island. It was just after 6:00 P.M. when a cougar suddenly raced out, grabbed Eva's leg in its teeth, and pulled her from the swing. The lion then attempted to drag the girl toward the woods. It had pulled the screaming child more than four feet toward some brush growing at the end of the road when Mary Leowen came outside to call the Walkus children in to supper, saw what was going on, and quickly responded. She grabbed a broom, then ran up to the cat and started beating on it. The animal dropped the child and ran away. Ms. Leowen then picked up young Eva and rushed her indoors. Thanks to Ms. Leowen's quick thinking, Eva Walkus suffered only puncture wounds in her legs. Another report indicates she was treated for shock and given shots for rabies. She remained in the hospital for four days before being discharged. Had Ms. Leowen not responded in the way that she did, the cougar probably would have gotten away with the child and killed her.

"[I] couldn't be frightened," Leowen later said. "Five minutes later and it would have been too late. All we thought about was saving the child."

B.C. Wildlife Control officers later destroyed the cougar, a small female that appeared to be starving.

1981: A man on a horse was attacked by a spotted adult cougar. He was not hurt. One month later, a wildlife control officer killed a spotted cougar in the same area, presumably the one responsible for the attack. The physical condition of the one-and-a-half-year-old female cougar was not noted.

1983: A teenage boy from Holberg was riding his bicycle when he was attacked by a cougar. The 16-year-old boy had been riding along a Canadian Air Force Base entrance road. Although the cougar was able to slash the boy, it was scared away by an oncoming vehicle. The boy suffered only minor injuries. Wildlife control agents later were able to track down the cougar and kill it.

1983: A man on a bridge near Esperanza was attacked by a cougar. The man managed to get away without serious injury. Wildlife Control Officer Dan Lay killed the cougar.

1983: Three boys were chased by a cougar through second growth brush on a hill above Port McNeill (some reports say Port Alice). One boy was mauled on his arm, another was mauled on his leg. Both boys were treated as outpatients and released. The cougar was later killed.

May 28, 1985: Johnny Wilson, 12, from Island Park, Idaho, was backpacking on Vancouver Island with his mother, his aunt, and his aunt's neighbor, Kelly Connor. After hiking the West Coast Trail on their way to Port Renfrow, the four had set up camp on Darling Creek. It was their second night on the trail. "Camping is a way of life for us," said Alissa Wilson, Johnny's mother. "I work for the forest service in Idaho, and John and I are outdoors all the time."

While the women bathed in the creek after a day on the trail, Johnny went a short distance upstream, where he planned to play with some of his toy soldiers. As the boy hunched over the creek's bank to move his toy soldiers, a cougar that had been hiding in a nearby logjam jumped him from behind.

"We heard a bloodcurdling scream," Johnny's mother said. "We ran over and saw the lion on John." The animal's jaws had clamped down hard around the boy's head and blood was already gushing from his nose and mouth. The boy was silent. "He was already in shock with a deep puncture wound in his throat," said Debbie Maher, the boy's aunt. The cougar then began dragging the boy back up the bank.

The two women started screaming as they approached the cat. This action apparently disconcerted the lion enough so that it dropped the boy, but the animal would not leave. "It watched us all the time, just pacing," said Maher.

The women grabbed young Johnny and pulled him away from the cougar. They carried the still-conscious but heavily bleeding boy across the creek to their tent, where they began administering first aid. Johnny presented a frightening sight: Blood was pouring out of his throat and mouth, while air was bubbling from one of his throat punctures. The mother knew that to staunch her son's bleeding throat, she would have to press down very hard upon his neck until help arrived. What made the ordeal even more frightening was that while the women were working on Johnny, the cougar continued to prowl outside the tent, despite the fire they had made before the attack. According to reports, the cougar hung around for at least an hour. "The cougar wouldn't go away," Debbie Maher said.

Debbie Maher was undeterred. She ran almost three miles to the Pachena Point lighthouse, where the lighthouse crew summoned help. The crew then brought rifles and accompanied Maher back to the campsite.

A U.S. Coast Guard helicopter medical crew based at Port Angeles was dispatched to the scene and arrived in a matter of hours. Johnny was treated for numerous scalp lacerations and puncture wounds to the neck. Next upon the scene was a shore party from the destroyer-escort HMCS MacKenzie. A Canadian Forces helicopter then arrived with a doctor to pick up the boy for delivery to Victoria General Hospital. Johnny was admitted to the hospital suffering from shock, puncture wounds, and lacerations to his head, neck, and shoulder. A surgical team was assembled to stem severe bleeding in the boy's throat. Wilson was then placed in intensive care, and spent seven days in the hospital before being released.

The cougar, which was reported to have been an "odd gray color," was not located again.

August 3, 1985: Alyson Parker, 10, was walking with two other girls on a trail near Camp Thunderbird, a YM/YWCA camp in the Glintz Lake area of Vancouver Island. The girls were campmates at Camp Thunderbird; the time was shortly before 7:00 P.M. This was the second night of her group's two-day outing away from the main camp.

When a cougar rushed out, threatening an attack, the girls started to run, screaming. Their screams alerted 19-year-old Lila Lifely, one of the counselors, who had been building a campfire to make the children's supper. Lila came running out to see what was wrong. When Lifely appeared on the scene, the cougar had already pounced on Alyson, and was trying to drag her away.

Armed with nothing but a quarter-cut of a log, Lifely charged at the cougar and beat it over the head. The cougar backed away a few feet, stared at Lifely, then pounced onto Alyson again. Lifely screamed for help, then charged the cougar again, fighting it off with a tree branch. Again, the cougar backed off.

With the child on the ground, bleeding profusely from the head and neck, Lifely made a dash to get her first-aid kit. As she did, the cat attacked and tried to drag Alyson away again.

Lifely returned and struck at the cougar's head with the branch. The animal retreated, but not very far. It continued to keep its eye on its victim and her rescuer from its vantage point in the bushes just a few yards away.

Lifely now climbed a tree so she could keep an eye on the cat, since it wasn't visible from where she had been standing on the ground. The struggle had by now attracted other camp personnel to the scene. When the cat would make a move to come in again, Lifely would yell to camp director Jim Legatt that the cat was approaching. Legatt would then grab a shovel and bang it on the ground. The cat would back off.

To keep the other children safe, Lifely had the presence of mind to send them scurrying up a nearby ridge and away from the lurking cougar. Within 30 minutes of the initial attack, two more men from nearby camps arrived. Soon afterward the cougar was again spotted stalking nearby, despite the noise the group was making in attempts to scare the animal.

Once help arrived to spell Lifely and Legatt, Alyson was whisked to a nearby hospital, where she was treated for skull punctures, scalp lacerations, and fifteen puncture wounds to the neck. She was released after eight days in the hospital.

The young tom cougar was killed three days later. Jim Walker, director of the provincial wildlife branch, reported that the attack did not appear to be motivated by starvation.

When Lila finally called her mother after rescuing Alyson, she couldn't speak because she was crying so hard. A nurse finally got on the phone and said, "Your daughter is a very brave girl."

May 15, 1988: Jesse Sky Bergman, 9, was out walking with his uncle and the uncle's three-year-old daughter when Jesse became separated from the two. Jesse, who during the week lived with his mother in Tofino, had been staying with his father, Frank Harper, for the weekend. Mr. Harper lived near the southerly tip of the Catface Mountains, not far from Tofino. The last time anyone recalled seeing the boy was around 4:00 P.M.

When the boy failed to return home that evening, a search ensued. The boy's light coat and trousers were found near the shoreline. Then his body was discovered about 200 yards away in the thick rain forest. All evidence indicated that Jesse had been attacked and killed by a cougar that had stalked him from behind. Reports stated that the boy had been badly mauled about his head and neck.

Speculation surrounds the circumstances of the boy's death. Dick Nimmo, of the provincial emergency program based in Ucluelet, said he believed the boy may have gone swimming because his clothing was not ripped. The boy had apparently removed his clothing of his own accord. Had Jesse gone swimming, or even if he had simply taken off his clothes, he had probably begun to suffer mild hypothermia. "You feel warm and stop shivering," Nimmo said. "That's a normal hypothermic reaction." Nimmo believes the cougar attacked the boy when the youngster's defenses were down.

Remarkably, Rod Burke, principal of Jesse's school, where the boy had been in third grade, commented on Jesse's skills in bushcraft and woodcraft. "He felt very comfortable in the woods. He had spent a lot of time out there exploring, hiking and camping," said Burke.

After Jesse's body had been removed the following day, one of the family's neighbors returned to the scene with his rifle. Mike Wright suspected that the mountain lion would return in expectation of feeding on the boy's body. Wright began moaning, as though he were injured. Within a short time, a large cougar appeared upon the scene, and it appeared to be looking for Jesse. Wright promptly shot the big cat.

Another version of the story has the cat standing guard over Jesse's remains when they were found. That Mike Wright shot the lion appears to be undisputed.

In both scenarios, human remains were found in the animal's stomach. The cougar, a large male that weighed 153 pounds and was estimated to be five years of age, was in excellent condition.

January 20, 1989: Ralph Lucas, 28, of Ahousaht, which is on Flores Island off the western coast of Vancouver Island, was gathering firewood when he was pounced on from behind by a cougar. The mountain lion bit Lucas on the head and inflicted a number of scratches on the man's arms before Lucas was able to struggle free. The cougar broke off its attack and dashed back into the woods. Lucas was rushed to a Tofino hospital.

The cougar was shot by a reserve resident minutes after the attack. Conservation Officer Ralph Escott investigated this incident.

July 1991: Two children were attacked by a young cougar as they played on the bank of the Fraser River near Lillooet. The children suffered severe cuts and lacerations.

May 5, 1992: Jeremy Lucas Williams, 8, was sitting on the grass near the playground of the Kyuquot school. The freckle-faced, red-haired youngster had no inkling of danger when a one-and-a-half-year-old female cougar rushed out from the forest bordering the area and grabbed the boy from behind.

The cougar killed Williams almost instantly. Children who saw the attack raced inside the school's gymnasium where the boy's parents were playing badminton with the school custodian. The custodian, Peter Skilton, grabbed his .30–06 rifle from the school workshop and raced toward the animal.

"The cougar was lying there with Jeremy. The boy wasn't moving," said Skilton. "He must have been unconscious at the time." Skilton shot twice, killing the small 60-pound animal. Williams was rushed to Kyuquot Red Cross Hospital, but was pronounced dead at 8:30 P.M.

July 2, 1992: Jill Sherman, a 29-year-old Washington State woman who had been observing orcas off the coastline of West Cracroft Island, just opposite Robson's Bight, was walking back to her campsite when a cougar attacked her. The animal had been waiting at the edge of the beach. At first, the woman backed away from the cat. Unfortunately, she tripped over a log, at which point, the cat pounced and started biting and clawing her. Sherman screamed, and the cougar backed off, then jumped up on a log and simply sat there, watching, appearing as though it was ready to resume its attack at any minute.

Sherman's screams had alerted another woman from her nearby group of campers and observers, many of whom were marine scientists. When this woman arrived upon the scene, she encountered the cat crouching on the log. Although at first reluctant to approach because the cat had positioned itself between the two, the second woman eventually walked right past the animal to tend to her wounded friend.

Both women later recalled how they had seen three children playing in that exact spot just an hour earlier. Sherman speculated that the cat may have been lurking there, waiting for an opportunity to get closer to the children, when Sherman walked past instead.

A few days after this incident, another camper discovered several mats of loose fur in a rock cut directly above their camp. That unleashed speculation that the cat had been paying close attention to the group ever since they had first arrived on the small island.

After the attack, Sherman and the other woman walked toward the camp kitchen, even though the cat was still crouching in the brush. Two other campers were left to stand guard in the event the cougar should decide to attack again. Sherman suffered numerous lacerations, scratches, and puncture wounds to her face, back, and thighs. When rescued, she was bleeding from her shoulder, leg and head.

Despite its attack upon her and its generally threatening behavior, Sherman requested that the cat not be destroyed. When the Canadian Coast Guard arrived with a doctor soon afterward, they removed the woman to the Port Hardy hospital for treatment. Sherman's scalp was sutured shut that afternoon; she flew home to Washington the next day.

A camper shot the cougar soon after the attack, but the shot was off center and did not kill the animal. It wounded the cougar in its face—perhaps its jaw—and the animal ran away. At the sound of the shot, some women campers started to cry. No one had wanted to see the cat killed.

Two subsequent searches by conservation officers with hounds turned up no trace of the cougar, even though they combed a large area of thick salal and second-growth fir and cedar. What was uncovered, at the place where the cougar had been shot, was bone, teeth, a bullet, and fragments of porcupine quills, which led to speculation that the animal may have been unable to eat because of a mouthful of porcupine quills.

Jill Sherman would later write in Jim Nollman's "The Incident at Boat Bay," a narrative of the attack and its aftermath published in the 1993 *Interspecies Newsletter,* "Humans have a hard time being threatened. We believe in health and life insurance. Then we visit a place for its wildness, to commune with nature, which includes a genuine risk. But in reality, nature is at risk from our visit. The shooting of the cougar is best understood as an insurance killing."

The last word on this attack is this report, also from "The Incident at Boat Bay:" "Five months later, a friend visiting the area was informed that a cougar had been killed on Christmas day just a mile north of our camp, shot by a man as it stalked his two daughters. The cat was a large female with a mangled jaw."

May 9, 1994: Gold River: Seven-year-old Kyle Musselman of Gold River was walking with some school mates down an embankment stairway that led to a highway when an 80-pound male cougar leaped at Kyle from the bushes. It knocked the boy to the ground and quickly dragged him screaming into the brush. Although the boy's friends threw rocks at the animal, they were unable to scare it away. The attack on Kyle was especially frightening since it occurred just 45 yards away from Ray Watkins Elementary School.

When Linda Dahl, a friend of the Musselman family, arrived on the scene, all she could see was thrashing bushes. She stood there frozen, holding some rocks in her hand, and she said she believed that the cougar sensed her presence, too, since the thrashing stopped.

When Kyle's father, John, arrived, he pulled apart the bushes. Dahl said she could see the cat sitting on the apparently lifeless boy. Kyle's father screamed at the cat, and succeeded in driving the cougar away. Ms. Dahl said it appeared as though the cougar had ripped the scalp off Kyle's head.

"All I could see was an empty scalp, no skin, no ears, nothing," she said, in comments published in the *British Columbia Report.* "Then I heard him say something to his father, so I knew he was alive."

Kyle's father scooped him up and raced into the school, where classes were just about to begin. Police arrived within minutes.

Kyle was airlifted first to Campbell River and then to Children's Hospital in Vancouver. The boy suffered serious head wounds that required extensive plastic surgeries on his ear, face, and scalp. Nothing could be done for Kyle's badly damaged eye, which was lost.

Constable Rick McKerracher of the RCMP, Gold River, shot the cougar minutes after the attack. Ten days later a second cat was spotted dragging a deer into the bushes near the place where Kyle was attacked. Since young cougars often travel in pairs, this second cat was thought to be related to the cougar that had attacked Kyle Musselman. Police treed the animal and shot it.

The cougar that attacked Kyle was apparently in good health, although Doug Turner, B.C. Environmental chief of enforcement for Vancouver Island, said that the animal looked as though it might have been recently struck by an automobile.

October 7, 1994, Gold River: Off-duty RCMP constable Rick McKerracher was riding horses with a friend not too far from the Peppercorn trailer park in Gold River. A cougar suddenly sprang from the bushes at McKerracher's horse. The officer kicked at the cougar, and the animal lashed back with its forepaw. McKerracher received five long scratches on his right leg above the top of his cowboy boot. Fireball, McKerracher's horse, was not hurt.

Conservation officers tried to locate the cougar, but could not.

July 8, 1995, Kitsukus Creek, Port Alberni: Lloyd Frederick Dayton, 32, had gone mountain biking along a well-used paved path about a half mile from the main highway to Port Alberni. When Dayton's tire went flat, the man apparently pulled off the trail so he could repair it. Less than 15 minutes later, a hiker discovered Dayton's body lying face-down in Kitsukus Creek, 100 yards from where his bike was discovered. Although the hiker, Mr. Stu Gibson, tried to resuscitate Dayton, his efforts were unsuccessful.

Gibson then ran for help. When the police arrived, they examined the body and found numerous puncture wounds on the right side of the man's neck, along with several scratches on his right arm and leg. Since Dayton's body was found so far from his bike, investigators concluded that he was either chased by the lion or for some reason had walked away from his bike before the attack.

Bloodhounds were called in by conservation officers working with the RCMP. The scent had dried up quickly, and the dogs were unable to track the killer lion.

Conservation officer Ralph Escott speculated that Mr. Dayton, a small man, may have been crouching when the cat pounced. "In most attacks, the cougar surprises whatever it's hunting," Escott said. "Cougars are opportunistic, secretive hunters. They strike when the odds are in their favor. They only attack for food, and it's very unusual for one to kill something [like Mr. Dayton] and not consume at least part of it."

Escott speculated that the cougar was an adolescent, "because that is the age when we tend to have problems with them."

February 12, 1996: A logger was attacked by a cougar while felling a tree near Little Espinosa Inlet. The cougar leaped upon the man's back just as he started moving away from a snag he'd just cut. The logger reacted by hitting the cougar with his chain saw, which was off, then ran one or two steps. Although the cougar remained on the man's back, the logger was provided some protection from his hat, neck coverings, and heavy clothing.

The man suffered a 2-mm puncture wound to his neck, as well as bruises to his back. When another logger arrived at the scene, the two men managed to scare the cougar away.

Conservation officer Ben York met a cougar hunter and his hounds at the site, but the search was unsuccessful. The area was extremely dry, making for poor trailing conditions.

July 20, 1999: A logger, age 50, was seated in his truck at 11:45 A.M. along the Fairservice Logging Road near Lake Cowichan, Vancouver Island, when a cougar raced out of the brush, leaped up and attacked his arm. Another man was in the truck at the time of the attack.

The victim received a single, three-quarter-inch-long cut on his wrist.

Conservation officers used hounds to pursue the cougar for two-and-a-half hours before losing the trail because of extreme heat.

February 9, 2001: Jon Nostdal, 52, was attacked by a cougar as he was bicycling. The *Vancouver Sun* reported the incident in their February 10th edition:

> Nostdal thought something was loose in his backpack as he bicycled in the dark. He kept hearing a clicking sound that became louder with each second. Nostdal was then hit in the back by something that knocked him from his cycle and to the ground. That something was a cougar, which bit into the back of his head. Luckily, the hood of his coat had been pulled up, so the cat only bit into the hood's material. Nostdal rolled around on the ground with the cat for long minutes until Elliot Cole, who was driving home late from work, drove by in his truck and noticed the struggle. Cole got out of his truck and saw that a cougar had wrapped its claws around the man and was chewing on his neck. Cole began yelling. Cole then hit the cougar with a bag loaded with heavy binders. The cougar continued its attack. Cole punched

the cougar repeatedly but had no effect. He then grabbed Nostdal's bike and pinned the animal to the ground. "I shoved the cougar to the ground to the point where I thought I was choking it," he said. "It put its paws through the spokes and hit me. I pinned it down again and punched it again.

"I yelled at the man to wriggle free and run to my truck . . . then I smoked the cougar one more time . . . [and] ran to the truck. "I was just re-acting. I had no time to think if it was stupid, dumb or anything else."

Nostdal was admitted to Port Alice Hospital [on Vancouver Island] where he was treated for bite marks on his head and lacerations to his face.

8

Washington State Attacks

The year 1924 brought with it large numbers of cougar complaints from people across the state of Washington, particularly from the northern areas close to the British Columbia border. The situation was considered serious enough to hire a professional cougar hunter, one Charles Shuttleworth, who moved from British Columbia to assume his duties. Shuttleworth set up headquarters near the town of Wenatchee.

On December 24 of that same year, at 11:30 A.M., a 13-year-old boy named Jimmie Fehlhaber was sent to a neighboring ranch to pick up a team of horses. The ranch was in Oleava, Washington, not far from British Columbia. The boy, who was wearing snowshoes, decided to take a shortcut that followed a winding trail and which, at one point, dropped down into a coulee. Tracks in the snow later revealed the full story of what happened to Fehlhaber. The cat apparently had been following the boy for some time, staying out of sight in the brush off to one side of the trail. When Fehlhaber finally realized that the cougar was stalking him, he apparently panicked and ran to a small tree, perhaps with the idea of climbing it. Running, however, was the worst course of action he could have taken, as the cougar well understood that prey animals run. Jimmie had managed to cover the 100 yards that separated him from the tree, but before he could climb up, the pursuing cougar leapt onto the boy and knocked him to the ground. The boy fought back, stabbing and slashing the lion with a small jack-knife. But the cougar was too strong and too hungry to be deterred.

When Fehlhaber failed to return home, search parties were formed. One of them soon discovered the remains of his body, which the cougar had been feeding upon. The cat had made an attempt to cover the body, as cougars often will. The boy's hands had been badly chewed up, and his thigh partially consumed. Recovered at the site were the open jackknife, a good luck charm the boy carried, and the animal's left front dew-claw, which the boy had managed to cut off before he died.

A bounty was offered to anyone who could kill the cat, but the searchers soon obliterated what good tracks remained at the scene. The hunt that followed failed to deliver up the offending cat, although a considerable number of cougars were killed.

Reports differ considerably as to the outcome of this story. According to Beier, the killer was a 13-year-old male cougar. Stanley P. Young and Edward A. Goldman in *The Puma: Mysterious American Cat* (1964) reported that it was a three-year-old female that had been caught in a trap by a local rancher some four and a half miles from where Jimmie Fehlhaber had been killed and partially devoured. Charles Haley, who had been on the scene and inspected the bodies of all suspect cougars, said that Fehlhaber's killer had been an old and gaunt female. According to the *Journal of Mammalogy,* two cougars were responsible: an old female and a three-year-old male.

Further evidence remains inconclusive. Both the *Journal of Mammalogy* and Young and Goldman reported that the killer cougar's stomach contained a small undigested mass which, under examination, proved to be hair from the boy's head, two bits of blue jean material, and an empty brass cartridge shell, which Fehlhaber had been known to carry in his pocket. However, their agreement on this matter is only partial: the *Journal* reports that the stomach contents came from the three-year-old male; Young and Goldman claim it was from the trapped three-year-old female.

Attitudes toward cougars all over the West have been in something of a state of flux since 1924. Opinions seem most likely to vary in those areas most attractive to Easterners displaced from large urban areas, and to Californians. These citizens generally carry notions quite different from those of the traditional Westerner on how wildlife should be managed. Many believe they're instant wildlife authorities if they've seen a special on the Discovery channel. Even if they're really not authorities, it is *good* that they have become involved in what was formerly only the province of biologists, ranchers, sheepmen, and hunting enthusiasts. Their attitudes have led all to a tightening up of restrictions on the way cougars are hunted over the West, and even if the animals legally may be hunted at all.

"Since 1996 we've noticed that the complaints are coming in from marginal cougar habitats, those that are butted up against areas of high human density," said Donny Martorello, the state's cougar biologist for the state's Department of Fish and Wildlife.

Where there were about 1,000 cougars inhabiting the state of Washington in the early 1980s, the state now conservatively estimates there are more than 2,500. Despite this, more than 60 percent of the state's voters voted for

Initiative 655, which banned hunting cougars with hounds as well as baiting bears. Most voters, while not against hunting cougars *per se,* felt there were better methods by which hunters could take the animals.

Not so, said Steve Pozzanghera, at the time carnivore section manager of the Department of Fish and Wildlife. "Hound hunting is the most efficient, most effective way of taking cougars." Dogs can follow scent, as well as pursue at speeds and distances that people on foot can't.

Still, more hunters are now going after the big cats. Since the initiative passed, game officials have eliminated the state's permit hunt, lengthened the season from August to mid-March, and dropped the price of a cougar tag from $24 to $5. "We've increased the number of hunters by going from a permit hunt to an open season," Pozzanghera said.

No matter. The state's cougar harvest has tanked. In 1995—before the ban—283 cougars were taken. In 1996, 178 cats were harvested. And only 132 cats were killed in 1997. These figures seem to support a report compiled by the Department of Fish and Game, which concluded that nearly 85 percent of the cougars killed by hunters between 1987 and 1995 were taken while using dogs.

"The population of cougars is growing faster than we can control it," said Pozzanghera. "If we're unable to control populations through hunting, you're going to have more interactions between the animals and people. It's just a given."

Washington's legislature, reacting to increasing numbers of reported conflicts with cougars—particularly near the state's most populated areas— passed a law in 1999 that stated once a public safety need had been established, the use of hounds would be allowed "within a narrow area," despite a previous statewide referendum that had banned the use of dogs for hunting the big cats. "If the number of complaints from a particular area reaches a certain level, we will establish boundaries, determine the quality of the habitat, and make the decision to remove a certain number of cougars," stated Martorello.

With a growing cougar population and fewer animals being killed, no wonder a state that hadn't seen a human fatality from a cougar in 76 years can now lay claim to so many attacks and near attacks over the past ten years. It's a disturbing trend, showing no evidence of slowing any time soon.

June 25, 1977: Cherie Lee and Don O'Neal, with their 8-year-old son Neal and 4-year-old daughter Keri, were camping in the Weyerhaeuser Park on the Greenwater River 24 miles east of Enumclaw. The word Enumclaw's original Native American meaning is "evil spirit," and it could be said that an evil spirit was busy along the Greenwater that day. What made the incident unique was that it was the first reported mauling by a cougar in Washington State in more than 50 years.

"Thank God that Keri and I are alive and able to be here," Mrs. O'Neal remarked from her south Seattle home after the incident. "I was sunbathing on a log near the river while Keri was wading nearby," she reported. "Neal, our eight-year-old son, was on one side of a deadfall fishing. Don, my husband, was about 40 yards upstream, out of my view.

"I'd been lying on my back for quite a while, so I turned onto my left side." That's when Cherie noticed the cougar, which had stalked to within two yards of her.

"It pounced, pulled me off the log and onto the ground," she said. "I fought off the cougar with my hands. I must have tried to put them into its mouth to keep it from getting to my head.

"The cat and I wrestled, then it leaped over the log and at Keri, who started screaming. The cat knocked Keri to her knees and was on top of her, trying to bite her neck." Don O'Neal heard Cherie and Keri screaming. The cat broke off its attack and bounded into the brush at the man's approach.

After she'd plunged her hands into the cold river water to help staunch the flow of blood, Don bandaged Cherie's hands. "He grew up on a Wyoming ranch," Mrs. O'Neal explained. "He always carries a first-aid kit."

Okie Sinclair of Burnett, Dan McBride of Tacoma, and Paul Kitchen and his son Don from Puyallup volunteered the use of their dogs to track the cougar. Hounds picked up the scent near the attack scene. The cougar had climbed a fir tree just 100 yards away. Bruce Richards, a state wildlife agent, shot and killed the animal.

The male cougar's age was estimated to be one and one-third years. It weighed 69 pounds and seemed to be quite thin. Its teeth were in good shape, but its stomach was empty. Some porcupine quills were found in the animal's mouth.

Mrs. O'Neal suffered bites and scratches to her back, thigh and arm, as well as a mutilated left thumb. Keri was not seriously injured.

June 15, 1992: Michael Vanney, of Arlington, was walking down to the shore of Lake Wenatchee with his five-year-old daughter, Jessica, and nine-year-old son, Matthew, to find some sticks for roasting marshmallows. The three were on a path near a campground in Lake Wenatchee State Park.

"I saw some movement out of the corner of my eye," Vanney said later. "Then a cougar ran from behind a tree and jumped on Jessica. Its front paws just wrapped right around her head and shoulders."

Vanney wasted no time. He grabbed his hunting knife and tackled the cougar, hitting it so hard that he knocked it right off the girl. He then yelled for his wife, who was back at the campsite, to bring his pistol. The cougar raced up a tree when Vanney's wife came racing up with the gun. Vanney fired at it twice, but missed both times.

The cougar was kept cornered in the tree until wildlife agents arrived with a tranquilizer gun. The cat was captured and held for fourteen days to make certain it didn't have rabies. The animal was then destroyed. "Throughout the nation, the policy has been that cats which attack humans are destroyed," said Harry Morse of the Washington Department of Wildlife.

Jessica, meanwhile, was taken to Cascade Medical Center in Leavenworth, where she was treated for scratches and small puncture wounds and released.

The family stayed one more night after the attack upon Jessica, but the girl refused to sleep in the kids' tent. "She slept right between my wife and me last night (in a motor home) and she didn't budge all night," said Michael Vanney.

After the attack, wildlife agent Jim Mares said Jessica probably surprised the cat. "They are curious animals," he said. "They'll follow people. Had it actually been attacking the girl, she would have had more injuries."

At the time, this was only the third known attack by a cougar on a human in recent Washington State history. That situation was going to change, however.

June 29, 1992: A young cougar jumped on a two-year-old boy who was camping with his family along Huckleberry Creek in the White River area. The boy's parents were able to drive the cougar away, and the boy was not seriously injured.

The cat's age was estimated at about five months. It weighed 25 pounds and, according to Rocky Spencer, biologist for the Department of Wildlife, was somewhat undernourished. "It's a cat that should have still been with its mother. I suspect it was separated from its mother."

The young cougar was captured and euthanized. The necropsy revealed that the cougar had a tennis shoe in its stomach.

Autumn 1993: A Stevens County rancher shot two cougars he said were chasing his young children.

August 20, 1994: Five-year-old Andrew Braun was throwing rocks into the Dungeness River about three miles upstream from Camp Hardy in Olympic

National Forest when a cougar rushed out of the brush and attacked him. The attack was especially unusual because the boy's father, Mike, was standing next to him when the cougar rushed in. Andrew's eight-year-old brother, Stephen, backpacker Bob Laschinski of Scandia, and Matthew Demaray, 12, were all nearby, playing by the river about 50 yards upstream. The Brauns, who were from Kitsap County, were on a camping trip.

"I heard a sound behind me and when I looked down, I saw my son lying on the ground with the cougar on top of him," Braun said. Braun yelled at the animal and chased it into the river, onto a small island.

Braun followed. "All I could find to hit the cougar with was a stick in the river," he said. "I swung it at him as hard as I could, and I think I hit him in the leg. The end of the stick broke off. Then the cougar ran off into the bushes."

Laschinski tended to Andrew's wounds with his first-aid kit while Braun and his other sons kept the cougar at bay in the bushes. "We were heaving rocks into the bushes as fast as we could," Braun later related. Andrew, meanwhile, was going into shock.

Braun and Laschinski took turns carrying the youngster back to camp, which was almost three miles downstream. Two other campers, who turned out to be nurses, came to the boy's aid. Then, using a jerry-rigged pack with holes in the bottom, Braun and his group carried the boy out to the trailhead. Once they reached their cars, they hurried Andrew to Harrison Hospital in Bremerton, Washington, where he was treated for two puncture wounds to the chest and a gash on his back, and released.

Fish and Wildlife agents returned to the scene with dogs on Sunday. The dogs tracked the cougar, treed it, and the agents shot it. The animal weighed 55 pounds and was thought to have been about eighteen months old.

"They told me it was learning to hunt," Mike Braun said. "They said it probably didn't know the difference between a small deer and a human."

August 1994: Melodie Gates and Nancy Sjoblom of Tumwater had hiked about four miles along the Dry Creek Trail near Lake Cushman in the Olympic National Forest when Gates heard a twig break behind her. "I turned around and saw this cougar walking down the hill toward the center of the trail. I said to Nancy, 'Do you see it?' and she said she did. Then we wondered, 'Now, what do we do?'"

The cougar stopped just seven feet from the women. Then it slowly advanced.

Gates, who was in the lead, did not budge. "I said, 'Please go away,'" she said. "It kept advancing. It opened its mouth and hissed. It came to within four feet of us." Gates then tapped the cat in its jaw with her walking stick. "It snarled and showed its teeth. It stepped ahead again, so I whacked it on the shoulder. It twisted its head and mouthed the stick. It snarled, glared at me, and stopped. Then it turned and went back the way it had come."

When the cougar was well away, the two women let out a huge sigh of relief and hugged. Sjoblom had snapped several photos of their close call.

"The key is not to take your eyes off the cat," said Rocky Spencer, a North Bend–based state biologist who has studied cougars. "They did the right things, although it might have been better to yell instead of talk. I would have let that cat know immediately that I was there," he said.

Gates was wise to stand her ground, Spencer explained. To flee might have triggered a predatory response from the cat.

"It could have been an adult female with kittens nearby," Spencer speculated. "The cat could have been protecting its young. Or it may have been simple curiosity, and that was this cat's response to these two-legged creatures walking through the woods."

Summer 1995: Rosalind Wallace and Gretchen Roffler were employed to do spotted owl surveys in Olympic National Park. As they trekked through one of the park's more remote reaches, searching for the endangered raptor, they walked right up on a mountain lion. Knowing their lives could be in danger, they made all the right moves.

"We raised the pitch and volumes of our voices," said Wallace, "then took a small step in his direction." The cat crouched slightly, laid back its ears, and hissed. "It showed us its teeth, but then it backed off." The women stayed in an upright stance, upslope from the lion. They stood their ground, and running never entered their minds. They looked directly into the cat's eyes. And when the lion backed off, it proved that it had made the connection: These two weren't acting like prey animals.

"At least not that day," Wallace later said.

June 6, 1997: Roy Parks, who lived near Peshastin in Chelan County, went out into his garage to feed his dogs. When he entered through the door, he was astounded to see a cougar on top of one of his dogs inside the garage. As Parks watched, the cougar quickly attacked the other dog. Fearful of losing his pet, Parks jumped onto the cougar and started punching its head, receiving a swipe from the cougar's forepaw as he did so. Parks succeeded in making the cat break off its attack, but the animal now felt trapped as it prowled around the garage, looking to escape. It finally leaped through a glass window, but inexplicably re-entered the building.

Later, Officer Grant and Sergeant Ward of the Washington Department of Fish and Wildlife immobilized and removed the cougar from Parks's garage. It was later euthanized. The two-year-old female cougar was suffering from malnutrition, but did not test positive for rabies.

Parks suffered scratches on his right arm, but declined medical attention.

May 1998: A cougar slinked out of the forest behind Wes Collins' house one evening and started chasing the family's Lab around the yard. The cat soon cornered the dog by the back deck.

Clamping its jaws on the dog's neck, the cougar quickly killed the dog and dragged it into the woods. It gnawed the dog's head and shoulder, then buried the rest to eat at a later time. Then it stretched out for a nap.

Two of Collins' children had witnessed the entire episode from the doorway of their house, which is on five acres outside Issaquah, not far from Seattle.

The next day, state game warden Rocky Spencer arrived with a hunter, Ed Mahany, and two hounds to try to track the cat. The hounds found the cat just 100 yards inside the woods. It turned on the dogs in a fury, sending both hounds cowering back to the truck. New hounds were brought in, and they quickly cornered the cougar in a hollow stump.

Mahany next moved in and shot the animal. It proved to be a 145-pound male.

"That was the most aggressive [lion] I've seen," said Spencer.

"This cougar wasn't sick or injured," added Mahany. "It didn't concern him to be around people, and dogs were just lunch."

The four Collins children—ages 8 to 14—were no longer allowed to play outside alone. Collins bought a can of pepper spray and cleared trails behind his house "to make our presence known."

August 4, 1998: At 4:00 P.M. five-year-old Carmen Schrock, of Chewelah, was trying to catch up to her younger sister and grandmother, who were on their way to use an outhouse at the Noisy Creek Camp Ground, where Carmen's family was camping with a large church group. Back at the campground, which is about eight miles southeast of Metaline Falls in Pend O'Reille County, Carmen's mother, Carolyn Schrock, was changing her infant daughter's diaper. As Carmen hurried down the trail, she suddenly spotted a cougar. Although friends and family call the child a "little tomboy," Carmen wasn't old enough to comprehend that what she was about to do may have been the absolute worst thing she could have done, at least in the presence of a predatory animal like a mountain lion. The girl screamed, then turned and ran. The cougar chased the girl and pounced on her from behind.

The girl continued to scream as the cat grabbed her head in its jaws and tried to drag her into the brush. Carolyn Schrock heard the commotion and came running, her baby in her arms. She saw the cougar with Carmen's head in its mouth, and yelled at the top of her lungs. The cougar dropped the child and retreated.

The child was eventually taken to Sacred Heart Medical Center in Spokane, where she underwent surgery. Her skull had been fractured, she had puncture wounds and lacerations, and she sustained some brain damage. Despite all the damage, the doctors told the Schrocks that the girl would probably make a full recovery, adding that "she's lucky to be alive."

"We should never have let her out of our sight," said Jeff Schrock, Carmen's father.

The day of the attack, Ione Marshal Rob McKay and rescue worker Keith Saxe shot and killed the young male cougar, which reeked of skunk scent, just 100 yards from the campground. The cat was 12 to 16 months old.

Rick Reiber, marshal for the nearby towns of Metaline and Metaline Falls, stated in a *Spokane Spokesman-Review* article that the lack of hound hunting has contributed to an increase in the number and boldness of cougars. "It's just a matter of time before something happens [at the edge of Metaline Falls]," he said.

"We're getting more and more sightings of cougars . . . getting more and more brave," agreed Pend Oreille County Sheriff Doug Malby.

August 1998: A U.S. Forest Service worker was taking an inventory of timber and other vegetation in the Tiger Meadows area south of State Highway 20 between the towns of Ione and Colville. The man was walking along when he saw a cougar come out of the forest and start to follow him. The cougar followed the man wherever he went, always keeping a distance of perhaps thirty yards between the two of them.

The employee, whose name was not released, was armed with a hatchet and a can of pepper spray. He made a lot of noise, plus kept in radio contact with the ranger office.

The cat continued to shadow the man for about thirty minutes. It eventually lost interest and left the area.

The incident took place just fifteen miles northwest of where five-year-old Carmen Schrock was attacked on August 4.

September 29, 1998: Bruce Deane of Lake Quinault Outfitters was leading a string of five packhorses north on the Elwha River Trail in Olympic National Park. Deane had just ridden beneath a tree more than three feet in diameter when he heard a snarl from above. The man immediately knew it was a cougar, and turned in the saddle just in time to see the lion leap from the tree limb and land on the back of the second packhorse. Fortunately, the cougar landed on the pack saddle and did not injure the animal.

The horse panicked, ran off the trail, then rolled down the hill for more than 300 feet before landing in creek, taking another horse with it. Packsaddles, food, and gear were either lost or destroyed. Both horses suffered injuries from the fall. Not only that, but the slopes on both sides of the drainage were so steep that the horses could not climb back up to the trail without help. Five park employees spent most of the day cutting and clearing a small section of trail back up the hillside so that the horses could regain the trail.

The cougar, meanwhile, fled when Deane yelled at it. Deane described the cougar as being young, and about five to five-and-a-half feet long from nose tip to tail tip.

Biologists speculated that the young cougar might have mistaken the horse for an elk.

November 12, 1998: William White, 38, was elk hunting at the Packwood Game Management Unit in Lewis County when a cougar charged out of the brush and knocked him over. White suffered a concussion, bruises, and abrasions, and was unable to seek help for himself. Confused from the effects of the concussion, he spent four days wandering in the woods without food or shelter before he was able to find his way back to civilization. White then spent two days in the hospital where he was treated for his injuries, as well as for hypothermia.

July 11, 1999: A cougar approached a group of five people while they were hiking through the woods after fishing the Quinault River in Olympic National Park. The group remained calm and shouted at the cougar. One member waved his fishing rod at the animal. After several minutes, the animal retreated.

July 16, 1999: A man was taking photographs along a gravel bar in the Quinault River. He heard noises behind him, and turned around just in time to see a cougar dashing toward him. The man shouted, and waved his camera gear and tripod at the animal. The cougar stopped ten feet away, paced back and forth for several minutes, then left.

The man began to walk back to his car at the Graves Creek stock camp. The cougar followed him, but never came closer.

August 24, 1999: Four-year-old Jacob Walsh was attacked and mauled by a cougar while playing with a five-year-old cousin in their grandparents' yard. The home, which belongs to Darrell and Karen Shute, is on U.S. Highway 395 not far from Barstow, and 11 miles northwest of Kettle Falls. It was 2:30 P.M., and the kids were playing in a shallow creek close to the house. The cat lunged at Jacob, perhaps knocking him unconscious because the child's body went limp. It chewed on him, then dragged him into the woods.

"I heard my daughter screaming," said Vicki Baker, Jacob's aunt. "When I looked out the window, I saw the cougar on top of Jacob. I ran to the creek screaming at the lion to let him go. The cat was holding Jacob in his jaws by the throat. He just stood there and looked at me."

Baker yelled again, and the animal dropped the boy and ran away. "I went to pick up Jacob and his neck flopped like a newborn baby's. His arms were limp. I remember thinking that if he weren't dead already, that I had just killed him. Blood was pulsating from his throat," Baker said.

Baker called authorities while another relative pressed a handkerchief and towel against Jacob's wounds. They then rushed Jacob to Mount Carmel Hospital in Colville, where he was operated on for a fractured collarbone and 30 puncture and tear wounds, some several inches long, which required more than 200 stitches. The injuries were to his head, throat, and shoulder, and included a severed nerve that surgeons were able to repair. Jacob was given two pints of blood.

A houndsman arrived at the scene of the attack not long after the boy was mauled. Two hours and fifteen minutes later, the two-and-a-half-year-old male cougar suspected of mauling the boy was killed. The cougar weighed between 90 and 100 pounds and was said to be in good condition.

Young male cougars are involved in most cougar attacks on humans, according to Madonna Luers, spokeswoman for the Department of Fish and Wildlife. "They tend to be the kind of bold, exploratory animals that this happens with."

Sometimes. But, as you can see from these accounts, as well as several others detailed in the appendices, not always.

9

Montana Attacks

Montana is Big Sky country, wide, open, with a wealth of sweeping vistas. Federal and state-owned land provides recreationists with plenty of wilderness opportunities. But the very things that make this state so appealing are also causing it to be filled up with tract homes and three-acre ranchettes, each with small corrals and tiny pastures. The wide-open spaces are still there; they've just been diced and sliced until it's difficult to travel unimpeded through many of the wildlife corridors and areas of critical winter range that border the state's truly wild country.

Critical winter range is where ungulates congregate for the forage they need to carry them through a winter. Large predators such as cougars, grizzly bears, black bears, and even wolves predictably follow them to those areas. Add people to the mix, and you can bet that problems will occur.

There is a long tradition of hunting mountain lions with hounds in Montana, which has kept cougar numbers at a manageable level. How long that sport will survive with the influx of urbanites and suburbanites is anybody's guess. Restrictions on hunting would result in an increase in the number of cougar-human conflicts. As you can see, conflicts are already beginning to occur at an alarming rate.

September 14, 1989: Residents of Evaro Hill, on the Flathead Indian Reserve near Missoula, had been having problems with mountain lions. Two dogs had been killed recently, one of them at the home of David and Rose Gardipe, and mountain lions were blamed for the deaths. Still, there were no indications that cougars would begin stalking humans.

Jake Gardipe, 5, was playing in his yard on September 14 when he disappeared. He was last seen at about 3:00 P.M., riding his bicycle not far from the trailer house he shared with his parents. When the boy's parents could not find him later that afternoon, fish and wildlife officials for the Confederated

Salish and Kootenai tribes, as well as the Missoula County Search and Rescue team were contacted.

One of the teams spotted a lion near the boy's home. Combing the area, the searchers finally located the boy's body later that night. The boy had been attacked and killed just 40 feet behind his home, which is about 100 yards east of Route 93. Later that evening, search and rescue teams spotted a 52-pound yearling within 100 yards of the boy's body. The cougar was treed by hounds, then killed. Fresh blood was found on the lion's mouth and paws. The dead lion proved to be a young female, between thirteen and seventeen months old.

Francis Cahoon, one of the searchers, who was also a trapper and wildlife biology student, was later quoted in *The Missoulian* that he had found the pawprints of two lion kittens, as well as the scat of an adult lion, near the Gardipe home. "We know the cat we killed was not the only cat to have attacked the child," he said. Tribal game wardens directed Cahoon to shoot any mountain lions he treed or trapped, even though the animals were plentiful in the Evaro area.

Kerry Murphy, a biologist who has studied mountain lions in western Montana, said, "Human-mountain lion encounters are uncommon in Montana, Idaho, and Wyoming. The problem . . . [in this instance] was a child playing in brush. The child, essentially, became the lion's prey. The child would not have had to provoke the animal." According to Murphy, the Evaro area is a travel corridor for all sorts of large animals, including mountain lion prey such as deer and elk, reason enough for the area to be a cougar troublespot. The problem is compounded by the fact that lions are not hunted on the Flathead reservation.

Murphy further stated that homeowners with heavy cover such as brush and trees around their homes run a "greater risk" than those who clear out surrounding brush.

Murphy encouraged homeowners to "reduce the food supply available to lions in backyards." He said he had heard of lions feeding at dog bowls, as well as lions congregating near apple trees where deer come to feed.

The necropsy report verified that the yearling lion's stomach contained hair and clothing belonging to Jake Gardipe. The animal did not have rabies.

Surprisingly, considering the numbers of mountain lions inhabiting Montana, this was the first documented cougar-caused human fatality in the state.

June 30, 1990: Skip Goerner was fishing at Quartz Lake in Glacier National Park when a mountain lion approached. Goerner fended off the lion with his fishing rod until the animal eventually lost interest and left.

July 11, 1990: Montana game warden Mike Quinn responded to a complaint about a cougar stalking a horse on a ranch east of Bigfork. Prior to this call, Quinn said he had rarely been contacted concerning problem lions. "We'd just started getting calls," Quinn said, " and then this one came in. I told the people to fire a shot over the cougar's head and it should leave. They did, and the cougar took off.

"But they called back an hour later," Quinn continued, "and told me the cat was back. So, I decided to take a trip out there to see what was going on." When Quinn arrived at Swan Sites, where the complainant's house was located, the cougar was nowhere to be seen. The warden decided he'd check the property.

"As I was walking around, I suddenly had a funny feeling," said Quinn. "I turned around and there was this cougar, thirty yards away, crouched real low to the ground, its tail twitching. I started walking backwards, talking to the cat, and it kept creeping toward me, keeping about 25 yards between us. I had brought along both my service revolver, a Model 66 Smith & Wesson .357, and my service shotgun, a Remington 870 pump short-barreled riot gun. I almost never take the shotgun, but something had told me to pick it up. I first fired my revolver off to the side of the cat to try to frighten it off. Instead, it acted like a starter's pistol! The cougar took off, straight for me, running fast. I didn't have much time to think. I dropped the handgun, leveled the shotgun, and fired from the hip. The load of Double 0 buck hit the cat in its face and chest while it was in mid-air. But there was no stopping it. Its momentum carried it all the way to me. Its carcass brushed right past me, and it piled up dead five yards away.

"I was very lucky, and I knew it. My knees started shaking afterwards. There had been no time to act, simply to react."

The cougar that attacked Mike Quinn was a healthy four-and-a-half-year-old female. The animal did not have rabies.

"There was a time when you never saw a cat when you were riding patrol," said Quinn. "They were such secretive animals that just seeing one was unusual. That's all changed. From 1990 until the present day, I've seen at least 25 cats while out riding around," Quinn said during a July 2000 interview. "One day, my son was visiting from Missoula. He came riding patrol with me and he asked if I ever saw cats. I said, 'No, not usually.' Then, an hour later, a big tom crossed the road right in front of us. When it comes to lions in Montana, things are definitely changing."

In the early 1990s, the times were definitely changing for Montana and its lions. As the lion population increased in response to the growing deer population and less competition from other large predators, more lion-human conflicts were being reported. Wildlife conflicts were nothing new to state biologists, who often had to tranquilize and relocate problem bears, both grizzlies and blacks. Bears were a known quantity whose behavior could often be modified through conditioning. But lions, it was soon discovered, are a different matter, and are not so easily swayed from the path they've chosen to follow. If a cat starts regarding humans as prey, it will do so from that point forward, no matter what. Rubber bullets, pepper spray, and blasts of loud music will rarely convince the mountain lion to amend its ways.

For that reason, many states—Montana included—have a "zero-tolerance policy" toward mountain lions. If a lion gets in trouble, particularly near Kalispell or close to Bozeman or Missoula, game officials take a hard line. The animal is captured and euthanized, period. Erik Wenum, the state's wildlife conflict specialist, has removed cougars from people's homes and backyards. Big cats that become that fearless, are, in the state's mind, to be feared.

"We simply cannot take chances with lions," explained Gary Olson, wildlife biologist for the area north of Great Falls. "With bears, we can. But a lion has a fixed search image in its mind for meat and meat alone. A bear is an omnivore. When it sees a human, food is not the first thing that pops into its mind. Everything a lion eats moves. People move. That correlation just about eliminates a lion's ability to adapt and change.

"What's more, even if we tried aversive conditioning and radio-collared a problem lion and it later killed someone, then what? The department is in trouble. We can't afford to take that chance."

July 23, 1990: Scott O'Hare, 9, was playing with Chadd Flanagan, a relative, on the beach of Lake McDonald near the Apgar Lake picnic area. Scott's parents, Merry and Richard O'Hare, of Dayton, Wyoming, were nearby with a group of other parents. No warning was given when a mountain lion slipped into the area, then rushed up and attacked Scott.

Scott later told authorities that he had been taught to play dead if ever he encountered a wild animal. That's good advice if a grizzly bear is attacking you, but not such a great idea when the animal in question is a cougar. Scott yelled, then played dead, but the cougar continued to bite him and drag him along the shoreline. Alerted by his screams, the group of parents now appeared upon the scene. Reports indicate that the boy's uncle, Michael Flanagan, rushed up and kicked gravel at the cougar. The cougar dropped Scott and bounded away.

Scott received numerous lacerations and puncture wounds to the head, face, neck, and right arm. He was flown in a U.S. Forest Service helicopter to the Kalispell Regional Hospital, where he was admitted in stable condition. After surgery, he was taken to St. Patrick's Hospital in Missoula for observation.

Tracker Mike Clanton of Coram, Montana, brought his dog to the scene shortly after the attack on the boy. Clanton was joined in the search by park rangers. The cougar was found and destroyed at about 3:00 P.M., within 100 yards of the beach.

Biologist Keith Aune, of Montana's Department of Parks, Wildlife and Fish, noted that the young male cougar weighed only 40 pounds. Aune said that although that is "light," the cougar was not emaciated. Aune further stated that "yearlings will often be thinner [at] this time of year."

August 12, 1992: Nathaniel Moore, 12, of Cornville, Arizona, was sitting on a log at about 4:30 P.M. in Glacier National Park, waiting for his father, Romano Scaturro, who had hiked a short distance into the woods ahead. The father and son had climbed a 20- to 30-foot-high embankment above the Going to the Sun Road, about three and a half miles from the foot of Lake McDonald. As Scaturro was walking, he heard Nathaniel cry out, "Hey!" He turned and saw a cougar on Nathaniel. Racing to his side, Scaturro kicked and yelled at the mountain lion until it broke off its attack. It retreated a short distance and watched the pair from a crouched position. Scaturro quickly picked up the bleeding boy and carried him back to their truck.

The Scaturros drove toward West Glacier seeking help. Park rangers, who noticed the vehicle being driven erratically and at a high rate of speed, pulled Scaturro over. When they learned of the incident, they rushed Scaturro and his injured son to a relief station for emergency medical care. The boy was then transported by A.L.E.R.T. helicopter to a hospital in Kalispell. Nathaniel's injuries included severe facial lacerations, numerous other lacerations, and puncture wounds to his chest, arms, back, and leg. He also had broken bones in his jaw and sinus cavity. The youngster underwent several hours of surgery at Kalispell Regional Hospital. Afterwards, one eye was swollen shut, his mouth was full of stitches, and a titanium plate had been installed to hold part of his skull together. All this the result of an attack that lasted no more than a minute.

"The cat came at me from the side," Nathaniel said later. "I heard something coming through the bush, and then it attacked me. [The next thing I knew] I was down on the ground struggling with it."

Trackers Mike Clanton and Dave Twamley, both of Coram, Montana, assisted park rangers with tracking dogs. The mountain lion was located near the attack site and was shot and killed at about 7:00 P.M. The lion, a 98-pound male, was not rabid.

July 31, 1998: Dante Swallow, 6, was hiking in the Marshall Mountains near Missoula with other campers and counselors from a nearby camp. For some reason, a cougar singled out young Dante and attacked him. Aaron Hall, a 16-year-old counselor from Missoula, rushed to the boy's defense. "I don't remember kicking the animal," Hall said. "I was just using my hands. I was waving and [trying] to get him off." Witnesses later said that Hall not only kicked the cougar vigorously, but screamed at it as well.

"It was like my brain was standing still and my body was moving 100 miles per hour," he said. "I didn't really know what I had done."

Hall's efforts were rewarded when the animal released Dante and ran off. Hall next tended to the numerous puncture wounds on Dante's neck and the scratches on his back and abdomen. Dante was eventually taken to Missoula Hospital, where he was treated and released.

The cougar was tracked, treed and killed by game wardens and deputies who brought in lion hounds.

Hall received numerous awards and honors for his courage. The Hellgate High School junior received $3,000 and a bronze medal from the Carnegie Hero Fund Commission, a board founded in 1904 by Pittsburgh industrialist and philanthropist Andrew Carnegie to reward rescuers who go above and beyond the call of duty. Aaron Hall also earned a trip to Washington to meet President Clinton. The Discovery Channel produced a television show about the rescue, and paid Hall $1,000. The unselfish young man gave half the cash to Dante Swallow.

Hall still doesn't like to be alone when he hikes or camps. "It's not that I'm afraid of cats, but I prefer not to be by myself," he said. Who could blame him?

Summer 1998: A group of pre-schoolers looking at flowers in the Rattlesnake National Recreation Area saw a cougar in the shrubs, just three feet away. The animal backed away.

Not long afterward, 25 day campers and their counselors were stalked by a pair of subadult lions on the same trail.

A similar thing happened to a family hiking Grant Creek a week later.

Then a mountain lion pounced on Dante Swallow as he played with other children at a day camp in the Marshall Mountains.

"From a public safety standpoint, we don't like to see so many incidences," said Joe Kipphut, a resource forester for the Missoula Ranger District in which the Rattlesnake recreation area lies.

The Forest Service's worries translated into a modification on its restrictions against dogs and firearms in the Rattlesnake Recreation Area, to allow lion hunting. The hunt was restricted, with only houndsmen selected by the Montana Department of Fish, Wildlife and Parks and the Forest Service being permitted to chase lions in the Rattlesnake. Only one houndsman was to be allowed in the drainage at a time. A sign was posted at the trailhead, telling area users that a hunt was in progress. Houndsmen were also limited to killing adult female lions and subadults. Handguns were the only weapons allowed.

"We are not after trophy toms with this hunt," said John Firebaugh, Montana Department of Fish Wildlife and Parks wildlife manager. "We are trying to manage the lion population by removing some females."

The hunt was considered a preemptive strike to prevent further incidents in an area popular with many of the state's residents.

August 1, 1998: It was Saturday evening at 8:10 P.M., and six-year-old Joey Wing was walking along a two-track road in the campground at Swift Reservoir, about 20 miles west of Dupuyer, Montana. Joey was walking behind a friend, who was mounted on a pony. The two children had been trading positions: One would walk while the other rode, then they would switch places. It was Joey's turn to walk. The boys were with three other chldren.

The Swift Reservoir campground consists of an upper camp and a lower camp. The upper camp lies upslope, some 300 yards away from the lower camp. The 300-yard stretch between the camping areas, which lies adjacent to the road upon which Joey and his friends were playing, is grown up in timber and thick brush. As Joey Swift walked past some especially thick brush, he noticed a mountain lion in the bushes. He started backing up and hollering, "No!

No!" Then he made a big mistake: He started to run. Aroused, the lion darted from the brush, leaped upon the boy, and knocked him to the ground. It bit him on the back of his head and his back, then grabbed him by the skull and dragged Joey almost 30 yards back into the timber and undergrowth. The lion singled out Joey despite the fact that the children were playing close to at least 50 adults and horses that were gathered at the campground for an outing.

When the lion pounced on Joey, the boy started screaming, and continued to scream and fight back as the lion dragged him into the brush.

The boy's mother, Melissa Wing, of Missoula, together with Frosty DeBoo and Kyle Sinclair, a tribal officer for the Blackfeet tribe, responded immediately when they heard Joey's screams, arriving at the attack site in less than thirty seconds. The mother rushed in and drove the cougar away from her son. They then picked up Joey, removed him from the brush, and took him to a private vehicle, which transported Joey and his mother to Dupuyer. An ambulance took them from there to the hospital in Conrad, Montana.

DeBoo and Sinclair, who was wearing a sidearm, went back into the brush to search for the lion. They found one, too, not fifteen feet from where it had dragged the boy. The men said that the cat was crouched low, its ears laid back. Sinclair fired his 9mm pistol at the cat, hitting it in the side of the head, but doing little damage. The cat ran off. The men didn't pursue it, since they believed that they had wounded and perhaps even killed it.

Houndsman Clint McAlpine of Valier was called in to track the wounded animal. When McAlpine arrived, he released his two dogs onto the blood trail. The dogs quickly treed a lion within 500 yards of where the boy had been mauled. The treed cat had a clearly visible wound on its head.

State game warden Tom Flowers killed the lion about two hours after the attack with a 12-gauge shotgun slug. The young male cougar weighed between 90 and 110 pounds.

Joey Wing was admitted to the hospital with bite wounds, claw marks, and lacerations and contusions to his head, shoulders, and abdomen (from when he had been dragged across the ground). Approximately 200 stitches were required to close the boy's wounds.

10

Arizona Attacks

In 1937, biologist Frank Hibben completed a study of cougar scat collected from various types of habitat in Arizona and New Mexico. To no one's surprise, the analysis of this scat revealed that deer are the cougar's preferred prey in all habitats within these two states. Surprisingly, small mammals formed a smaller percentage of the cougar's overall diet than was anticipated. Although jackrabbits, cottontails, gray foxes, skunks, porcupines, and badgers were all occasionally eaten, deer were preferred by a lopsided margin.

Arizona cougars will also target sheep and cattle, as will cougars anywhere. About 35 percent of all cougar kills documented by wildlife biologists during research studies conducted both during the mid-1970s and in a later study in Aravaipa Canyon, were calves. According to Harley Shaw, "Where ranchers run year-round cow-calf operations in Arizona, losses to pumas are very real and significant." Even though Arizona law allows ranchers to take whatever measures are necessary to protect their stock against cougars, the big cats are still numerous. In fact, lion sightings have become common in the suburbs just outside Flagstaff, Phoenix, and Tucson, where pet predation by cougars is a real problem.

In 1997, the Arizona Department of Fish and Wildlife estimated the state's resident population of cougars at more than 3,000 animals. With so many mountain lions, an increase of human activity in prime cougar habitat, and the occasional drop in deer numbers, especially during times of drought, it's inevitable that the number of lion-human encounters will rise.

Cougar sightings, especially near the Madera Canyon area just south of Tucson, had become common as long ago as 1988. Things became so bad that the U.S. Forest Service closed several popular hiking trails near Mount Wrightson in the Santa Rita Mountains for nine days in late May and early June. When a hunter employed by the Arizona Game and Fish Department eventually killed a young, emaciated male mountain lion that had reportedly not only stalked a camper but also attacked a number of dogs, the trails were reopened.

All was well for exactly one day: Then another hiker reported having been stalked by a mountain lion in Madera Canyon. Game and Fish officials visited the site, and stated that they believed two young lions, possibly siblings, had been responsible for the stalkings.

Arizona has had its share of cougars attacking humans. Here is a roundup of some of the most recent attacks.

May 28, 1988: It was Saturday of Memorial Day weekend. Sarah Fuller, 6, was playing with her sister Amy, age 8, just fifty yards away from the cabin their family had rented for the weekend. The location was the Rim Trail Ranch Resort in the rugged Mogollon Rim country of Arizona. Sarah and Amy were so excited to be on vacation that bright May morning that they hadn't even bothered to change out of their pajamas.

The two girls were trying to catch a lizard near an old tree. It was early—about 7:30 A.M.—and their stepfather, Greg Egnash, and mother, Lisa, of Mesa, Arizona, were still inside the cabin.

As the girls continued to play, they didn't notice the mountain lion crouched in the bushes. When the animal decided to make its move, it crept slowly ahead in the low stalking posture so familiar to anyone who has ever observed a house cat hunting. As the cougar stalked closer, the girls suddenly noticed its approach and began to scream. Inside the cabin, Greg and Lisa heard the screams and headed out the door—perhaps at the very moment the cat was launching itself onto Sarah Fuller.

Forty pounds of muscle, bone and tendon drove the youngster down onto the ground. By the time Greg Egnash had burst out the cabin's door, the cat was trying to grab onto Sarah with its jaws.

Egnash raced toward the struggling child with one thought in mind: To get the girl away from the cat. Meanwhile, Lisa ran back to the cabin for the .22 rifle inside. As soon as Egnash reached Sarah, he hurled his body at the lion and knocked the animal off the girl.

Egnash now grabbed the injured child with one arm, caught hold of Amy's hand with his other, and began running for the safety of the cabin. Lisa ran from the cabin, handed the loaded gun to her husband, and pulled the two girls back inside with her.

The lion recovered its footing and just stood there, staring at the man. Egnash didn't hesitate: He started shooting. Seventeen times he fired into the cat's body. He shot until the rifle finally jammed. The .22 had done its job, however. The female lion was dead.

Egnash loaded the dead cat into the trunk of the car, then gathered his family and rushed Sarah to a hospital in nearby Payson, Arizona.

After three hours in the emergency room, Sarah was released. Her injuries included puncture wounds of the shoulder, neck, and body, as well as a badly torn ear.

According to a June 1991 *Outdoor Life* article written by Nick Worth, Greg Egnash reported that when he gave the lion's carcass to the Arizona game and fish officials, "the first thing they said was that the lion had been starving." The one- to two-year-old female cougar weighed about 40 pounds, less than half what its normal weight should have been.

Lee Fitzhugh, a wildlife extension specialist for the California Fish and Game Department at the University of Southern California at Davis, disagreed with the Arizona Game and Fish Department's appraisal of the lion. In his paper titled "The Biological Status of Mountain Lions in California," Fitzhugh wrote, "It is possible that young transient animals in good health may have been misclassified as 'emaciated' because of their low weight and youthful configuration. Claims that mountain lions are starving based on estimated weight often are wrong. Young lions are naturally lean-appearing," Fitzhugh concluded.

Reports that an offending animal had been a "captive" lion that was recently released illegally into the wild often crop up after incidents such as these. This very rumor circulated after the attack upon Sarah Payson, but was never substantiated. To date, no lion involved in an attack on a human in the wild has ever been proven to have been a captive lion.

May 1, 1989: Arizona's Superstition Mountains are said to be where a crazy Dutchman lost the richest gold mine ever uncovered in this country. The mountains loom above Canyon Lake, 30 miles northeast of Phoenix. Canyon Lake was the destination Tim Walsh had in mind that weekend when he and his two sons, Joshua, 5, and Eric, 6, arrived at the Palo Verde boat ramp, which is situated in an open and well-used area of the lake. Walsh was also accompanied by a female companion and her 8-year-old son. The time was 6:00 P.M.

"The boys were hiking up a little hill," Walsh said. "All of a sudden, this mountain lion came out of nowhere. It came bounding out and knocked Josh over, grabbed him by the head, shook him, and started to drag him off." Walsh, who had taken a brief hike to a nearby embankment, sprung into action. He jumped down off the embankment, picked up the nearest large rock he could find, and threw it at the lion. Walsh's aim was true, and the rock hit the cougar in the head. The lion promptly dropped Joshua and went bounding down the lake's shoreline. Walsh and his companion gathered up the children and ran for the safety of their pickup truck. What makes this attack so incomprehensible is that it took place near a parking lot and a boat dock crowded with people. Yet it happened so quickly, few were aware. The cougar, for some reason, simply zeroed in on young Joshua and attacked.

Joshua was airlifted to the hospital, where doctors operated to suture shut the boy's extensive scalp wounds. It took surgeons 90 minutes to repair his right ear, which was nearly severed from his head. Overall, Joshua's wounds required more than 100 stitches to close.

The cougar was estimated at about four feet in length and 100 pounds in weight. State Game and Fish officials later stated that from its description they believed it to be a one- or two-year-old animal.

After the attack, Joshua underwent a series of rabies shots in the event the attacking animal was rabid. County Rabies Control officers did not search for the animal, however. "We're not trackers," commented one authority, according to an article in *The Phoenix Gazette*. The Maricopa County Sheriff's Office unsuccessfully searched for the animal after the attack. They felt hindered by not knowing which animal they were after, or even where to start looking.

Donald Van Driel, a spokesman for the Tonto National Forest, the entity responsible for managing Canyon Lake and its facilities, said that from descriptions of the animal, he doubted it had rabies. "The mountain lion probably had no water to drink elsewhere on its range, and when it came near the lake went after the first prey he found," Van Driel said. "They will take anything they can catch."

Van Driel further stated that because of its age, the cat might not have learned to hunt properly. There had been no previous reports of the mountain lion having had any run-ins with people.

Tim Walsh was ready to hunt down the mountain lion on his own simply to determine whether the animal had rabies. When he went back to retrieve his truck, after having been airlifted from the attack site to the hospital with Joshua, Walsh found that the blue rubber thongs he had left behind in the excitement had been chewed up by an animal. One thong, nearly torn to shreds, was discovered where the attack occurred. The other, with numerous puncture marks, was found 300 yards away, near where the pickup truck had been parked. Walsh feels certain the frustrated cougar vented its rage on his thongs. "He was mad that I took his meal away," he said. "And it's obvious that this animal came back. It's a very disturbed animal."

August 21, 1993: Merlue Irwin, a ranch woman, had just located a colt that had been missing on her 70-acre ranch, which is about a mile north of Wickenburg, Arizona. The colt had somehow managed to snag itself on a barbed-wire fence. Irwin freed the colt, patched the hole in the fence with some cedar fenceposts, and then headed back to her house, taking one of the posts with her as she walked.

As Irwin walked through the gathering dusk, she couldn't help but notice that her horses were acting spooky. She was only about 1,500 feet from her home when the unexplained spookiness of the animals, together with the sounds of dry twigs snapping behind her, caused the woman to spin around in her tracks.

"I couldn't believe what I saw," she later recounted. A mountain lion was running directly at her. When the animal was about five feet away, it crouched and lunged at the 53-year-old Irwin.

Imagine the animal's surprise when, instead of landing on its intended prey, it was hit in midair "across the snout and the top of the head," as Irwin described it, with the cedar fence post. "I kind of stunned it," she said.

The animal, noticeably dazed, lay in the dirt at Irwin's feet. The woman began to slowly back away, screaming as she did so. She didn't run, as running triggers the predatory chase response in animals such as cougars and bears. When she backed into a tree, the lion hissed, slowly got up, and started to approach. Fortunately, the lion stopped, seemed to think twice about things, turned around, and crawled back into the undergrowth.

Irwin backed up the remainder of the distance to her home. Once inside, she called the sheriff's department. The officers arrived with a dog, and quickly treed the cat. When the animal continued to act aggressively, a deputy shot it.

The cougar that tried to take down Merlue Irwin was a young female. The cat had been spotted prowling just outside Wickenburg in the days leading up to the attack, but no one had actually complained about the animal.

"There is no [other] choice [but to dispatch it]," said Harley Shaw, a mountain lion expert and biologist, in a *Phoenix Gazette* article. "You can't capture the cat and relocate it. You'd just be moving the problem into someone else's back yard. A mountain lion that isn't afraid of humans is one that will get into conflicts with them."

July 17, 1994: The summer of 1994 was hot and dry in Arizona, and it seemed as if mountain lions were on the prowl everywhere. Near the town of Fort Huachuca, a cougar pounced upon a child's pet goat that was only a few feet from its five-year-old owner. The lion was pursued, found with the injured goat, but allowed to escape since it was just "doing what mountain lions do."

Another bold lion pawed at the window of a Tucson home before deciding to head back out into the desert.

Then there was the cougar of Apache Lake.

Apache Lake lies within the Tonto National Forest, outside of Phoenix. The lake's smooth, broad beach appeals to campers who like to roll out their sleeping bags on its rockless shores. The night of July 17, two-year-old Jesse Humphreys was camping with his parents, Suzi Humphreys and Jocy Day, when a mountain lion snuck in under darkness and tried to drag off the boy while he was still in his sleeping bag. Day, the boy's father, pulled the boy away before the lion could drag him off.

That didn't end the ordeal, as the lion continued to stalk the family for the next 20 minutes. The three people huddled inside their beached boat, on the bank of the lake, using their water skis to fend off the mountain lion. Finally, the lion wandered away.

Jesse's injuries included scratches and a gash in his ear that required 10 stitches.

Officials later decided that the cougar probably was attracted to the campsite by food scraps left near the fire, although the boy simply moving about within his sleeping bag could have been enough to trigger the cat's curiosity.

April 29, 2000: The site was Bartlett Lake in Arizona's Maricopa County. The time, about 8:30 P.M. A family fishing at the lake was camping at one of the area's campsites. A burnt-out fire-ring could be seen close to the family's tent, and the father had recently lit two lanterns to illuminate the camp. Although the family's name was reported in the newspapers at the time of this attack, Arizona Game and Fish officials have asked this writer to refrain from revealing the name of the family in any accounting of cougar attacks.

The victim, a four-year-old girl, and her seven-year-old brother had been outside, chasing bugs away from the family's large aluminum frame tent. Inside that tent, the girl's father and mother were preparing their gear for the night. They had originally intended to return home, but had changed their plans to spend one more night at the lake. When the tent was ready, the parents called for their children to come inside.

Each child came around the tent from a different direction. As the four-year-old girl walked past some palo verde trees, a mountain lion suddenly jumped out and grabbed her. The girl screamed, and a loud commotion followed. When the girl's father peered out of the tent to see what was going on, he saw a mountain lion dragging his daughter away by the back of her head. Shaking the child violently, the animal headed east, away from the tent. That was all the man was able to see before his daughter was dragged beyond the glow of lantern light and into the darkness. The man and his wife scrambled out of the tent and immediately chased after the lion. Screaming and yelling as they searched for the child, the parents soon located their daughter wedged in a thicket of ironwood and acacia, only 15 yards from the tent.

The man looked around anxiously, but the cat was nowhere to be seen. He believed that their yelling had made the animal nervous, causing it to drop the girl and run. He retrieved his daughter from the thicket, cutting himself numerous times on the acacia thorns in the process. Then he held his daughter close to his chest while his wife flagged down an approaching camper. The camper agreed to take the mother and daughter to an aid station at the campground for medical assistance while the man and his son stayed behind. Their vehicle was still hooked up to their boat. They decided they would need to unhook the boat in order to make the best possible time to the hospital.

Officers Kevin Bergersen and Brian Anthony of the Arizona Department of Game and Fish had meanwhile arrived at Bartlett Lake. The father was still wearing a shirt covered in his daughter's blood. The two officers sent for an air tracking unit that had (FLIR) infrared radar capabilities, but the unit was detained.

While waiting, the officers decided to go with the victim's father to the attack site. The man pointed out the tent and also the direction in which the cat had dragged the girl. The officers were able to locate six or seven big lion tracks, approximately four inches in diameter, leading from the tent to the thicket. When the officers neared the thicket, they noticed blood on the branches and ground and also some human hair. Reluctant to go into the thicket, one officer went to the projected exit from the bushes and found another four-inch-diameter lion track. Large clumps of blond human hair were scattered about, along with mountain lion hair clinging to the acacias.

The officers decided to kill the cat if they found it, not only to check it for rabies, but also because any cougar that bold is a definite threat to people.

As the officers were examining the scene, a woman from nearby campsite approached. She said a mountain lion had gotten into a fight with her dog about twenty minutes before (10:40 P.M.). Officer Anthony immediately left with the camper. As Officer Bergersen was discussing with a Maricopa County sheriff's deputy how to preserve the scene for the next day's tracking effort, he suddenly noticed an animal's eyes glowing within the thicket right where the hair and blood had been found. "As I looked in with the spotlight, I saw two orange eyes looking back at me," Bergersen later said. He called out to Anthony, and the mountain lion emerged from the thicket. Bergersen pulled out his service pistol and aimed it at the lion. The deputy, meanwhile, had gone off to get his rifle. When Anthony returned, he used the deputy's .30–30 to kill the mountain lion with one round to the chest.

Upon examination, the lion was found to be a healthy 140-pound adult tom. The animal had three inches of abdominal fat. Multiple lead pellets were embedded in its hind quarter, but they were completely healed over. There was speculation that the animal may have been marauding near humans or their dwellings, which would explain the shot, although it is just as likely that a quail or rabbit hunter simply flung some lead its way when the cat was encountered in the field.

The victim's injuries were substantial. The attending physician said that had the injuries been just a fraction of an inch to the right, or lower, they would have been fatal. As it was, the doctor was unable to say how many times the victim's skull had been punctured. The scalp had been avulsed (skinned off) severely about the rear of the head, then displaced to either side and atop the wound. The skull had been compressed and the dura—the brain-covering membrane—had been compromised, which exposed the brain to infectious fluids from the lion's mouth. The neurosurgeons had to flush and clean the brain, patch the dura, then lift the section of skull that had been depressed. A plastic surgeon then had to mend the massive scalp avulsion. Doctors also had to cleanse and drain six deep claw wounds, three on each side of the chest. From the position of these wounds, it appeared as though the mountain lion had grabbed the victim from behind with its claws and then used the leverage to grab the victim by the skull with its incisors.

The surgery went very well. The victim also was given preventive treatment for meningitis. She will probably need many additional reconstructive surgeries as she grows.

Mountain lions will often return to the scene of an attack, particularly if they know they have injured their prey. Since it had been successful once in attacking a small child, there was every reason for authorities to fear it might do so again.

When the son asked his father why the attack happened at all, the man replied, "We're in his [the lion's] house." Nothing more could be added to such a profound statement, remarkably uttered during extreme duress.

11

Texas Attacks

After years of hostility by ranchers and others toward mountain lions, the Texas Department of Parks and Wildlife undertook a five-year telemetry study of radio-collared lions in south Texas. Completed in 1998, one of the study's most important findings was that mountain lions in south Texas have little effect on cattle. Of 69 carcasses identified as possible mountain lion kills, 50 percent were white-tailed deer, 22 percent were javelina, 9 percent were feral hogs, and 16 percent were other species, including seven domestic sheep, two bobcats, one mountain lion, and one lone calf.

Researchers also learned that mortality of Texas lions is high. Of the 19 cats collared for the study, two were shot by hunters, two died after getting caught in neck snares in fences, and two died of unknown causes.

The big cats roam most of south and west Texas, but are only protected—as is all wildlife—in the jewel of the state, Big Bend National Park. The park is named because it's located at the big bend made by the Rio Grande River as it snakes its way southward between Texas and Mexico. The park covers more than 801,000 acres of west Texas. It is in this park, this oasis of life erupting from an arid landscape, where all of Texas's modern-day cougar attacks upon humans have taken place. Here are some of the most dramatic:

April 14, 1953: An unnamed man was walking along the Lost Mine Trail when a cougar rushed up and grabbed him by his pants leg. The man's shouts and aggressive behavior drove the cat away. G. Sholly, park ranger, shot the cougar the next day.

November 11, 1978: Mr. T. Rives and his family were hiking along the Lost Mine Trail in the early afternoon. The family reached the upper end of the trail and had just left it when a "large, purring, tail-waving lion" ran toward Rives's three-year-old son. The father raced toward the charging cat, pushed his son behind him, and faced the lion. He stood in the trail face-to-face with the "lion inches from him." The lion soon tired of this stand-off and walked off the trail, although it remained in nearby bushes. The family was able to leave with no further incident.

April 4, 1984: Ranger Susan Roe was hiking along the South Rim Trail close to where it intersects with the Blue Creek Trail when she glanced up and saw a cougar ready to spring. Without further warning, the cat leaped and slammed into the woman's shoulder, knocking her onto the ground. Roe fell and twisted an ankle. The cat ran away.

Roe later said that the cat was a male that weighed about 65 pounds. She also believed it was a juvenile because she was able to make out faint spots on its pelage.

August 3, 1984: Kim and Chris Brown who lived in Garland, Texas, a suburb of Dallas, had been married for less than a year. The couple had just arrived at Big Bend National Park for a visit. The family—Chris, Kim, and Kim's children, David Vaught, 8, and Justin Vaught, 4—was eager to do some exploring, and set off along the popular Basin Loop Trail. This particular trail starts out near Big Bend's park headquarters, makes a loop around the Chisos Basin, and winds up back near park headquarters.

The Chisos Basin comprises about 60,000 acres. Oak Spring provides the basin with a reliable source of water, and the surrounding habitat remains lush even under drought conditions. White-tailed deer, mule deer, and javelina are common here; so are mountain lions.

Kim, Chris, and her two children were thinking about none of that. David was having great fun yelling, "Snake!" to frighten his mother. But his attempts soon wore thin. In fact, Kim had stopped paying any attention to David after she found herself getting bitten by some fire ants that had crawled inside her pants leg. David had hurried ahead of brother Justin, so when he rounded a bend in the trail he was the first to see the cougar crouched and ready to spring.

"Mountain lion!" David yelled.

The cat was on the uphill side of the trail. Kim and Justin paid no attention to David's yell. After all, he'd been crying "Snake!" ever since they'd started hiking. When Chris glanced up, he was horrified at what he saw.

In an instant, David was racing toward him, the mountain lion close on his heels. When David glanced back over his left shoulder to see if the cat was gaining, the cougar leaped up at him. Jaws wide open, the cat made contact with the boy, its hind claws digging deeply into David's thigh while its front claws scratched into both shoulders. The lion now clamped down on

David's skull with its powerful jaws. As it did this, it relaxed its grip with its claws. The cat's weight, or inertia, catapulted it over David's body in a move calculated to break the boy's neck. David and the lion dropped to the ground.

Kim Brown screamed in terror at the sight of her son lying limp upon the earth. Even as Kim screamed, the lion refused to give up, and continued to bite down on her son's head. Chris Brown raced at the cat, yelling, in an attempt to frighten it away, but the cougar wasn't intimidated. It turned and snarled, then went back at the boy's skull. Brown now ran up and started kicking at the lion, but fell on the slope. As the man slid down next to the cougar, he tried to grab onto the animal. His touch caused the cat to pause and turn its head. When it did so, Chris grabbed onto the cougar's head with both hands and pulled for all he was worth. He yanked it across his legs and threw it down the hill, the animal screaming as it was torn off the boy. The man was now between the cat and David.

Kim Brown remembered the sounds of the cat screaming as Brown pulled it from its prey. Certain that her son was dead, she now watched in horror as the cougar landed on her husband. Chris was lying on his back, trying desperately to keep the cougar's fangs away from his face. The animal's hind legs raked Chris Brown's legs as the two wrestled on the ground. With what seemed to be his last bit of strength, Brown finally managed to hurl the cat six feet down the slope.

The cat wouldn't give up. As Chris lay on the ground, the cougar gathered itself and sprang at the man. Chris was ready: He pulled back his legs and then kicked as hard as he could as the springing animal hit him. This tactic had the desired effect, and made the cat retreat one or two steps. When it did, Chris jumped to his feet, grabbed a big stick that was on the ground, and brandished it at the cougar, screaming like a banshee as he did so. The cougar hesitated, screamed once more—probably in frustration at being deprived of its prey—and then ran into the bushes.

Chris hurried to David, who was lying motionless on the ground. A big patch of David's scalp was missing; what remained was hanging loosely from the boy's skull. Fang marks had scratched at the bare skull, but remarkably, had not penetrated. David's eyes were full of blood, but appeared uninjured. Chris wrapped his shirt around the boy's head, then picked him up and started running toward park headquarters.

Kim thought she heard something moving along with them, paralleling their progress in the nearby bushes. Chris heard it too, but wouldn't admit it to his wife. To keep her calm, he told her that he heard nothing.

Reaching park headquarters, David received first aid from park rangers, then was transported to a nearby hospital. No one there was qualified to perform the intricate surgery required for David's wounds. Sgt. Carl Bierman, a police officer from nearby Alpine, Texas, helped David and his family in an ambulance, then drove them 600 miles to Dallas. They made it in the amazing time of seven hours!

Meanwhile, the mountain lion continued to roam free. Clayton McKinney, a Texas Ranger, heard about the attack on his radio and called his nephew, state predator hunter Bill McKinney, at about 7:30 P.M. McKinney, who was not far from the attack site, loaded his hounds into his vehicle and headed to Big Bend.

When McKinney arrived, no one at the park could authorize him to hunt down the cat. By the time a decision was made, it was too late to start on the cat's track that night.

McKinney asked Doug Waid, a biologist who had done considerable work with lions, to join in the chase. The two men were ready to go before 5:00 A.M. the next day. They knew they would have their best luck before the sun rose and burned out any lingering scent from the lion's trail.

Instead, the rangers asked them to wait until other personnel arrived. As additional rangers and help showed up, McKinney's anxiety mounted. He knew how fleeting scent trails could be, especially when they had been laid down many hours before.

At 7:00 A.M., Bill freed Missy, one of his two best lion dogs, and two others. Amazingly, she ran in the same direction that the Browns had taken after the attack. The lion *had* followed them! Disgruntled at being deprived of its prey, perhaps it had been stimulated at the sight of the fleeing family. In any event, the cougar had paralleled the family's path for about 150 yards before it made a 90-degree turn that took it away from the hiking trail and across Laguna Meadow.

The cat was headed for 7,000-foot Ward Mountain, a formidable obstacle, especially when viewed from the perspective of a lion hunter and a biologist on the track of what could easily become a man-killer. The dogs quickly raced up the mountain and beyond the men's ability to hear them. McKinney turned on a portable receiver so he could electronically track his hounds. In that manner, he was able to stay on the trail.

Overcast skies had helped keep the temperatures down, which aided the hounds immensely. McKinney also carried water to refresh the dogs' drying mouths and noses, either of which might easily spell failure to the trackers. At 10:30 A.M., the dogs located the remains of a skunk the lion had apparently killed and eaten.

At 2:00 P.M., the clouds cleared and a warm wind destroyed what was left of the cat's scent trail. Foiled, at least for the time being, the men looked around them. McKinney noticed a thicket up ahead, and instinctively felt that that was where the cat had headed.

The men led the hounds toward the thicket. Even before they reached the brush, the dogs began showing signs of having detected a scent. When they gained the brush, Missy immediately began to bay. The two other dogs joined in. The chase was on. Remarkably, the cougar headed back toward the foot trail where David Vaught had been attacked. About a quarter mile up the Laguna Meadows trail from the junction with the Basin Loop Trail—and less than one quarter mile from where David Vaught had been attacked—the dogs barked treed.

At first the two men were uncertain. Did they have the right cougar? The lion biologist dispelled Bill McKinney's doubts. "It has to be," Waid said.

McKinney drew his revolver and shot the cat through the lungs. The cougar leaped from the tree, ran 200 yards, and climbed up another. This time McKinney aimed for its head and fired. The cat died at 5:30 P.M., less than 200 yards from where it had attacked David Vaught.

The cat had a strange reddish-colored coat. Later estimates put its age at between 16 to 24 months. The animal weighed 85 pounds, about right for a Texas puma of this age. Laboratory analysis proved that this was the right cat. David Vaught's hair was found in the animal's lower intestinal tract. The cat was not rabid.

The cat was in good condition. It had no discernible injuries. The animal wasn't even particularly hungry, having fed on a deer shortly before it attacked David. David Vaught had not even ventured close to the lion's kill, as the carcass was found at least 200 yards from where the boy had been attacked. This particular lion was a member of that most dangerous and unpredictable grouping of pumas, the adolescent male; forced out by his mother and relegated by older, more dominant males to marginal habitats.

David Vaught had numerous plastic surgeries performed on his face and head. The Dallas Cowboy Cheerleaders even gave a benefit performance for the boy, to help raise money his mounting medical bills.

Big Bend National Park biologists have tried, without success, to use aversive conditioning on offending mountain lions. After a near attack, an offending animal is shot at close range with a load of rock salt. If the animal returns to its aggressive mode of behavior within two weeks, it is shot.

What follows is an incident that occurred after a failed attempt at aversive conditioning:

April 19, 1987: At 12:15 P.M. Linda Burt was hiking with her husband, Steve, and her son along Big Bend National Park's Basin Loop Trail. She was wearing a daypack in which she was carrying apples, peanut-butter crackers, a granola bar, and peanut patties. She was holding a grape drink in her hand.

The family had traveled to a point on the Chisos Basin loop cut-off about one quarter mile east of the Laguna Meadow Trail when they saw two deer running down the hill. At first they thought that they had spooked the animals. They continued along the trail, and five minutes later ran smack into a mountain lion, standing in the middle of the trail. The family was uncertain what to do next, so they just stood where they were. The cougar stared at them. Steve Burt warned Linda not to run. He then scooped up their two-and-a-half-year-old son, and the family began to back slowly down the trail. The lion followed. The couple stopped once again. Steve slowly bent over to pick up a rock. Linda, however, panicked, and started to run. Steve told her to stop, and she did, but it was too late as the lion rushed up and leaped onto Linda's back. Steve hurled the rock at the animal, then both he and Linda started to yell. The lion jumped off the woman after only a few seconds, ran into the woods, and stopped. It turned and looked at the family.

Steve Burt checked his wife to make certain she was all right, then told her to start back down the hill. The lion was only about twenty feet away at this point. As Linda began to walk away, Steve picked up another rock, then began backing down the hill after his wife. The lion followed the Burts for about 100 feet, then stopped and allowed the family to move out of sight.

The family arrived back at park headquarters at 12:25 P.M. First aid was administered to Linda Burt, who had six puncture wounds to her left thigh and two scratches across her right buttock.

At 1:10 P.M., trackers Mike Fleming, Steve Stinnett and Dale Thompson were directed to the spot where Linda Burt had been attacked by the lion. All trail heads had been closed by this time. As Thompson was inspecting the area, he heard something behind him. He turned and saw a mountain lion just ten feet off the trail, perhaps 25 feet from Thompson.

Thompson threw up his .223 and shot. The lion started running downslope, and Thompson was able to shoot twice more before it disappeared from view. Fleming shot his 12-gauge shotgun three times. The lion began favoring its left foreleg.

An hour and twenty minutes passed before several rangers on horse-back arrived with Billy Pat McKinney of the Texas Parks and Wildlife Department and his pack of hunting dogs. The dogs were released, and barked treed almost immediately.

The lion was shot by Bill McKinney. The cat, it turns out, was not rabid. It was later learned that four months prior to this attack, the yearling cougar had been chased, treed, drugged, and radio-collared. Whether this contributed to the animal's aggressive behavior is unknown.

May 24, 1998: At sunset, a man hiking Pine Canyon Trail in Big Bend National Park came over a rise and suddenly found himself face to face with a mountain lion. The cougar was close, too—no more than ten or fifteen feet away. When the hiker attempted to frighten the cougar away by waving his arms and yelling, the lion merely hissed. It wouldn't budge. When the hiker waved and yelled even more aggressively, the lion responded by closing the distance between them to three feet. The hiker now struck the lion with a tree limb, and then a rock. The hiker slowly retreated, all the while throwing rocks at the lion. When the hiker could no longer see the lion, he continued back to the trailhead uninterrupted.

May 25, 1998: Mary Jane Coder, who lived with her family in the South Texas town of Harlingen, had taken her three daughters hiking in Big Bend's scenic Chisos Mountains. The girls, Jessica, 9, Dallas, 8, and Meagan, 6, had paused along the Pine Canyon Trail so their mother could take a photograph of the trio in the starkly beautiful surroundings. Coder had daughter Dallas in the viewfinder when she saw that the child, who was sitting upon a boulder, was not smiling. Then "she started screaming, 'Mommy, Mommy, get me down from here,' " Coder later recalled. "I turned around and saw a big mountain lion getting ready to pounce." The cougar was on a rock about four feet from the family, its haunches up, as though ready to leap or lunge at them.

Coder, thinking fast, pulled the children behind her to protect them. She told them to get her pocketknife out of the backpack. She also threw a rock at the lion to try to scare it away. Unintimidated, the cat hissed back.

Now Coder shouted at the lion, and waved her knife. In response, the cougar charged at the girls, first at one, then at another, trying to cut them out of the group like it might a fawn deer out of a herd. "My kids scattered, which was the worst thing they could do," Coder said. "[The cat] would go toward one of them, and I would run toward it and it would veer away. I kept shouting at the girls to come to me, while shouting at the cat to go away. It was chaos."

At one point, the mountain lion came so close to the defending mother that it reached out with a forepaw and whacked her right hand. "It was like it was batting me to get to my children." One of the cougar's claws punctured the woman's hand.

After fifteen minutes, Coder pushed the girls under a rock ledge. The big cat promptly positioned itself on a boulder just above them, and waited. She told the girls to pray.

"That was the most fear I have ever known," Coder said.

Coder thought that if she remained where she was, the lion would consider it a challenge and eventually attack. She also knew that if she got into a fight with the animal and it went badly for her, then the lion would kill her children. She decided the only course of action was to get her girls out of there. She told them to walk quickly back up the trail, in a tightly bunched group, toward their car. Since the vehicle was two miles away, she knew they were probably in for a long, dangerous walk. The girls obeyed her and Coder, now walking backward while holding the small knife, followed warily, keeping an eye on the lion until, at last, she could no longer see the animal.

They had traveled a few hundred yards down the trail and, seemingly, beyond harm's way when Meagan suddenly screamed. Coder now saw the cougar crouched down, waiting in the bushes up ahead. The cat had circled around in front of the family to reach its new ambush site. Coder now walked in front of her girls, brandishing the knife and shouting at the lion. "I yelled, 'Get out of here! No!' like you would with a dog," she said. The cat remained hunkered down in the bushes while the Coders moved past it and down the trail. The vegetation was sparser here, providing the cat with much less cover than it had been able to use farther up the trail. The family covered the remaining distance to their car without further incident.

Coder was provided first aid by a park official, who also suggested she obtain a tetanus shot. Arrangements were made for the woman to visit the health clinic in Terlingua, Texas.

Park rangers later told news reporters that a severe drought in the area had made food scarce. Pine Canyon Trail, on which the Coders were confronted by the cat, as well as the Lost Mine Trail and Pine Canyon 4 campsite were all closed down because of the incident. The animal was not hunted down or killed, however. Coder approved of this action. She said, "[the cat] was doing what mountain lions do."

12

New Mexico Attacks

January 20, 1974: Two brothers—Kenneth Clark Nolan, 8, and half-brother David Cordry, 7—were playing near the village of Arroyo Seco, which means "Dry Canyon" in Spanish. The small town is on U.S. Highway 285–64 between Santa Fe and Espanola, New Mexico. The boys were in the rabbit brush and gullies about two miles east of the town's several occupied houses when they suddenly glanced up and saw a mountain lion getting ready to pounce. The boys started to flee, but the cougar caught Kenneth and started biting him on his back. David turned to help him, and tried to push the lion away. Instead of being discouraged, the cougar now grabbed for David with its forepaw. It tore the boy's coat and inflicted superficial scratches on his body, then went back to mauling Kenneth.

David knew he had to get help, and ran off to get his father, a State Police Patrolman also named David Cordry.

When young David reached his home, he was hysterical, almost incoherent, and unable to give his father accurate directions to the spot where his brother was possibly dying. More than twenty minutes elapsed before the man was able to calm the boy down, get him loaded up onto his motorcycle, and drive back to the attack site. Cordry also brought his dog, a mixed German shepherd. Getting off his motorcycle, the elder Cordry quickly climbed a nearby ridge to see if he could see Kenneth. Then he heard the dog baying at the lion. The cougar stood its ground, refusing to leave the boy's lifeless body, all the while clawing and snarling at the dog. As Cordry drew closer, he saw the animal crouch over the boy and lick blood from his face. Holding his .357 Magnum service revolver in both outstretched hands, the man fired at the cat from twenty five yards. The lion was hit, and jumped sideways as the bullet ripped through its stomach. Two more shots found their mark. Trailing blood, the still-snarling wounded lion fled the scene and headed north down the arroyo. Mr. Cordry, knowing his boy was dead, sat down and wept.

James Meyer, one of Cordry's neighbors, took up the chase. The lion was bayed about half a mile from the attack site, then killed with a .30/30 rifle. Meyer turned the carcass over to the state police who, in turn, gave it to New Mexico Department of Game and Fish personnel when they arrived on the scene.

The lion turned out to be a female. It weighed 47 pounds and appeared to be emaciated. Its appearance was "bony, . . . particularly in the pelvic region . . . Probing indicated little of flesh overlying the skeletal structure," according to the New Mexico Game and Fish News dated January 24, 1974.

Post-mortem examination of the animal was conducted at the Bernalillo County Medical Center. The animal was not rabid. Its digestive tract was empty except for human remains and several small hair balls. There was no fat anywhere on the lion's body. Its bone marrow was red, not the creamy white usually associated with healthy animals, which indicates a possible white cell deficiency, severe infection, or other potentially fatal conditions. The lion was otherwise normal. There were no old injuries, fractures, or disabling diseases. Wear on its foot pads led investigators to believe it may have traveled extensively. It appeared weak, and was probably well below normal in both stamina and strength. The diagnosis was of an animal in a "starvation condition." The female was estimated at no younger than eighteen months of age. The necropsy report was inconclusive as to whether the cat had ever been a pet or captive. Analyses included a fluoroscopy to test for tetracycline, an antibiotic commonly used to treat respiratory ailments in domestic cats, and also on the hair balls to determine whether any domestic animal hair, human hair, or synthetic fibers were present. Dog hair was found, plus some cardboard. A follow-up letter from Ladd S. Gordon, director of the laboratory that analyzed the hair balls and fecal matter, stated the following:

> . . . the identification of cardboard, in particular, might indicate that the cat had been captive at some stage, but we do not believe much emphasis can be placed on it. Even across the Pecos Wilderness area in New Mexico, the amount of litter scattered could be a source of this type of material in the fecal samples. For this reason, these tests did not conclusively answer the question to which we hoped to get the answer. Was the animal ever captive?

The boys' father later investigated the scene on his own. He was able to track the boys' movements from the top of a nearby ridge to the bush where the attack took place. He then backtracked the lion and found where it had circled down from the Santa Fe Mountains to the north and then along the top of the ridge down to where its tracks intercepted those of the boys. The lion tracks then traveled from bush to bush, down into the arroyo, crossing the boys' tracks several times. The lion then circled and approached the rear of the bush beneath which the two boys were sitting. Kenneth had run about 18 feet before the lion brought him down. The animal then dragged the boy back into the brush. The boy had died almost immediately, as his autopsy would show, of a severed carotid artery.

Cordry told investigators that the year before he had seen a "hippie-type girl hitch-hiking in the Pojoaque area with what he believed to be a young lion on a leash." Cordry's comment could not be substantiated. Despite this, rumors persisted that the animal had been starving, and that it had been released back into the wild to fend for herself.

January 31, 1974: Mark Chopilote, 26, was tracking a flock of wild turkeys across the snow when he was attacked by a small mountain lion near Las Vegas, New Mexico. The man had just bent over to examine a turkey track in the bottom of a small canyon when a cougar attacked him from behind, sinking its claws deep into his shoulder and attempting to bite his neck. Chopilote hurled the animal off to the side and fired at it with his .30–30 rifle. He didn't hit the animal, but he did scare it away.

The victim, who received scratches on the top of his head and on his back, did not immediately report the attack.

Investigators were able to find enough turkey feathers scattered near the attack site to at least suggest that the cat may have been defending its kill.

13

Colorado Attacks

Colorado has not yet gone the way of California, with its "mountain lion off-limits" attitude. Cougars are still classified as game animals in the state. Despite this, people still debate whether hunting removes aggressive lions from the population, or if it even puts the fear of humans in the hearts of those mountain lions chased by hounds or shot at by hunters. Paul Beier says, "No," in fairly certain terms. "Attacks by cougars are rare but increasing," he wrote in "Cougar Attacks in the United States and Canada" (1991). "It is unlikely that sport hunting will remove enough cougars to reduce the risk.

"There is no evidence that cougars are more likely to attack humans in unhunted areas," Beier continued. "Indeed, 57 percent of attacks occurred in British Columbia, where about 200 cougars are killed annually by hunters and predator control agents."

Beier's statement is true, up to a point. And that point is most succinctly made by Lee Fitzhugh, wildlife specialist with the University of California, who has noted that most of British Columbia's attacks occur on Vancouver Island. Although hunting *is* allowed on Vancouver Island, most hunting takes place on the island's *eastern* shore, while the most the attacks occur on the sparsely populated and lightly hunted *western* shore.

"I'm not arguing in favor of hunting [cougars], but when they were hunted regularly, they had a good reason to fear us," said Todd Malmsbury of the Colorado Division of Wildlife.

Indeed, the state's wildlife officials say there are more lions—well over 3000—in Colorado now than at any other period since World War II. This is largely because their traditional prey animals—elk, deer, and raccoons—are more plentiful, which in turn begets more lions. In 1965, Colorado removed bounties on cougars, reclassified them as game animals, and established a legal hunting season. Lion numbers have since rebounded to the point where it is now no longer unusual to see a mountain lion. At the same time, legal hunting kills have also been on the rise. Unfortunately, hunters take most lions on the western slope of the Rockies. Most human/cougar confrontations—including the state's two fatal ones—occur on the eastern slope, where many residents frown on hunting.

Another consequence of the new attitude toward cougars is that ranchers have had to deal with escalating predation by mountain lions. Lynn Sadler of the California-based Mountain Lion Foundation admits that adult sheep killed by cougars in Colorado rose from 60 a year between 1984 to 1993, to about 1,200 yearly in 1996—which translates into $500,000 in damage to sheep and lambs. Not surprisingly, in 1997 Colorado raised its legal hunting quota for the big cats. Utah and Wyoming, suffering similar problems, followed suit.

Following are some of the many attacks and near attacks that have been reported from the state of Colorado:

1970: A cougar attacked a two-year-old boy while the boy was playing in the garage of his home in Lewis, which is a small town of 250 inhabitants in the southwest corner of the state. The boy sustained minor injuries.

December 22, 1976: Thane Morgan's family owned a weekend home near Rye, Colorado. Thane, 14, was on Christmas break from his high school, and decided to go snowshoeing on the trails of the nearby San Isabel National Forest. While he was preparing for his trip, Thane decided to take along with him a small hunting knife. The teenager tossed it in his backpack and thought nothing more of it. It would save his life.

Reaching the trail head, Thane strapped on his snowshoes and started up the trail. He hadn't traveled far when a cougar sprang out of the cover and bounded right up to him. The animal crouched low, just a few feet away from the boy, then leaped onto him, biting at his skull and head and digging its claws into his body. Although the boy weighed only 120 pounds and was just five feet six inches tall, he fought back with every bit of his strength. Somehow he managed to get free of the cougar, reach into his backpack, and grab his hunting knife. He now used that knife to slash at the cougar, wounding it and causing it to lope off into the forest.

Thane made his way to a neighbor's house, where he got help. Later, at the hospital, he received several hundred stitches to close up the wound to his head and back. Although Thane Morgan would always remember how he spent his Christmas vacation of 1976, he also knew that the outcome could have easily been much worse.

June 2, 1990: Linda Walters, 28, a medical student, was jogging on a forested path near Fourmile Canyon Drive and Poorman Road west of Boulder. It was early morning—6:00 A.M.—as Walters approached a creek near a deer crossing.

Walters, five feet four inches tall, didn't see the two lions resting in a shady area adjacent to the creek until she was only 10 feet away; then she only spotted one of them. She immediately stopped jogging, then raised her arms above her head and began shouting. She threw sticks. When that didn't scare off the lion, she decided to retreat. As she started to leave, she turned to check her backtrail and discovered one of the cats following her.

Normally, lions will run when confronted with such tactics. These didn't. Instead, the first lion seemed almost curious as the woman did her best to prove that she was the larger, more menacing animal. The second lion now joined the first, to Walters' dismay. When the lions edged closer to her, she scrambled up a nearby embankment. The lions continued to close the distance, so Walters climbed into an evergreen tree. As she clambered up the tree limb, the larger lion caught up with her, took a swipe, and struck her in the leg. Walters kicked the lion in its face, and it dropped to the ground.

When the smaller lion started up the tree, Walters broke off a tree branch and struck it as hard as she could. This lion also dropped back to the ground.

The two cats milled around the evergreen tree for the next 20 to 30 minutes, glancing up occasionally at the by-now terrified woman. They finally left the scene.

Walters later told a reporter from the *Boulder Daily Camera,* "They just stare you down. I was quite terrified. I don't think they were trying to kill me, because if they wanted to, they could have. But when an animal keeps coming at you, that's more than curiosity."

Kristi Coughlon, Colorado Divison of Wildlife district manager, did not consider Walters's encounter an "attack," but rather "curious apprehension," which is rather curious in itself. The animals were thought to be an adult female and her nearly grown kitten.

July 27, 1990: A family living on Magnolia Road, just west of Boulder, repeatedly tried to scare off a young male lion lurking about their property. That evening, while the husband was taking his 4-year-old son to an outdoor toilet, the lion confronted the pair. The lion was watching the boy so intently that the father got a gun and shot the animal.

January 14, 1991: Scott Dale Lancaster, 18, who was on his high school's ski team, decided to go jogging during lunch time on this cold January day. When Scott set off from Clear Creek High School, in Idaho Springs just 40 miles west of Denver, it would be the last time the young man would be seen alive.

Lancaster jogged along his favorite training route, a trail that snaked around the nearby mountains' steep, snowy slopes. He was listening to music with his head phones, enjoying himself, perhaps even contemplating his imminent graduation from high school and what that might bring. Not far along the trail, Lancaster ran by a mountain lion. The cat had probably watched from hiding as the boy ran by, and equated that action in its predator's mind with the fleeing of escaping prey. The animal ran up and pounced on Lancaster from the rear. A battle to the death ensued. Investigators later found an area where sagebrush was flattened and brush was shredded. The young man's glasses were found at the scene. The lion prevailed. It had the element of surprise on its side, and it simply overwhelmed and overpowered the teenager. The lion then dragged the teenager's body off the trail, to a secluded location where it could feed. Lancaster never had a chance. He became the first human in recorded Colorado history to have been killed by a mountain lion.

When Lancaster didn't come home that Monday night, his mother became concerned, but felt that Scott had probably decided to spend the night with friends and had forgotten to call. When school called the following morning, however, that concern quickly became desperate worry. She reported her son missing to local authorities. An Alpine Rescue team was dispatched to the area where Scott had been going when he was last seen. Bloodhounds joined in the search, but the searchers came up empty-handed, possibly because the wind was blowing any scent the wrong way, according to Robin Schmutzler, mission leader for the rescue effort.

The next attempt was more fruitful, as the young man's remains were discovered underneath a juniper tree. The body was still clad in the now-torn sweat suit he'd worn when he left on his jog. Drag marks led to the body, which had been covered with twigs and brush. After following bloody paw prints across the snow, an Idaho Springs police officer found and shot the mountain lion, which was crouching just 100 feet away from the body.

"That's just the worst way to die," classmate Eryn Osterhaus, 18, said in the *Rocky Mountain News*. "It would have been easier to accept if he'd . . . hurt his leg and hypothermia set in. To get killed by a mountain lion, that's unbelievable."

The two- to three-year-old male lion's carcass was removed to Colorado State University to be tested. The cat was later determined to have been in good condition, with no obvious abnormalities. Human hair, bone, and cartilage were found in the lion's digestive tract. The animal weighed 110 pounds.

June 1991: Arboles County, southwestern Colorado: Bob Swanemyr, a farmer, was out walking his dog when he was jumped by a cougar which he later estimated to weigh about 100 pounds. Recovering quickly, the man and his dog chased the cougar up a tree.

A hunter with dogs was called in, but there is no information stating whether or not the cat was ever killed.

November 1994: Fred Champagne was hunting up East Elk Creek near New Castle, Colorado, when he was followed and attacked by two mountain lions. Defending himself, Champagne was able to kill both of the animals. A judge later found that Champagne had acted in self-defense.

December 13, 1994: Suzanne Groves, at five feet nine inches, was a tall, physically fit woman who enjoyed working in the outdoors. On this brisk early winter day, at about 10:30 A.M., Groves was taking a water sample in the Mancos River in the Ute Mountain Ute Reservation. Clad in hip boots, fleece jacket and a fly-fishing vest, the woman was standing in the shallows downriver of the Grass Canyon Bridge when she heard some twigs breaking up on the bank. Looking up, Groves saw a lion standing on top of the river's north bank. The two made eye contact, and the lion immediately came down to the edge of the stream.

Groves, who was about two thirds of the way across the river toward the north bank, began moving back toward the south bank, where her vehicle was parked. The lion followed, entering the foot-deep water without hesitation. Groves now angled across the river toward the north bank again, always looking at the lion. She yelled at the animal, and splashed water at it. Nothing seemed to scare the creature, which continued to parallel the woman's path, always easing in closer. The lion never showed its teeth, nor did it assume any threatening pose such as crouching. It just stared at Groves intently.

The pair went back and forth across the river three or four times. Then Groves slipped on some rocks and lost her balance just downstream of the bridge. When she fell, the animal reared up to attack. Groves later said she thought the lion was trying to grab her by the neck, but since she was falling, the animal's jaws instead closed on the back of the woman's head. Groves fell into the water and was on her back beneath the surface for perhaps 10 seconds. Then she jumped out of the water and started to run toward the south bank, away from the lion. She reached the bank, but must have slipped because the next thing she remembered was being on her back, and shoving her arm out in front of her face in a defensive gesture. The lion bit down on her arm. Then, somehow, Groves managed to get on top of the lion. Her arm was still in the animal's mouth, but she no longer cared. She shoved her arm as far back in the lion's throat as she could, in effect pinning the animal down. Then she grabbed for the forceps (hemostats) that were dangling from her fishing vest and stabbed the lion in the right eye. Suzanne meant business. In the Division of Wildlife incident report, she would write, "my intent [was] to kill her by reaching the brain."

As soon as Suzanne stabbed the lion, it growled and clamped down even harder on her arm, all the while fighting to get back up. This went on for five minutes, until the lion, still being stabbed, finally released Groves's arm. The woman was not about to let the cat get back up and attack her again, and was able to keep the animal pinned beneath her for what she estimated to be another five minutes. The lion finally pulled itself out from beneath Suzanne, who stood up immediately and faced the animal. The lion just stood there, staring back. Groves lunged at her, to see what the animal would do, and it continued to stand there, not moving. Groves then started backing downstream, to a place 20 yards away where the river's bank wasn't very steep. She climbed up the bank and followed a cow path back to her truck.

Suzanne Groves sustained bite puncture wounds to her head and right arm, massive bruises to her right arm and right thigh, plus scratches and lacerations to her thigh, back, and arm. She was treated at Southwest Memorial Hospital in Cortez and released the same day.

The next day the Colorado Division of Wildlife's Robin Olterman, district wildlife manager, received permission from Ute tribal officials to locate a houndsman to track the lion. Animal Damage Control specialist Justin Ewing arrived at the reservation with some dogs at 4:00 P.M. Ewing was able to track down and kill the cougar that evening. The animal was only 600 yards from the attack site, lying by the streambed when Ewing shot it. The lion had a wounded eye.

The lion was an old female, with worn teeth and a graying face. It weighed 63 pounds and was, according to Olterman, "very near starvation."

September 13, 1995: Moses Street was jogging on the Tonahuto Trail in the Rocky Mountain National Park's Big Meadows area when he happened to glance over his shoulder. Street later couldn't recall why he'd looked back, whether by chance or by some atavistic instinct warning of impending threat, but he did just in time to see a cougar racing toward him, in the final stages of attack. Street swerved, waved his arms, and started to yell, causing the cougar to back off. Then the animal charged the man again. This time Street was able to counter its attack by swinging a tree branch at the cat. Street then scrambled up onto a tumbledown shack where he then had to rebuff a third attack, again by swinging the tree branch at the lion. By now it was getting dark, and Street was afraid to sleep on the cabin ruins. When the cat wandered off a bit, Street ran to a nearby tree and climbed as high as he could. He then prepared to wait until morning, hoping that by then someone would come looking for him. After many frigid hours spent in the tree—all the man was wearing was a T-shirt and running shorts—the mountain lion came back and began to climb the tree.

"I could hear him," Street said. "If you've ever heard a squirrel scramble up a tree, magnify that. He'd put a claw in and there would be a crunch." Street waited until the cat got closer and then swung his stick, hoping to connect. It did, and the animal worked its way back down.

Meanwhile, Street's girlfriend had notified park rangers when the man failed to return from his jog. The rangers found the man at about 2:00 A.M., still perched high in the tree, wondering where the cat had gone and what it would do next.

Early June 1996: Linda Austin, an employee of Rocky Mountain National Park, was attacked by a mountain lion near the park's North Inlet Trail, a popular hiking spot. The woman was jogging when the cougar charged her. Austin reacted by dodging off the trail, yelling at the animal, and waving a stick at it. The cat went away, and Austin escaped without injury.

July 14, 1997: Two sightings of a mountain lion were reported the previous week in the Park Point Lookout area of Mesa Verde National Park in southwest Colorado. Park personnel closed the Park Point Lookout Trail for several days, in hopes that the animal would move on. Visitors who reported seeing the lion near the trail said the animal did not appear to be aggressive.

Rangers pepper-sprayed the area and fired guns into the air in an attempt to scare off the lion before reopening the trail after the weekend. Why rangers felt the need to pepper-spray the terrain is unknown, since the repellent has been proven to work only when sprayed directly onto the mucous membranes of bears. The jury remains out on whether pepper spray works when used against mountain lions. In fact, Tom Smith of the U.S. Geological Service has demonstrated that pepper spray, when used the way the rangers used it in Mesa Verde National Park, could very well encourage bears—and perhaps other large predators as well—to visit the scene. Indeed, it may act as a curiosity lure instead of aversive conditioning. The lesson here is "when in doubt, don't!"

A lion attacked four-year-old Rafael DeGrave, a French boy, along Mesa Verde's Park Point Lookout Trail at 10:30 A.M. on the first morning of the park's re-opening. The incident took place near a parking lot close to the park's northern boundary. Park ranger Bob Erner, Park Point lookout, was escorting a group of visitors, including Rafael and his parents, back to the parking lot after another hiker had reported seeing the lion along the trail. Some in the group, walking ahead, spotted the lion crouched in the undergrowth several feet from the trail. Young Rafael immediately screamed and ran, which triggered the lion into giving chase. The cat quickly grabbed the child by the head and started to drag him into the brush before the family was able to chase the animal away.

Rafael received first aid from rangers and was then transported to Southwest Memorial Hospital in nearby Cortez, Colorado, where he was treated for lacerations of his nose, shoulder and neck. His left ear had to be surgically reattached. He was listed in fair condition.

The lion, a young male that weighed 60 pounds, was killed shortly after the attack by park rangers. A necropsy determined that the cougar was in good health.

July 17, 1997: The Miedema family had traveled from their home in Lakewood, Colorado, to Rocky Mountain National Park near Estes Park for a three-day camping trip. The family loved the outdoors. They owned a canoe and often went on hiking or camping trips such as this one. On this particular day, the family—parents Dave and Kathy, Mark, 10, and Rachel, 6—had been hiking the park's North Inlet Trail in the Summerland park area. When the family entered the trail, they undoubtedly noticed the sign warning backcountry travelers that they are "entering lion country" and that hiking or jogging alone is "discouraged." "Although rarely observed and not usually a threat to people, hazardous encounters with wildlife have occurred," the sign reads. "Unsupervised children and lone adults are especially at risk."

The family was working its way back down the trail at about 4:30 P.M. when Mark ran up ahead to check on some nuts he'd put out earlier along the trail for the animals. Three minutes later, his parents and Rachel approached an open area. They were only about two and a half miles up the trail from the town of Grand Lake when they saw Mark's feet and legs extending out from the bushes. At first, the Miedemas thought the boy was fooling around, like 10-year-old boys so often do. But as they moved closer, a mountain lion came out of the brush, picked up their son, and started dragging him off the trail and into the heavy vegetation.

The horrified parents began to scream, and their screams soon chased the lion off into the underbrush. The Miedemas rushed to their son. Mark had suffered puncture wounds to his neck and head, and was bleeding profusely. Worse, he had no discernible pulse or respiration. Kathy Miedema, who was trained as a nurse, immediately began CPR. Meanwhile, Chris and Joe Kafka of Westminster, Colorado, who were hiking nearby, heard the family's screams and came rushing over to see what was going on. Chris, a registered nurse, began to help Kathy. The two women began two-person CPR on the child while Joe ran to the trailhead to summon help.

Kafka made it to the trailhead in what seemed to him to be record time, and called 911. But by the time park medical officer Harry Canon arrived on the scene and the two men made it back to the Miedemas, there was almost no hope. After more than an hour of resuscitation efforts, Mark was declared dead.

Chris Kafka later commented, "When we first heard what they were saying, we thought they were joking. It was just so unreal—a mountain lion! Joe's a big hiker. He's been all over, and he never sees mountain lions."

Park spokesman Doug Caldwell theorized that "Mark came along at the wrong time when the lion was in a hunting mode." He added that "Mountain lions don't distinguish between humans and deer and elk." Perhaps Caldwell was right. After all, one side of the trail where the boy had been attacked is heavily forested. On the other side is a meadow where deer and elk can frequently be seen grazing. Caldwell continued, "My best guess . . . is that [Mark] walked between the mountain lion and where she was used to hunting.

"Lions are opportunistic hunters," he added. "We feel that the young fellow probably had no chance, no warning, that he was attacked from behind, perhaps after he walked by the lion without seeing it."

Rangers speculated that if the child had remained with his parents, the lion would not have attacked. That is something no one will ever know.

Park officials radioed the medevac helicopter that was enroute and told it to return to base. Ranger Chris Philippi then arrived at 6:00 P.M. with a team of rangers, who spread out along the trail to warn hikers about the lion. Philippi stayed at the attack site.

The lion returned and jumped at Philippi at 7:00 P.M. "She was crawling to her prey," Philippi said. "We looked eye to eye." The ranger shot the animal, hitting it in the shoulder. He shot twice more and may also have wounded it in the hindquarters.

The wounded lion ran away. Three park rangers—Jim Richardson, Jeff Hodge, and Chris Ryan—plus Lyle Willmarth and two other professional trackers and their hounds now converged on the scene. The dogs treed the lion at 8:04 P.M., less than a quarter of a mile from where Mark Miedema was attacked. The three park rangers fired at the same time, killing the lion instantly.

An adult pregnant female, with no kittens, was deemed responsible for the attack on Mark Miedema, the first death in Rocky Mountain National Park known to have been caused by an animal since the 415-square-mile park was established in 1915. Miedema was only the second person killed by a lion in Colorado history. The lion weighed 88 pounds and did not suffer from rabies.

An autopsy was performed on Mark Miedema, to determine the real cause of his death. Grand County Coroner Dave Schoenfeld reported that the boy died of respiratory failure brought on by "massive asphyxiation." Mark did not die of his wounds. Rather, he choked to death, tragically, on his own vomit.

October 20, 1997: Todd Dunbar, a mountain biker riding alone on Walker Ranch Open Space near Flagstaff Mountain just outside Boulder, got the surprise of his life when a mountain lion lunged at him from beside the trail.

"After the lion realized the biker wasn't typical prey, like a deer, it stopped and began snarling at the man with its ears laid back," reported Rick Basagoitia, district wildlife biologist for the Colorado Division of Wildlife.

According to Basagoitia, the biker positioned his bike in front of him until the lion backed off. The man then slowly and warily proceeded along the trail, but the lion wasn't ready to give up. It continued to follow Dunbar in a posture that suggested it was going to attack. "The lion didn't attack, and eventually went its own way," said Basagoitia. The encounter took place about one and a half miles from the parking lot in the valley. Dunbar had been riding his bike on a secondary trail at the time.

Mountain bikers and hikers may run a higher-than-normal risk of being attacked, suggested several Colorado Division of Wildlife experts. A mountain biker's heads-down posture while riding might stir a lion's curiosity, especially if the animal is actively searching for prey. A lion might also interpret the movements of hikers, trail runners and mountain bikers on forested trails as fleeing actions, which can stimulate a predatory attack response.

"From what we understand, the biker did everything he should have when people encounter mountain lions," concluded Basagoitia.

April 30, 1998: Andy Peterson, 24, had noticed lion tracks in the area of the Carpenter Peak Trail in 3,245-acre Roxborough State Park near Louviers three weeks earlier. Peterson hiked this particular trail on the average of once a week. On April 30, he had already finished hiking to the end of the trail, had turned around and, at about 3:00 P.M., was well on his way back down when he noticed a mountain lion lying about ten feet off the trail, chewing on a log. The lion, facing downslope of Peterson, did not appear to see him. When it did, the man and the cougar stared at each other for long seconds. Peterson slowly backed up. He prepared for the worst by picking up a rock and removing a Swiss Army knife from his pocket and opening it. Peterson also removed his shirt and dangled it in front of him in an effort to appear larger to the lion. The lion got up and stood there, staring at the man. This stand-off continued for about twenty minutes. Peterson then backed slowly up the trail until he was out of view of the lion. That's when his memory fails him.

The next thing he remembers is swinging his backpack at the lion and yelling, "It's going to be you or me!"

The attack occurred as he was backing down the trail. He knew there was a drop-off nearby, and glanced around to see where he would be stepping next. When he shifted his eyes for the merest moment, the lion took advantage of his lapse of attention and attacked, knocking the man over. The two rolled over and over down the hill for ten yards. Peterson landed on top of the lion, but the lion had the man's head in its jaws. Peterson could hear a crunching noise on his skull. Luckily, he had not lost his knife. He now used it to stab the lion. Although he couldn't see where the blade hit, he thought he probably cut the animal on the right side of its throat and on top of its head. He then reached over, behind his head, and felt for the lion's eyes. Then he gouged an eye with his thumb. The lion screamed, and released its grip.

The lion retreated a few yards, giving Peterson the chance to get up. Wisely choosing not to run, he headed slowly down the trail. The lion started to follow him. Peterson picked up a large rock and threw it at the lion. The rock hit the lion in its side and knocked the animal off the trail. Peterson didn't wait to see what would happen next. Close to panicking, he hurried down the trail, almost running. As he rushed downwards, he drank from his bottle of water, then tossed the bottle aside. He lost his knife farther down the trail. When he encountered a group of hikers, he threw his backpack at them and told them to call 911. "I've been attacked by a lion," he said, as he continued down the trail. He later told investigating officers that, "I didn't want to bleed to death on the trail, so I kept on running." Andy Peterson made it to the visitor center with the help of some other hikers.

Peterson was transported to a hospital for medical attention, then airlifted to Swedish Medical Center near Denver, where he went into surgery at 6:30 P.M. The man had lacerations and scratches all over his body. He had a three-inch long laceration under his left eye, a six-inch laceration on his forehead near the hairline, a 12-inch laceration on the back of his head, and a cut on his index finger. His back was scratched, and his knees were badly scraped and bruised. Although the cougar had clamped its jaws on his skull, it fortunately had not fractured. Peterson also had to undergo rabies vaccinations.

Four Division of Wildlife officials converged on the scene. They swept the area for sign or tracks but could find none, even though they did find Peterson's Swiss army knife and water bottle. Both had blood on them. They also found a regular trail of blood drops leading from the attack site, where they soon located the victim's hat and T-shirt. They noted the broken brush and the disturbed ground litter. They also found lion hair on the ground next to the clothing. Peterson's sunglasses were another 100 yards up the trail.

At 7:00 A.M. the next morning, houndsmen and dogs met the wildlife officers at the park. Let loose, the dogs occasionally picked up scent, but were unable to hold the trail. The weather was dry, warm, windy, and sunny, poor conditions for tracking.

When questioned later, Andy Peterson estimated the lion's weight at about 100 pounds. Peterson, who at the time was a seasonal ranger for Bear Creek Lake Park and was studying for a degree in natural resources management, had seen the mounted cougar at the park where he worked, and had a good idea of what full-grown lions look like.

Although trackers continued to search for the lion, the animal was never located.

July 19, 1998: At 10:30 P.M., Timothy Morris, of Lyons, Colorado, went outside to check on his dogs. The dogs were barking, and some coyotes were yelping, and Morris had become curious about why there was such a racket going on. Morris walked outside and noticed some motion in the trees about 75 yards from his house. He went over to see what was going on, and had just walked under a tree when a mountain lion dropped onto him, knocking him to the ground. Morris was now lying face to face with the lion. He grabbed one of the lion's paws with one hand, and gripped the animal's neck with the other. The lion tried its utmost to free its paw, swinging it back and forth, but Morris held on. The man had the distinct impression that the lion wasn't fighting nearly as hard as it could have been. Now Morris's Australian blue heeler—a Labrador-sized dog—jumped onto the lion's back and bit down on the animal's tail. The lion went after the dog, and Morris was able to crawl away. When he was free of the lion, the man got up and ran into the house. He returned with a knife, looking for the lion, but could not see it.

Later, Morris's brother and roommate returned to the house. All three men armed themselves with shotguns and went looking for the lion. Again, they were unable to find it. They shot several rounds into the air to scare it off, just in case the animal was still in the area.

Morris suffered only superficial scratches from his cougar encounter, and did not seek medical attention. His dog was unhurt.

September 19, 1999: Bowhunter Jess Ring of Bakersfield, California, was cow-calling for elk near Yellow Jacket Pass, in western Colorado, not far from Meeker. As Ring called, he became aware of a mountain lion slowly creeping up behind him. The lion was less than 12 feet away when the man first detected its presence.

Ring first tried to frighten the animal away by waving his arms. All he succeeded in doing was making a tense situation somewhat tenser, for the cat now laid its ears back.

"I have a house cat that does the same thing just before it pounces," Ring said in a *Denver Post* article. "I decided I didn't want to play this game any more." Ring shot the cat through the neck with an arrow.

The two-and-a-half-year-old mountain lion weighed 125 pounds. The pelt was made into a rug, and is used to educate schoolchildren about wildlife.

October 2, 1999: Jaryd Atadero, 3, and his sister, 6, were hiking with eleven adults up the Big South Trail in Poudre Canyon just north of Fort Collins. The group, which included several of Jaryd's relatives, had covered about one and a half miles when someone noticed that young Jaryd was missing.

A search and rescue team was assembled, but after an extensive four-day search, the only solid clues searchers had uncovered was a small child's footprint about 175 yards from where they found definite evidence of a mountain lion.

The trackers found the small footprint about 1,000 feet off the east side of the trail on which the group had been hiking. They were also able to determine that Jaryd had climbed up a steep, rocky slope. No other clues were discovered, but a cougar could easily have picked up a youngster like Jaryd and run a long way before killing the boy.

The worst was feared. As Sergeant Justin Smith of the Larimer County Sheriff's Department commented, "It's certainly consistent with why there have been no solid signs of Jaryd."

14
California Attacks

The story of mountain lion bounties in California comprises just one chapter in a long and sometimes checkered history of man's attempts to control these animals. The idea of bounties originated with sixteenth-century Spanish Jesuits who had traveled to the southern part of the state to minister to indigenous peoples. The good Jesuits would provide a bull to any Native American who killed a puma. A bull offered incentive enough to send almost anyone scurrying into the hills to bring back any cougar they could trap or kill.

The bounty system persisted in one form or another well into the twentieth century. In 1907, the state promised a bounty to hunters of $20 per puma. In 1917, the reward for taking a female lion was raised to $30, a princely sum in those days. Bounties were later raised again for both sexes of the big cats. Between 1907 to 1963, California doled out an incredible $389,345 to trackers and hunters for killing 12,461 lions.

California's mountain lions have been managed in a political fashion for many years. These management decisions are more often based on prevailing attitudes toward mountain lions than on biology. For example, from 1907 to 1963, mountain lions were bountied. A monetary reward was offered as an incentive to kill all mountain lions, mainly because of pressures from cattlemen and sheep ranchers.

The bounty program ended in 1963, but lions remained unprotected until 1969, when they were classified as a game animal. From 1969 to early 1972, two hunting seasons were held. During these two seasons, 118 lions were killed. A legislative moratorium in 1972 effectively ended the hunting of mountain lions in the state. In 1990, Proposition 117, a ballot initiative, prohibited mountain lion hunting.

Yet, from 1972 until 1999, 1,401 mountain lions were killed in California under the depradation permit system. In 1994 alone, lion hunters hired by the state killed 121 lions—four more animals than were taken in the last two *legal* hunting seasons by people who had purchased California lion permits. Ordinary hunters once paid money to the state to take mountain lions. Today—and ever since Proposition 117 passed in 1990—the state pays out money to contract hunters to kill mountain lions.

Proposition 117, a referendum passed in 1990, "specially protected" cougars from hunting. Meanwhile, depredation permits for lions attacking livestock and pets have risen steadily from the early 1970s. According to figures compiled and released by the California Department of Fish and Game, more cougars are now killed annually than in the days when sport hunting was allowed. An average of 200 depredation permits have been issued each year since 1990. About 40 percent of those permits result in the death of a lion.

In California, especially, the lengthy ban on hunting—when lions are stalked, shot at, hounded, and chased by hunters—may mean that an animal that once was shy and retiring has now become increasingly emboldened. California lions today have little or no experience with humans as predators. Nor do they have to worry about grizzlies, which once inhabited the same range as cougars but are no longer there to challenge them. The lion must no longer compete for its kills with wolves, either. In fact, the only natural enemies these animals now face, save for the occasional depredation hunter, who, we must remember, is successful just 40 percent of the time, are other cougars. No wonder mountain lions begin to feel like the toughest critters on the mountain. Who can blame them? Humans, after all, have made a decision that seems designed to place human lives in serious jeopardy, at least when viewed over the past ten years.

Cougar researcher and authority Harley Shaw doubts that the lions of today have become any more emboldened than their predecessors. Rather, Shaw said, "[In former times] any lion caught or confronted, died. Those that weren't [killed] probably had little experience with humans. I find the hunter harrassment idea hard to buy. Note, also, how many juvenile pumas [are involved in attacks.] These are individuals that would probably not have encountered humans when human populations were at much lower densities.

"Finally, I think one of the big changes is in the kind of humans that are out there. Historically, most folks afield carried a gun. A puma approaching them would have been shot as a matter of course. The event would have never made the media—it might have made the rounds of neighbors as an interesting story. Possibly, the cat would have been bountied, possibly not. I still carry a gun afield. I have no desire to kill a puma, but I wouldn't hesitate if one showed aggressive behavior. Folks in California seldom carry firearms afield, unless they are hunters. They have to stop and think about the legal repercussions of shooting a cat. They are likely to report anything they see that looks like a puma to authorities. The whole complexion of cat-human relationships has changed."

Steve Torres, the California Department of Fish and Game wildlife biologist in charge of mountain lion management, said, "There is no biological reason not to hunt mountain lions. Lions in California are not endangered or threatened and are not in jeopardy." With the current California cougar population estimated somewhere between five and six thousand animals, the "animal" most threatened in the state is probably the individual human who chooses to walk or jog alone into a situation from which he or she may not return alive, or in one piece.

Yet resistance to the resumption of licensed hunting of lions continues, unabated. An even greater percentage of the population disapproved of the practice than that which approved Proposition 117 in 1990. In 1996, Proposition 197, which would have allowed licensed hunting, met with resounding defeat. Statements such as those attributed to Brooks Fahy, executive director of the Predator Defense Institute in Eugene, Oregon, fan the antihunting flames. Fahy believes that there is no evidence that hunting puts the fear of people in mountain lions, pointing to the numbers of cougar attacks in British Columbia—and particularly in Vancouver Island—as his rationale.

University of California–Davis extension wildlife specialist Lee Fitzhugh believes the data from British Columbia shows just the opposite, as stated in an earlier chapter. Fitzhugh quotes a paper by Daryll Hebert and Dan Lay that analyzed the Vancouver Island/British Columbia lion attack data. According to Hebert and Lay, nearly all the mountian lion attacks in British Columbia occurred on the western side of the island, where few humans reside. Lions on the east side of the island, according to Fitzhugh, "even in areas where they are treed only for scientific purposes, seem to learn to identify people as predator rather than prey." Lions on the west side of the island would move freely into and around towns far more readily than those on the east side, where they are hunted. In contrast, lions on the east side would actually change their territories and move on after being treed several times by hounds. According to Fitzhugh, "The lessons from Vancouver Island seem to be that where people and lions live together, there are fewer attacks when lions are hunted than when they are not."

Other respected biologists and researchers, such as Harley Shaw, disagree. "During my years as a field researcher, we used dogs to tree individual lions as many as five times," Shaw said. "We never noticed any tendency among lions to desert their established ranges. Too many variables are involved here for one to arrive at a simple or easy explanation of what appears to be an increasing number of attacks. These include human encroachment upon habitat; varying densities of prey during different years; habitats that tend to be sources, rather than sinks (or prey-deficient). Easy explanations—as much as we'd like to accept them—simply won't work."

One emergency measure that recently passed in the California legislature permits the department to take any mountain lions that threaten the endangered California, or Sierra Nevada, bighorn sheep or the Peninsular, or Baja, bighorn sheep.

Another change in the state's program of information and education is that the department no longer says that mountain lions are "secretive, solitary, and avoid people." "We can't," said Terry Mansfield, deputy director with the Department of Fish and Game. "Not when people are seeing them in daylight all the time. Solitary? It's common out here to see females with young. And with habitat loss and fragmentation, mountain lions can't help but inhabit areas in close proximity to people. There's a disturbing and increasing trend for mountain lions to be seen around urban settings."

Californians have been attacked and killed by mountain lions throughout the state's history, although the number of incidents has increased since the early 1990s—so much so that Steve Torres's analysis of attacks in the state shows them occurring at a rate equal to that of British Columbia over the ten years since Proposition 117 was passed.

The recorded history of cougar attacks in the state began in 1890 with an entry for 7-year-old Arthur Dangle of Quartz Valley in Siskiyou County. In July, 1909, Earl Willson, 10, and Isola Kennedy, 22, were next, succumbing not to their wounds, but to the rabies carried by the attacking animal. That attack took place near Morgan Hill. In 1917, a farmer named Boheim was killed in Strawberry Valley in the San Jacinto Mountains when he tracked a pig-stealing cougar at night. A long period of calm settled on the state before the next death by cougar occurred in 1988. This case has still not been resolved to everyone's satisfaction, however.

In 1988, the body of Lucy Gomez-Dunton, of Butte County, was discovered after she had been missing for several days. By the time the body was located, it was in such an advanced state of decomposition that it was difficult to determine the exact cause of death. Enough evidence existed to put the blame on one of the state's increasingly numerous mountain lions, however. Bite marks to the woman's neck, evidence that a cougar had been feeding on the woman, plus the fact that the victim had gone off by herself, all pointed to the possibility that the woman had been attacked and killed by a lion. Still, some doubted this conclusion. Reinforcing that doubt was the fact that no person residing in California had been killed in a verified lion attack (one recognized by the California Department of Fish and Game) since 1909. The case was eventually filed under "death by unknown causes." Six short years later, however, another incident occurred that left no doubt as to its origin.

It's not as though Californians had had no warning about the biological powder keg upon which they were sitting—indeed, upon which they had *chosen* to sit. It was just a matter of time before that keg blew up.

April 23, 1994: Barbara Schoener, 40, of Placerville, went jogging early this Saturday morning on a trail in the Auburn State Recreation Area near Cool in remote Eldorado County. Despite numerous reports at the time of her death indicating that she was a small, 120-pound woman, Schoener was instead a muscular athlete. Husband and friends said she was five feet eight inches tall and weighed a muscular 140 to 150 pounds. Schoener was no tiny morsel of mountain lion snack. The lion that attacked this woman would have a fight on its hands.

And it did. Evidence at the scene indicated that the jogger struggled desperately with the mountain lion that had pounced upon her back. Investigators reconstructing the events leading to her death believe the cougar was lying atop a rock shelf on a steep, brush-covered hillside when the woman jogged by on the trail beneath it. The mountain lion quickly arose, jumped onto the path about 20 feet behind the jogging woman, and attacked her from the rear.

The force of the animal's attack knocked the woman off the trail and about 30 feet down a slope. Schoener apparently struggled back to her feet, and was immediately attacked again. A brief struggle ensued, but the woman managed to get up once more, break free of the animal, and run about 25 feet before the animal grabbed her again. This time, the cougar killed Schoener.

The trail on which Schoener was jogging, located about 50 miles east of Sacramento, is part of the Western States 100-Mile Endurance Run. Runners, hikers, horseback riders, and motorcyclists are all frequent users of the popular trail. The attack occurred less than a mile from the Auburn Trails housing development, and about three miles from where Schoener had parked her car.

Investigators initially believed the woman had been murdered, but quickly backed away from that theory. Preliminary autopsy results "rule out any cause of death other than the cat attack," stated Lt. James Roloff of the El Dorado County Sheriff's Department.

Schoener, a mother of two children, ages 5 and 8, suffered wounds on her forearms and hands, indicating a desperate fight with the animal. She also sustained two massive wounds, either of which would have been fatal. The woman was bitten on the neck as well as on the head. The head wound—a crushed skull—was the likely cause of death, according to Roloff.

After partially consuming the woman's body, the mountain lion dragged her about 300 feet down the embankment. It buried Schoener's remains under leaves and twigs.

Schoener was reported missing by her husband the afternoon of the same day. Her body was discovered Sunday morning at 7:30.

Lion trackers using dogs sealed off a 4,200-acre portion of the recreational area to hunt for the cougar. Rain on Monday hampered their efforts, but the trackers finally tracked down and shot the lion. When it was discovered that the cougar was a lactating female, an all-out search was organized to find her kittens. That search was successful when rescuers found a shivering, malnourished and dehydrated six-week-old male kitten in its den. A contest was held to select a name for the orphan. Named Willow, it is now the resident mountain lion at the Folsom Zoo.

Schoener left behind two children. For a period of time following the attack, contributions to see to the orphaned kitten's well-being far outpaced those collected for the Schoener family. Once this ironic situation was brought to light by the media, including personalities such as conservative talk show host Rush Limbaugh, the public responded with such an outpouring of generosity that Mr. Schoener pleaded with people to stop sending contributions, saying his children were "taken care of for life."

Barbara Schoener is remembered by her family and friends. The site of her death is now marked by a plaque and a stone bench that serve not only as a memorial to the woman, but as a reminder to those who choose to follow this trail.

December 10, 1994: As if to reiterate the grisly point she was trying to make, Mother Nature struck again on this day. Iris Kenna, 56, an avid birdwatcher, was walking alone on a road near Cuyamaca Peak in Cuyamaca State Park in San Diego County, when at some point, she probably became aware of a mountain lion observing her, or perhaps even stalking her. Expert trackers later reconstructed the morning's events and concluded that Kenna had been facing the animal at first. Then, perhaps, as the animal's body language became more threatening or maybe as the animal started its charge, Kenna became more frightened. Evidence suggested that she turned, dropped her backpack, and ran. Thirty-five yards from where she had dropped her pack, the lion leaped upon her back, bit through her neck, and dragged her to the ground. According to the San Diego County autopsy report, her death was not instantaneous.

After Kenna was dead, the cat dragged her body into a brush-covered area some fifty feet from the fire road, and no more than a mile from popular Paso Picacho Campground.

Later that morning, at 11:00 A.M., two hikers came upon Kenna's bloodstained backpack and glasses on the fire road. They hurried back to Paso Picacho Campground for help.

Kenna's body was discovered by park rangers about fifteen minutes later. Shreds of clothing marked the trail to her body, which was lying face down. "Profound" gashes pierced her torso, and severe bite and claw marks covered her head and neck.

The area was quickly evacuated, closed to arriving campers, and cordoned off. Various state, park, and local officers swarmed over the landscape searching for the lion. It returned at 9:45 that same evening to reclaim Kenna's body, which had already been removed. Officials knew that they were dealing with an animal that was dangerous to humans, so they summoned houndsmen to tree it. Officers then killed the cougar, a five-year-old male that weighed 116 pounds.

"The lion was in good condition," said San Diego County veterinarian Dr. Hubert Johnstone, in the December 13th edition of the *San Diego Union-Tribune*. "There was nothing preventing this lion from bringing down deer or any other prey. He was eating up to the time he was killed. He had plenty of body fat." The necropsy found Iris Kenna's scalp and hair in the cat's stomach.

Dr. Mark Super, deputy medical examiner for San Diego County, said that Kenna had died of bite and claw wounds to the neck, head, and upper body, and that she had probably been attacked from behind while in the act of fleeing.

After Kenna's death, some of Cuyamaca's older rangers remarked that it wasn't too many years ago when simply sighting a mountain lion in the park was big news. Attacks and threatening behavior were unheard of then. No more. In recent years, Cuyamaca Rancho State Park has become known as a "lion hot spot" in more ways than one. The attacks here underscore just how divisive the issue of how to best ensure safe and peaceful coexistence between the human and feline populations has become. The mere mention of the park's name is enough to raise hackles on both sides of the issue—those who defend the big cats' right to live and to hunt unmolested by humans, and those who defend the human right to feel reasonably safe in our surroundings. As lion opponents point out, Article I, Section 1 of the California state Constitution states, "All people . . . have inalienable rights. Among these are . . . pursuing and acquiring safety." They believe that the $30 million of taxpayers' money that's set aside each year, by law, for the purchase of lion habitat harbors a species that, more than any other animal in the state, threatens this right. Other folks are pragmatic about the issue. "When you enter the park, you enter the food chain, and you'd better know the risks," said Bob Merigan, a rancher in nearby Descanso.

Many ranchers are aware of the risks to themselves, their loved ones, and their stock. A few don't wait for permission from state authorities to kill cougars they feel are either menacing their livestock or becoming too visible or threatening to general ranch operations. "It's not hard to bury a dead cougar," one resident remarked.

In 1994, the statewide cougar population was estimated at more than 6,000 animals. It is no wonder then, according to information specialist Pat Moore, of the California Department of Fish and Game, that some people become uneasy when speculating about the number of mountain lions that may be living in or passing through the former Mexican rancho's 26,000 acres at any given time.

Prior to the Iris Kenna attack, officials had killed six lions—including the four mentioned in an earlier section of this chapter—in the previous 16 months within the ten-mile-wide corridor that included Cuyamaca Rancho State Park. A collision with a vehicle on a nearby road killed a seventh lion.

Ron Woychak, resource officer for the nearby Cleveland National Forest, where deer hunting is allowed, could not recall a single human/mountain lion incident in that forest, other than sightings. "State parks like Cuyamaca serve as game reserves," Woychak said, in the December 13, 1994, edition of the *San Diego Union-Tribune*. The park is a magnet [with its no hunting restrictions] that draws in the deer the lions prey on." His message was clear. If you choose to recreate where cougars can choose from an unlimited supply of wildlife, don't be surprised when one of them decides you might be the delicacy he'd most like to sample.

The following attacks represent just some of the state's reported attacks, incidents of threatening behavior, and near attacks. More will undoubtedly occur in the years to come. About the best one can hope for is no further loss of human life.

March 23, 1986: Despite several mountain lion sightings in the months immediately before March, park officials at Ronald Caspers Wilderness Park, a 7,500-acre green space about 60 miles southeast of Los Angeles in Orange County, did nothing. Darrell Bennett, a state park ranger in Indio, said that at least twice before this date mountain lions had seemed to threaten hikers. On one occasion, a cougar charged at and circled two hikers, leaving only after they pelted it with rocks.

"The books that we were reading had said that [mountain lions] were secretive little critters that wouldn't hurt us and usually posed no threat to man," Bennett said. The books were right—most cougars don't pose a threat to humans—but wrong, too. A few pose a huge threat.

Laura Small, a five-year-old girl, was attacked by a cougar while visiting the Ronald Caspers Wilderness Park. The girl was attacked at about 2:00 P.M. as she was wading in a stream searching for tadpoles while her mother and father waited nearby.

After hearing some rustling in the underbrush, "I saw this thing—it looked like a big dog—come after her," said the child's mother, Susan Small. "It grabbed her by the head and ran off. There was no warning, no nothing." The animal had been hiding in thick brush by the side of the trail. When the child went by, the cougar sprang from of its hiding place and grabbed her. "I didn't know where she was, but I could hear her screaming," Small said. Laura later recalled, "I was being dragged on the ground and all these thorns were going into my legs. I thought it was a big dog."

Small frantically raced through the undergrowth to the source of the screaming. There she found the cat, its teeth dug deeply into her daughter's face and skull. The cougar held onto the girl's head for at least five minutes until a hiker, Gregory Ysais, 36, of Mission Viejo, heard the girl's screams and ran up to help. Ysais later said that when he arrived, he found the lion "sitting on its haunches" with the girl's head and neck inside its powerful jaws. Ysais grabbed a branch and swung it over the lion's head, hoping to frighten the animal into releasing its prey. The cougar reacted by swiping at Ysais with its paw, but it dropped Laura. Then the animal started lunging at the rescuer. Ysais kept the animal at bay until Susan Small could pick up her daughter and carry the child away. The cougar eventually fled.

Laura Small said the next thing she remembered was her mother and father taking turns carrying her back to the park's visitor center for help. She said she heard them talking about "how my face was all torn to pieces." Rangers, meanwhile, cleared about 250 campers from the park. A search for the animal was organized.

Laura was flown to Mission Community Hospital by helicopter. After hours of surgery, the girl remained in serious condition with bite wounds and deep lacerations.

Laura Small eventually underwent 15 separate surgeries in an attempt to patch her back together. The attack partially paralyzed her right arm and leg, blinded her in one eye, and left numerous other physical and emotional scars. The girl also suffered brain damage. To this day, she has trouble doing simple things such as tying shoelaces or picking up small objects. In 1991 a jury awarded the Small family more than $2 million in damages. The county appealed the verdict, and also ordered the park closed to minors.

A tentative settlement to the Small lawsuit, agreeable to both parties, was announced October 22, 1993. Under its terms, Laura Small will receive $1 million in payments from Orange County to be spread out over her lifetime.

After the attack, game warden Ronald C. Darnall said, "Mountain lions normally hunt at night." This attack, he stated, "goes against normal behavior patterns."

Perhaps up until that day. After all, the attack on Laura Small was the first documented attack upon a human in California in more than 60 years. With no previous experience dealing with lion aggression toward humans, California officials were about to become experts on the topic.

October 19, 1986: Authorities had just managed to talk themselves into the notion that the attack upon Laura Small was an isolated incident, one not likely to be repeated, when Justin Mellon, a six-year-old boy, was also attacked by a mountain lion, also while visiting Ronald Caspers Park. The attack upon Justin occurred just seven months after the vicious attack on five-year-old Laura Small.

Justin's parents joined with Laura Small's to criticize park officials for what they called "inadequate warning signs at the park." Justin's father, Timothy Mellon, said he was "furious and frustrated" at officials.

Recalling the attack, Mellon told a news reporter that "I could see the mountain lion on top of Justin. It was trying to get him in a position where it could drag him away, but Justin was fighting him on his back for dear life, and rolling down [an incline] at the same time."

The only signs at the park, according to Mellon, was one that said, "Respect the Animals." Ten minutes after reading this sign, Justin was attacked by the cougar. According to Mellon, "The sign should say, 'Enter at your Own Risk.'"

Justin's father quickly jumped into the fray and was able to chase off the attacking lion with a knife.

The boy was admitted to Mission Community Hospital for treatment. He required more than 100 stitches, and still suffers from mental injuries and emotional anxieties.

June 25, 1988: Two mountain lions chased a German couple and their small son in the Green Valley Campground of Cuyamaca Rancho State Park. The local game warden found the two lions together. Neither animal budged as the man approached. The warden shot an 80-pound male lion first; when the smaller lion stayed where it was, the warden shot that lion as well. It proved to be a 63-pound male. (Adapted from Tom Chester's Internet list of Mountain Lion Attacks).

March 1992: A mountain lion mauled a nine-year-old boy who was hiking with his family in Grass Valley State Park in Santa Barbara County. The boy was hospitalized with 50 puncture wounds, according to information posted to the Internet's Mountain Lion Attacks on People in the U.S. and Canada by Tom Chester. (http://tchester.org/sgm/lists/lion_attacks.html) There is some question as to whether this is actually a different attack than the one that follows, since it is not listed in the roundup of cougar attacks upon humans provided by the California Dept. of Fish and Wildlife:

March 12, 1992: Darron Arroyo, a nine-year-old boy, was mauled by a mountain lion in Gaviota State Park in California. The boy's father, who was hurried to the scene by the boy's brothers, "hit the cougar on the head with a rock, causing the cougar to retreat." The boy recovered from his injuries.

April 5, 1992: Near his Sacramento home, turkey hunter Arthur Eichele, 27, was dressed in full camouflage, crouched near a turkey decoy, and using a turkey call when he heard something big land behind him. "It was fast, very fast," Eichele said. "I turned just in time to see it hit me right in the head."

"It" would be the mountain lion that obviously thought it was pouncing on a turkey. The cat knocked off Eichele's hat, pushed the man down to the ground, then bounded away. "My hunting partner said, 'Was that a mountain lion? Did you see a mountain lion?' "

Eichele responded by saying, "Hell, it knocked me over!" Eichele then fired two shots into the ground, even though the cat by that time was long gone.

A truly dedicated hunter, Eichele continued hunting the rest of the day, even though he was bleeding from four or five long scratches on the back of his head. The man finally went to the hospital where he received three stitches. He then underwent a series of rabies treatments, including two injections to his head. The rabies treatments entail taking 10 injections.

"I think it was a case of mistaken identity," said Bill Clark of the California Department of Fish and Wildlife in Sacramento. "Once the cat realized it wasn't a turkey, it took off. I think it was probably as scared as [the hunter] was."

The cat was not hunted down and killed. It was behaving like a mountain lion, plus it had the cat sense to realize its mistake and let the hunter go. Eichele agreed. "Nothing's wrong with this lion," he said. "It just made a mistake."

September 6, 1993: In June, a young adult mountain lion had menaced a family hiking on Cuyamaca Rancho State Park's Azalea Glen Trail.

At the end of August, a lion matching that same description approached to within 40 feet of a group of campers barbecuing chicken at the park's Los Caballos horse campground. The cat growled, but left after campers shouted and threw rocks at the animal.

A week later, in September, Konnie Brooking, 36, of Julian was riding horseback with her father, Dick King, when the pair spotted a cougar right at sunset. Brookings and her father, neither of whom had any knowledge of prior mountain lion incidents in the 26,000-acre park, stopped their horses to admire the big cat. Brookings said she had never seen a lion there before, even though she has ridden on park trails and fire roads for nearly two decades.

"We'd been riding for five and a half hours and we were heading back up the fire road when we heard the bushes rustling," Brooking recalled. The pair were near Stonewell Creek when "the cat bolted out and was about 15 feet away. It was beautiful. I couldn't believe it," said Brooking.

Awe became concern when the cougar turned to stare at the riders. King yelled at the lion, but the puma walked toward the pair "like it was going to hurt us," the man said later.

According to Brookings, "Its hackles came up, just like when a house cat is hunting a bird. We [urged our horses] into a dead run, and it must have chased us more than a half mile before it stopped. The horse was frightened, too. You could feel it."

Brooking's husband rode by five minutes later. He also saw the cat. "It was about the size of a Great Dane," Billy Brooking said, "only a little longer." The lion, estimated later by authorities to have weighed about 90 pounds, did not follow the man. By all accounts, the cat appeared healthy and well fed.

"I felt like we were its prey," said Brookings. "That was exactly the look I got from that cat. It was pretty scary."

Rangers closed Cuyamaca Rancho State Park that evening. Thousands of campers and picnickers were turned away even though it was Labor Day weekend. Steel gates were installed at camground entrances and hiking trails and roadside parking areas were cordoned off.

Trackers and state wardens were led to the spot where the cougar had last been sighted, but the trail had gone cold.

The park remained closed until September 15.

September 17, 1993: Roger Fitzgerald of Escondido was fishing at Dixon Lake when he spotted a mountain lion watching him intently. The lion screamed and looked as though it was ready to pounce on the man, so Fitzgerald threw his stringer of fish at the cat. The man then waited on shore until park rangers, making their rounds, were able to help him out.

September 18, 1993: On this day, a writer for the *San Diego Union-Tribune* dedicated a column to the cougar described in the previous account. The writer interviewed people in and around Cuyamaca Rancho State Park, and mocked the signs posted by rangers within the park as foolishness. In this unbelievable account, the writer even has the cougar scoff: "Excuse me. But warning campers that they might encounter a cougar in this setting is like telling visitors to Alpine that they might bump into a pickup truck. This is my world. This is where I live."

In regard to the threatening behavior exhibited by the lion in the Brookings incident and the measures taken by officials, the writer quotes a man as sarcastically saying, "Watch out for those little kitty cats."

September 18, 1993: At about 10:25 A.M., rangers learned that a mountain lion had been spotted crossing a trail leading to the area where the Torrey Pines Ski Club of San Diego was holding its annual picnic outing in Cuyamaca Rancho State Park.

An hour later, a club member saw the lion emerge from a clearing and move toward a picnic area where a turkey was being roasted for lunch. Some of the club members took photos of the cougar, and then it disappeared into the bushes.

Lisa Kowalski, a fifth-grader at Chula Vista Hills Elementary School, was camping with her family in the recently reopened Paso Picacho campground, about 100 yards upslope from where the ski club was camping. She and her father, Bob, were playing catch. Her mother, Kathy, and two brothers—Brian, 8, and Michael, 8 months—were nearby. The girl had just caught the rubber ball when her father shouted, "Freeze!"

Lisa did, then slowly turned her head to see a mountain lion sniffing her. Suddenly, the cougar jumped forward and bit her buttocks. Lisa screamed.

The lion moved away from the girl. The Kowalskis, not knowing what else to do, freed the family's dog, Henry, in hopes that the dog might divert the lion's attention from Lisa and the other children. The lion went after the dog, clawing its shoulders. The pair tussled for a while, then the lion retreated to a tree 50 yards from the Kowalski's tent.

The family climbed into their van, and stayed there, videotaping the mountain lion, until it left the area ten minutes later.

Kathy Kowalski reported the attack upon her daughter to park rangers who were ordered to destroy the lion. It proved to be a 20-month-old female. Slightly underweight at 41 pounds, it was not rabid. Some of the rangers were quite bothered by the shooting, which one ranger described as "very traumatic."

Lisa Kowalski was rushed to an emergency clinic, where her wound was described as minor, nothing more than an ugly welt. The bite didn't even rip her blue jeans. The family dog also recovered from its wounds.

January 1, 1994: On New Year's Day, three mountain bikers were menaced by a mountain lion in Cuyamaca Rancho State Park. The cougar approached the three bikers near the Green Valley Falls campground. Rangers reacted by closing a 25-square-mile area of the park for four days. A lion was shot a few days later, after it menaced some livestock nearby.

May 9, 1994: A German couple and their young son, who were on an outing at Cuyamaca Rancho State Park, were terrified when a mountain lion approached their campsite. They threw rocks at the cougar, but it wouldn't leave. The family vacated the campsite and went to notify a game warden, who returned to the area, saw the lion, and shot it. He later discovered a deer carcass nearby that the 83-pound male had apparently been feeding upon.

August 21, 1994: A bowhunter was stalked by three cougars in the woods near Porterville. When one cat became particularly aggressive, the bowhunter shot it with an arrow. The arrow pierced the cat's body and the animal ran off.

California Department of Fish and Game officials later surmised that the three were a female lion with her two nearly grown kittens.

Hunters with dogs were then called in to search for and destroy the wounded puma. The animal was never found.

August 1994: Troy Winslow, 50, and his wife, Robin, were camping in the yard of their cabin near Dos Rios in Mendocino County. The structure was being refurbished. Kathleen Strehl, a friend, was with them. At about 4:30 A.M., a fight broke out between the Strehls' dog and a two-year-old female mountain lion. The group came to the dog's rescue and pelted the lion with rocks. The animal retreated under the cabin. At daybreak, the cougar came back and attacked Kathleen, puncturing her arm and knocking her to the ground. The others were able to jump on the cat and kill it. Troy Winslow's thumb was bitten off during the melee. The female mountain lion was later discovered to have been rabid.

January 1995: A mountain lion charged Michelle Rossmiller, 17, as she was unloading her books from her car outside her home on Vulcan Mountain in San Diego County. The girl reported that the lion came right at her, fast, but that she was able to get inside the car and slam the door before it could reach her. It hung around for a few minutes, then left.

March 20, 1995: Scott Fike, 27, was mountain biking near Mount Lowe in the Angeles National Forest above Pasadena when a mountain lion pounced on him from the brush. The cat bit him in the head and clawed his face before Fike was able to chase it off with rocks.

"I've never been that scared in my life," said Fike, whose injuries were cared for at a nearby clinic.

The cougar was tracked down and killed by authorities.

January 16, 1996: A woman was riding her horse in Cuyamaca Rancho State Park when a lion leaped out onto the trail, about five feet in front of her horse. Reacting quickly, the woman bared her teeth, growled like an animal, and stared at the cougar as it crouched in front of her. She then lunged at the animal with her horse, but the lion held its ground. The rider turned and rode back the way she had come.

The woman reported the incident, and two game wardens and an animal damage control specialist responded the following day.

The lion was still hanging around the same spot. When it saw the group of men, it charged them. It had closed the distance to just 15 feet when warden Bob Turner, of the California Fish and Game Department, shot it twice.

After a necropsy, department veterinarians reported that the male lion weighed 62 pounds. Its age was estimated at between one and a half and two years old.

February 18, 1997: A man was walking to a stream behind his home near Shingletown when a cougar charged out of the brush and pounced on his back. The pair wrestled in midstream until the man was able to pull out his pistol. He fired it to frighten the lion, and the cat ran away. The man escaped with nothing more serious than a ripped vest.

Searchers with tracking dogs were called to the scene of the attack, but failed to pick up the animal's scent. The search was eventually called off.

December 28, 1998: A cougar emerged from the brush and began circling a group of women and 5- to 8-year-old children at a day use area in Caspers

Regional Park in Orange County. Women in the group yelled at the cougar, but this seemed to infuriate the animal, which switched its tail, hissed, and then crawled forward on its belly, positioning itself to charge the children. One woman threw a hiking boot at the cat, and the cougar retreated. The cougar was later spotted by another group of people who reported on its nonchalant atttitude around human beings.

Eleven years earlier, an administrative decision had closed down this park to all minors following a spate of lion attacks on children. Ironically, the restriction had been lifted just two weeks before these incidents.

The cat was eventually tracked down and killed. No dogs were needed, because the cougar was in no way being furtive or stealthy. The female was in good health, and did not have kittens.

Orange County Supervisor Charles Smith said he would propose closing the park to minors again. "We have to decide if this is going to be a park for children to play in or a park for mountain lions. The two are not compatible," he said.

August 1998: Two women hikers encountered an aggressive cougar near Stonewall Peak in Cuyamaca Rancho State Park. When the lion came too close, one of the women pepper-sprayed it, causing it to retreat.

October 9 and 10, 1998: Four mountain lions were killed in Cuyamaca Rancho State Park by California Department of Fish and Game wardens. Two of the animals were killed on October 9th after menacing a riding club. The next day, a lion threatened a camper at Los Vaqueros horse camp by attempting to grab the man's leg. Authorities dispatched Lt. Bob Turner to the camp. When Turner arrived, the lion was lurking in nearby woods. As Turner approached and shot the animal, another lion came charging out of the brush at him. Turner shot that lion as well. This brought to 12 the number of mountain lions killed in the park since 1987.

In an interview during the battle for Proposition 117 in 1990, Mark Palmer, director of the Mountain Lion Foundation, a group dedicated to both the preservation of the mountain lion's protected status and the procurement of its habit said, "I'm still unwilling to admit that the mountain lion is exceedingly dangerous." This statement stands in marked contrast to the one made by Cal Hert, in his 1955 book *Never Go Unarmed Into the Hills*. Hert called the mountain lion the most dangerous of California predators, "a natural killer" that "kills for sport."

Most observers believe that the mountain lion situation in California—and, increasingly, elsewhere—boils down to a fight between those who live in the cities and suburbs, who relish the thought of mountain lions roaming the hills visible from their residences, and whose sentiments are clearly on the side of the animals; and those who actually live in those hills, and who must contend with lions and the threats they present on a daily basis. The advantages all belong to the people who reside in coastal cities. They have the votes, the campaign dollars, the media savvy (and support), and Hollywood mentoring. Thanks to their efforts, the mountain lion's future appears to be safe.

The people of California have spoken, at least for the time being. "We've pointed out the biological facts," said Idaho's Maurice Hornocker, the dean of cougar researchers. "California has viable, flourishing populations of cougars. And as long as it's based soundly in biology, there's nothing wrong with hunting cougars."

Many people don't care about the biology. They don't care that there are plenty of lions. They don't care that the population could withstand some hunting. They simply don't believe that it's right to kill a beautiful animal for "sport."

15

The Victims

A ccording to the analysis presented by Paul Beier in "Cougar Attacks on Humans in the United States and Canada," there were nine fatal and 44 nonfatal attacks resulting in 10 human deaths and 48 nonfatal injuries. Five of the attacks involved two victims.

Beier further states that 37 of the 58 victims (64 percent) were children (less than 16 years old); while the other 21 (36 percent) were adults (over 16 years old). Of 37 children, Beier stated that 35 percent were alone, 43 percent were in groups with other children, and 22 percent were with adults. Eleven of 17 adult victims were alone at the time of the attack. Of the victims classified as "alone," six of 13 children and four of 11 adults were within hearing distance of other people. Except for one adult and one child who probably died of rabies (California, 1909), all fatalities were children unaccompanied by adults. Beier's analysis was completed in 1991, before any of the well-publicized cougar fatalities of the 1990s had taken place. In the intervening years, the rate of attacks upon people seems to be escalating. Previously unknown attacks also continue to be discovered in old journals, letters and newspapers; while these statistics may no longer be current, pertinent information can still be gleaned from them.

Beier found that most victims in his analysis (24 of 32, excluding two who were injured after they came to a companion's aid) did not see the cougar before being clawed or bitten, so no preventive action was taken. The other eight victims failed to prevent the attack. Beier discovered that in all near attacks, the actual attack was averted because the potential victim had time to react to the cougar's presence. In some near attacks, the cougar was shot as it approached. In most others, however, aggressive behavior such as shouting, swinging sticks, throwing rocks, or waving arms were sufficient to deter the animal from carrying out its attack. Beier discovered only one credible near attack in which the intended victim escaped by panicked, headlong flight. That incident occurred on June 18, 1966, in British Columbia (see Chapter 6).

More recently, "Cougar Attacks on Children: Injury Patterns and Treatment," an article by K. M. Kadesky, C. Manarey, G. K. Blair, J. J. Murphy III, C. Verchere, and K. Atkinson that was published in the *Journal of Pediatric Surgery* (Vol. 33, No. 6: pp.863–5), approaches the seemingly disproportional number of attacks upon children by reviewing circumstances and injuries. Here are some of the findings from that paper:

- Cougar attacks on humans appear to be on the rise. A review of all attacks on children was performed to determine the method of attack and injury patterns so that a treatment regimen and possible preventative measures could be determined.
- There were 50 documented attacks [that they could find] on children, with a 25 percent fatality rate.
- Most children (92 percent) were not alone at the time of the attack.
- In many instances, adults were present or nearby.

The authors noted that the most common injuries were severe head and neck lacerations along with puncture wounds. Typical cervical (neck) injuries include "a nonfatal vertebral artery injury, phrenic nerve njury, a fatal internal carotid artery injury, and a fatal cervical spine injury." The cougar was rabid in two cases. *Pasteurella* (an infectious bacteria) resulted in late infections in two patients.

The study's authors recommend "aggressive evaluation for occult cervical injuries as well as surgical debridement. Antibiotics should cover orpharyngeal flora including *Pasteurella multocida*. Rabies prophylaxis is indicated."

The study's last statement is simply this: "Adult supervision in wilderness areas is not necessarily protective."

The discrepancies in numbers of attacks as well as ages of victims between Beier's and Kadesky's databases can be explained by noting that Beier's data only included attacks up until 1991, while Kadesky's includes many more recent attack accountings. Media coverage of cougar attacks and near-attacks has also become more intense during recent years.

In this latest accounting of cougar attacks, 41 fatal encounters have been documented from a variety of sources, while 185 non-fatal attacks have also been listed. This data has not yet been analyzed as scrupulously as Dr. Beier's was as to the actions taken by the victims, and whether those actions had any effect on the outcomes of the attacks.

16
Dealing with Lions

According to his records, written in the spring of 1871, Kansas pioneer Dr. N. C. Fancher was inspecting a proposed land claim in the south-central part of the state when he found himself being circled by a puma. Fancher picked up several nearby buffalo bones and began to yell and jump about while clacking the bones together. The commotion had little effect, as the puma crouched . . .

> down like a cat and started crawling toward me, . . . [but upon my] bellowing desperately" and whacking "the bones savagely together," the animal "stopped, raised its head and looked away from me for the first time. It then turned and started to trot away, just as a cat would trot. I watched it until it passed over the divide three quarters of a mile away.

Was the cat stalking the man? Possibly, but even if it wasn't, Fancher made the right moves for dealing with a nosy, perhaps aggressive, cougar.

Beier noted in his 1991 study that a person is more likely to be killed by a rattlesnake, bee, black widow spider, or common dog than by a cougar. Lightning strikes kill far more people each year than do cougars. Confrontations, however, will continue so long as people continue to invade cougar habitats.

Further, if a cougar is doing its predator job properly, the human victim will not even see the cat to know that he or she is being stalked. If the mountain lion has done its job efficiently, the human victim will not even realize he or she was attacked. That is how quickly a mountain lion can complete its kill.

Such a statement is not meant to frighten those who venture into lion country. Merely reaching the mountains or canyons where lions live involves risk. Death by cougar may even be preferable to death by truck or automobile, if we had to make such a ghoulish choice, yet most of us consider the eighteen-wheelers speeding over our highways and back roads an "acceptable risk." Short of killing off every cougar in the countryside, or refusing to allow humans access to any cougar habitat, we simply have to consider mountain lions in the same way we consider big trucks. They are out there, and they can kill you.

Should the unthinkable happen, and you find yourself confronted by a mountain lion, here are some tips for dealing with the animals:

Body Language

- A mountain lion conveys its intentions through its body postures, facial expressions, and distinctive vocalizations. Knowing the warning signals can help people to recognize an imminent threat.
- A lion may be expressing simple curiosity while standing or sitting, looking intently at the subject of interest, its ears perked forward and, perhaps, even sniffing the air.
- A lion approaching a person, pet, or animal in a half or full crouch with its ears perked forward and eyes riveted on the subject means serious business. An attack may be imminent.
- A lion lying on its belly with its four feet tucked underneath, ears perked forward, may be preparing to launch an attack. Its eyes will be focused intently on the subject of its interest, its tail will be twitching nervously. This cat is sizing up the situation. Such an animal can—and will—move with lightning speed.
- To express aggression, a lion may growl with its mouth closed, or "hiss" with its mouth wide open so that the teeth are bared.
- If a lion is cornered with no route for escape, it may express its fear by pinning its ears back and growling or hissing and baring its teeth. The lion may do this in either the standing or sitting position. The cornered animal may also bluff charge or attack whoever or whatever is cornering it.

There is a simple solution: Never approach a mountain lion. If, for some reason, you do, leave it a way out, an escape route to freedom. Never back it into a corner.

Here are precautions to be followed that may minimize your or your children's chances of being attacked, or that may lessen the severity of injuries should you be attacked:

Children

(12 years and younger, or teenagers and adults with slight frames and small stature.)

- Closely supervise children. Because of their size and their sometimes unsteady gait, which can resemble the tentative first steps of baby animals, they are more likely to be attacked than adults are.
- When in cougar country, instruct your children to play in groups when outdoors; always supervise them.
- Consider erecting a fence around play areas in mountain lion country.
- Install outside lighting. While lighting won't prevent a lion from entering an area, it could help you spot a lion should one wander close to your home.
- A dog can act as an early warning system when the animal is with the child at home. Since a dog can detect a cougar's presence before humans can, a dog could distract a cougar from attacking a child.
- Keep a radio playing when children are outdoors. Noise seems to discourage lions.
- Make sure children are home before dusk and that they stay indoors until after dawn. Realize, however, that some lions are active during the daytime.
- If cougars have been sighted near your neighborhood, escort children to the bus stop in the morning and pick them up in the evening.
- Clear shrubs away from your yard and close to your house. Clear shrubbery away from the bus stop so that there is a cleared area measuring at least 60 feet in diameter.
- Do not attract or feed wildlife, especially deer or raccoons. These animals are a mountain lion's natural prey. Inviting them into your yard means extending the invitation to mountain lions.

Pets

- Roaming pets are easy prey.
- Be wary of walking pets in mountain lion country. A dog running loose could even bring a lion back to you should a lion decide to attack it. A pet means "food" to a mountain lion.
- Bring pets inside at night. If they must be left out, confine them in a kennel with a secure top.
- Never feed pets outside. This will attract small animals, which may then attract cougars. Pet food is also a cougar delicacy.
- Lock domestic livestock in an enclosed shed or barn at night.
- Close off open spaces below porches or decks.

- Landscape your property with native plants, not highly palatable non-native species that may attract deer.

General

- Never hike, jog, or ride a mountain bike alone in mountain lion country.
- Make enough noise to prevent surprising a cougar.
- Keep children close at hand and under control.
- Should you smell the stench of rotting meat, do not move any closer. Should you see an animal carcass, back away. Should you come upon an animal carcass that has been partially buried beneath sticks, leaves, or dirt, back off slowly and do not return. It is likely that a large predatory animal has killed its prey nearby and might, at this very moment, be watching you.
- Watch for cougar tracks and sign.
- A daypack, backpack, or collared garment will protect vulnerable neck and throat areas.

If You See or Meet a Cougar

- Never approach a mountain lion. If you see one, stop. Most lions will try to avoid a confrontation. Provide them with an avenue of escape.
- Avoid placing yourself downhill of a cougar. Being downhill will leave you more vulnerable to attack since a mountain lion is a pouncing animal.
- Never approach cougar kittens. Do not attempt to pick them up! Leave the area immediately should you spot a kitten. A female mountain lion will defend her young.
- Speak loudly and firmly. You must convince the cougar that you are a threat, and not a meal.
- Although averting your eyes is wise when you are confronted by a grizzly, do *not* do so if a cougar approaches. Cougars, like all cats, do not like making eye-to-eye contact. Should you succeed in locking gazes with the lion, do *not* look away. To do so would be to signal submission, or weakness.
- If you encounter a mountain lion, stand and face the animal. Make eye contact. Pick up your child, but do not crouch or bend down to do so. A person crouched or bent over resembles prey to a mountain lion. If you must crouch, Lee Fitzhugh, wildlife extension specialist at the University

of California, suggests growling and snarling in a confrontational manner, as though *you* are the one about to attack. Gauge the cougar's reaction if you do. If growling seems to incite the animal, stop growling.

- Consider carrying a walking stick. Not only do walking sticks come in handy, especially when covering rough terrain, they can be used as weapons in the event of an attack. Should a cougar come too close, wield the stick like a sword. If it comes closer, whack the cougar on the head with the end of the stick. If that doesn't discourage the animal, keep the stick at the ready. Should it attack, hold it parallel to the earth and at 90 degrees to your body in front of you. Shove it into the cat's mouth to keep the animal from clamping down on you with its jaws. Use what leverage you can to force the animal back off from you.
- Never run. To do so will trigger the lion's predatory chase response.
- Do what you can to make yourself appear larger. Raise your arms over your head, open your shirt or jacket, wave your arms slowly, and yell.
- If you yell, try not to do so in a high-pitched voice. A scream that is high in pitch can sound like the cry of injured or dying prey.
- Do not turn your back on the cougar. Face the animal and remain upright.
- Pick up sticks or branches and wave them about.

Alternative Measures

- Carry a compressed air horn to frighten the animal.
- Carry pepper spray in a holster on your chest or waist. A chest holster allows you to spray directly into a cougar's mucous membranes—eyes, nose, inside the mouth—at the very last minute. If you're being attacked, it could cause the cat to disengage before even making contact. (Note: Two pepper sprays that meet or exceed the standards of bear researchers are UDAP and CounterAssault.)
- While carrying pepper spray may make you feel safer, the jury is out as to whether it would work on a determined lion. Studies have not yet been undertaken or completed on its efficacy against cats (if they have been done, this writer was unaware of them when this book went to press). Remembering that all animals are individuals with varying sets of behaviors, and that to use pepper spray may infuriate an attacking lion rather than cause it to flee, you may still choose to carry pepper spray into lion country. Several cougar authorities have stated that if a lion is charging and attack is imminent, you have nothing to lose. Spray for all

you're worth—just do so at close range. Pepper spray is most effective when sprayed from a distance of no more than two feet. This means waiting until the last possible moment before unleashing your spray into a cougar's mouth, nose, or eyes. Beware of incapacitating yourself, however, particularly if the wind is blowing back toward you. To be rendered helpless at the moment of a lion attack is like putting yourself on a silver platter and shouting, "*Bon appetit!*"

- Although no one, at least to my knowledge, has done any testing with stun guns on aggressive cougars, if you are in imminent danger of life or limb, a major shock should discourage the cat and cause it to leave. While I am unable to advise anyone to carry a stun gun, if a stick can beat off a charging cat, common sense says that a stun gun could do the same. Were you to stun a cat that was in contact with you, however, it is likely that you would feel some effects of the charge unless you were well insulated from the ground (still standing upright and with thick rubber soles).

- A gun is probably the best protection of all—preferably a large-caliber handgun in a holster that is easily accessible.

If a Cougar Behaves Aggressively

- If the lion starts to follow you, throw something at it: rocks, sticks, canned goods. Do *not* throw sandwiches or other edibles. To do so will reward its aggressive behavior and, once it has eaten the food, it will probably continue to follow you.

- Never play dead. A cougar is a prey animal that is used to killing animals. To play dead informs the animal that you are ready to be eaten. Whereas a grizzly or brown bear, for example, simply wants to remove the threat, or have you acknowledge your submission, predatory cougars must be defended against.

- If attacked, fight back with anything you can lay your hands on. Use rocks, sticks, your camera, even your bare hands. Poke the lion in its eyes. Should the lion grab on to your arm, bite its ear as hard as you can. Do anything to inflict pain on the animal. Hit it with your walking stick. Spray it with your pepper spray.

Source: New Mexico Department of Game and Fish: *Living With Wildlife in Lion Country.*

17
Whither the Cougar?

*P*uma concolor appear poised at the brink of an incredible comeback. After centuries of bounties, poisonings, traps, and even outright persecution, many populations of pumas once thought of as extinct may be anything but. That doesn't mean that everyone who has recently reported sighting a cougar has actually seen such an animal, but some eyewitness accounts ring so true that those who bear the news can hardly be disbelieved.

Reading in Robert H. Busch's *The Cougar Almanac,* for example, one comes across these sentences:

> In October 1994, Rick Hedders saw a ghost. He was hunting deer in upstate New York when a large cat bounded out of the trees. "I stared at this thing and thought, 'This isn't supposed to be here,'" he says. He looked away for a few seconds to call his dogs and the cat disappeared. "I'm sure it was a cougar," he says. "Nothing around here is that big."

Hedders's sighting is all the more remarkable when one considers that the last known Vermont cougar, for instance, was dispatched on Thanksgiving Day, 1881, near the hamlet of Barnard. Cougars were already so rare in Upstate New York and New England that the hunters had the cougar mounted by a taxidermist and then exhibited it around the state, billing it as the "King of the Brute Creation." Spectators paid 10 cents to view the cougar, and tourists can still see it today at the Vermont Historical Society Museum in Montpelier. The cougar snarls from a place of honor befitting a "King"—within a glass display case positioned in the museum's foyer.

It's a wonder the cougar lasted so long, considering that colonial governments started establishing bounties for cougar skins as early as 1650. Massive habitat destruction followed, as a burgeoning population spread up and down the coast. Then westward movement began, with more habitat destruction and degradation following. Deer populations plummeted in the face of few, if any, hunting regulations. By the end of the nineteenth century, the mountain lion was virtually extinct east of the Mississippi. Only a small population of the Florida subspecies remained, managing to hang on, barely, in the Everglades.

Today, the country is divided, as far as cougars are concerned. In the East, they remain extremely rare, if not extinct. Florida researchers, in fact, are attempting to save the cougar, to help its numbers grow. In the West, the situation is just the opposite, with too many cougars, and the numbers continuing to grow. It's gotten to the point where researchers at Colorado State University are pursuing the development of a contraceptive—recently proven to be extremely ineffective when used on deer—that can be delivered in a biodegradable cellulose bullet to control suburban lion populations.

But will such tactics be enough? How many human victims in the future will comprise an "acceptable loss" to those who live and work in or near cougar country? The mark has already been exceeded, according to some observers. Others, however, are willing to accept whatever mountain lions do, so long as they're not on the receiving end of those deadly claws and razor-sharp fangs.

"Twenty years ago, [a lion that was aggressive toward people] never got a second chance," said Tom Beck, carnivorous mammal specialist with the Colorado Division of Wildlife. "People killed him. Now people will be nervous about that lion, but they will tolerate him. Crossing that line scares me."

"The only species we have too many of is the human one," countered Sherri Tippie, founder of Wildlife 2000, a consortium of people whose goal is to preserve all wildlife in its natural state. The group believes nature knows best and adopts a hands-off attitude toward wildlife management. As long as enough people agree with Tippie and others like her, mountain lions will continue to expand both their numbers and their range. The result will be many more lions much more familiar with—and contemptuous of—the people attempting to share their habitat. More attacks will occur. The only questions are: How many? and Where?

In the meantime, the Great Lion Comeback continues. Mountain lions are being sighted regularly in South Dakota, where their numbers had once dwindled to almost nothing. They have been spotted in Nebraska, in western Oklahoma, in Arkansas, and even in places where even game and fish departments had long thought the creatures to be extinct, including Missouri, Illinois, the Carolinas, Pennsylvania, Tennessee, Pennsylvania, and New York. Whether escaped pets or bona fide immigrants from small, but established, populations, the lion is making its move and it's anything but furtive.

Coupled with the lions' apparent resurgence is an apparent resistance on the part of the citizens of several states to consider hunting as a legitimate management tool. Yet you have to search to find even one or two respected wildlife biologists to agree that cougar hunting should be stopped. We instead hear comments such as this one from Maurice Hornocker, cougar researcher and founder of the Hornocker Wildlife Institute in Moscow, Idaho. "Some 300 lions are killed during Idaho's six-month, controlled hunting season each year, but there are as many lions in Idaho now as there have ever been," he said.

Hornocker further states that, "We need to educate people [. . . about] lions. All you need to do is fly to Los Angeles and see all the new subdivisions on the finger ridges. Those ridges are wildlife corridors, critical grounds, and also where humans and mountain lions may run afoul of each other.

"Populations of lions may differ genetically," Hornocker said. "Some seem more inclined to live and interact with humans than others. We don't know why yet. We need to do DNA testing on lions in areas where there are consistent attacks and perhaps replace those lions with others that avoid humans."

We may be able to train people how to behave in mountain lion country, but when we design our own, less-fierce cougar, we will be taking some of the wild out of the wilderness. And that may be just one more step on the treacherous path that will deliver us to a world in which there will no longer be any truly wild places or truly wild creatures. And that world will be, by far, a much poorer place.

Bibliography

Acosta, Gilbert (as told to S. P. English, Jr.). "Lions Best Them All." *Outdoor Life,* May 1963.

Aristotle. *Aristotle's History of Animals.* Translated by Richard Cresswell. London: Geo. Bell & Sons, 1897.

Audubon, John James, and John Bachman. *Viviparous Quadrupeds of North America.* New York: J. J. Audubon, 1845–48.

Barnes, Claude T. *The Cougar or Mountain Lion.* Salt Lake City: Ralton Co., 1960.

Bauer, Erwin A. *Treasury of Big Game Animals.* New York: Harper & Row, 1972.

Beier, Paul. "Cougar Attacks on Humans in the United States and Canada." *Wildlife Society Bulletin* 19 (1991): 403–12.

Beier, Paul, and Stanley C. Cunningham. "Power of Track Surveys to Detect Changes in Cougar Populations." *Wildlife Society Bulletin* 24 (3) (1996): 540–546.

Beier, Paul, and Steve Loe. "In My Experience. . . .: A Checklist for Evaluating Impacts to Wildlife Movements and Corridors." *Wildlife Society Bulletin* 20 (1992): 434–440.

Bolgiano, Chris. *Mountain Lion: An Unnatural History of Pumas and People.* Mechanicsburg, Pennsylvania: Stackpole Books, 1995.

Bourke, John G. *On the Border with Crook.* Lincoln: University of Nebraska Press, 1971.

British Columbia. Fish and Wildlife Branch. Information and Education Section. *The Cougar in British Columbia.* By D. J. Spaulding. 1994.

Brunet, Robin. "She Gave Her Life for Her Son." *Alberta Report,* September 2, 1996.

Busch, Robert H. *The Cougar Almanac: A Complete Natural History of the Mountain Lion.* New York: The Lyons Press, 1996.

California. Department of Fish and Game. *Outdoor California* 61 (May–June 2000). Sacramento, 2000.

Caras, Roger. *Dangerous to Man.* New York: Chilton, 1964.

Chittendon, Hiram Martin. *A History of the American Fur Trade of the Far West*. 1935. Reprint. Stanford: Academic Reprints, 1954.

Clark, William, and Meriwether Lewis. *Original Journals of the Lewis and Clark Expedition*. Edited by Reuben Gold Thwaites. New York: Dodd, Mead and Company, 1904–5.

Clarke, James. *Man is the Prey*. New York: Stein and Day, 1969.

Cuvier, Georges (Baron), and Edward Griffin. *The Animal Kingdom Arranged in Conformity with its Organization*. 4 vols. Translated by H. M'Murtrie. Carvill, New York: G. & C. & H., 1831.

Danz, Harold P. *Cougar!* Athens, Ohio: Swallow Press/Ohio University Press, 1999.

Davis, Goode P. Jr. *Man and Wildlife in Arizona*. Phoenix: Arizona Fish and Game Department, 1982.

DeVane, Albert, and Park DeVane. *DeVane's Early Florida History*. N.d. Reprint. Sebring, Florida: Sebring Historical Society, 1978.

Dobie, J. Frank. *The Ben Lilly Legend*. 1950. Reprint. Austin: University of Texas, 1982.

———. "Tales of the Panther." *Saturday Evening Post,* December 11, 1943.

Dufresne, Frank. "Crazy Cougars." *Field and Stream,* December 1955.

Ellis, Don D. "Hound Man's Dream." *Outdoor Life,* November 1967.

———. "The Cougar Does Attack." *Outdoor Life,* September 1971.

Fergus, Charles. *Swamp Screamer*. Gainesville: University of Florida Press, 1998.

Fitzhugh, E. Lee. "Changing Dynamics of Puma Attacks on Humans." Unpublished data. Sixth Mountain Lion Workshop, San Antonio, Texas, December 12–14, 2000.

Fitzhugh, E. Lee, and W. P. Gorenzel. "The Biological Status of Mountain Lions in California." T. P. Salmon, editor. From proceedings of the Twelfth Vertebrate Pest Conference, University of California, Davis, 1978.

Froman, Robert. *The Nerve of Some Animals*. Philadelphia: J. B. Lippincott, 1961.

Goode, Monroe H. "Killers of the Rimrock." *Field and Stream,* June 1943.

———. "The Real Cougar." *Field and Stream,* August 1944.

Haley, Charles. "Killer Cougar." *Field and Stream,* March 1953.

Haley, J. Evetts. *Charles Goodnight: Cowman and Plainsman*. Norman, Oklahoma: University of Oklahoma Press, 1949.

Hall, Del. *Island Gold: A History of Cougar Hunting on Vancouver Island*. Victoria: Cougar Press, 1990.

Hibben, Frank. "Cougars Kill People: Terror at Arroyo Seco." *Petersen's Hunting,* March 1975.

Hilderbrand, E. Boyd (as told to Ken Crandall). "Cougar Nightmare." *Outdoor Life,* August 1915.

Hittell, Theodore H. *The Adventures of James Capen Adams.* New York: Charles Scribner's Sons, 1926.

Hornaday, William T. *A Wild Animal Roundup.* New York: Charles Scribner's Sons, 1925.

Howard, Charles B. "An Instance of a Mountain Lion's Attack on a Boy." *Outdoor Life* 36, August 1915.

Hunter, J. Marvin. *Pioneer History of Bandera County.* Bandera, Texas: Hunter's Printing House, 1922.

Jeffcott, P. R. *Nooksak Tales and Trails.* Ferndale, Washington: Sedro-Woolley Courier Times, 1949.

Journal of Mammology 6 (1925): 197–99.

Klassen, D. *Cougars in the Yukon.* Yukon Department of Renewable Resources Technical Report, 2000.

Kobalenko, Jerry. *Forest Cats of North America.* Willowdale, Ontario: Firefly Books, 1997.

Kurtén, Björn, and Elaine Anderson. *Pleistocene Mammals of North America.* New York: n.p., 1980.

Lawrence, D. H. "The Mountain Lion." *The Complete Poems of D. H. Lawrence.* Edited by Vivian de Sola Pinto and F. Warren Roberts. New York: Viking Press, 1964.

Laycock, George. *The Mountain Men.* New York: Sedgewood Press, 1988.

Lesowski, John. "The Silent Hunter." *Outdoor Life,* July 1967.

Lewis, Jerry A. *The Long Walkers.* Prescott, Arizona: Wolfe Publishing, 1995.

Lindzey, Frederick G., Walter D. Van Sickle, Steven P. Laing, and Clint S. Mecham. "Cougar Population Response to Manipulation in Southern Utah." *Wildlife Society Bulletin* 20 (1992): 224–227.

Mills, Enos. *Wildlife on the Rockies.* New York: Houghton Mifflin, 1909.

Moody, Charles S. "The Mountain Lion at Home." *Outing* 59, February 1912.

Mueller, Larry. "Cougar Attack." *Outdoor Life,* April 1958.

New Mexico. Game and Fish Department. *Living with Wildlife in Lion Country.*

Nickels, Sam H. "Never Trust a Lion." *Outdoor Life's Anthology of Hunting Adventures.* New York: Beaufort Books, 1986.

Nicol, James Y. "He Wrestled a Cougar." *True West* 5, No. 3, January–February, 1958.

Nollman, Jim. "The Incident at Boat Bay." *The Interspecies Newsletter.* 1993.

Outdoor Life's Anthology of Hunting Adventures. New York: Beaufort Books, 1986.

Parsons, P. A. "All over the Map." *Outdoor Life* 100, No. 2, August 1947.

Pattie, James Ohio. *The Personal Narratives of James Ohio Pattie.* N.p.: J. H. Wood, 1831.

People of the Desert. Alexandria, Virginia: Time-Life Books, 1993.

Perry, W. A. *The Big Game of North America.* Edited by G. O. Shields. Chicago and New York: Rand, McNalley, 1890.

Pike, Zebulon Montgomery. *The Journals of Zebulon Montgomery Pike, with letters and related documents.* Edited and annotated by Donald Jackson. Norman: University of Oklahoma Press, 1966.

Range, Lester A. "Stalked by a Cougar!" *Bowhunter,* September 1987.

A Reminiscent History of the Ozark Region. 1894. Reprint. Greenville, South Carolina: Southern Historical Press, 1995.

Roosevelt, Theodore. *Hunting Trips of a Ranchman and The Wilderness Hunter.* 1893. Reprint. New York: Random House, 1998.

———. *The Hunting and Exploring Adventures of Theodore Roosevelt.* Edited by Donald Day. New York: Dial Press, 1955.

Ross, P. Ian, Martin G. Jalkotzy, and John R. Gunson. "The Quota System of Cougar Harvest Management in Alberta." *Wildlife Society Bulletin* 24 (3) (1996): 490–494.

Russell Osborne. *Journal of a Trapper.* Edited by Aubrey L. Haines. Lincoln and London: University of Nebraska Press, 1986.

Seton, Ernest Thompson. *Lives of Game Animals.* Volume 1. Garden City, New York: Doubleday, Doran & Co., 1929.

———. *Wild Animals at Home.* New York: Grossett & Dunlap, 1913.

Shaw, Harley. *Soul Among Lions: The Cougar as Peaceful Adversary.* Boulder, Colorado: Johnson Books, 1989.

Smithwick, Noah. *The Evolution of a State; or, Recollections of Old Texas Days.* Austin, Texas: Gammel Book Company, 1900.

Southesk, James Carnegie, Earl of. *Saskatchewan and the Rocky Mountains: a diary and narrative of travel, sport, and adventure, during a journey thorugh the Hudson's Bay Company's territories, in 1859 and 1860.* In Robert H. Busch, *The Cougar Almanac: A Complete Natural History of the Mountain Lion.* New York: The Lyons Press, 1996.

Storer, Tracey I., and Lloyd P. Tevis, Jr. *California Grizzly*. Lincoln: University of Nebraska Press, 1978.

Tinsley, Jim Bob. *The Puma—Legendary Lion of the Americas*. El Paso: Texas Western Press, 1987.

Topsell, Edward. *Historie of Foure-Footed Beastes, Describing . . . Collected Out of All the Volumes of Conrad Gesner, and All Other Writers . . .* 1607. Reprint. New York: Theatrum Orbis Terrarum & Da Capo Press, 1973.

Torres, Steve. *Mountain Lion Alert: Safety Tips for Yourself, Your Children, Your Pets, and Your Livestock in Lion Country*. Helena and Billings: Falcon Publishing, 1997.

Townsend, John K. *Journey Across the Rocky Mountains to the Columbia River*. 1839. Reprinted in *Townsend's Narrative*, volume 21 of *Early Western Travels, 1748–1846*. Edited by Reuben Gold Thwaites. New York: AMS Press, 1966.

Treadwell, Joseph. "Cougar Encounter." *Bowhunting World* 39, No. 1, February 1990.

True, Frederick William. *The Puma, or American Lion: Felis Concolor of Linnaeus*. National Museum Report 591–608, miscellaneous document. Washington, D.C., 1889.

Turbak, Gary. "The Cougar Makes a Comeback." *Field and Stream*, January 1991.

Udall, Scott. "Encounter with a Cougar." *Field and Stream*, November 1971.

Vanderbilt, Amy. *Mountain Lion Injures Boy in Glacier National Park*. GNP News release: July 13, 1992.

———. *Apgar Mountain Lion Incident*. GNP News Release: July 23 and 25, 1990.

Ward, Doug. "Meet a Hero—Man Punches Cougar in Head, Rescues Cyclist." *Vancouver Sun*, January 10, 2001.

Wehausen, John D. "Effects of Mountain Lion Predation on Bighorn Sheep in the Sierra Nevada and Granite Mountains of California." *Wildlife Society Bulletin* 24 (3) (1996): 471–479.

Wells, William. "Cougar." *Field and Stream*, March 1932.

Worth, Nick. "When Cats Go Bad." *Outdoor Life*, January 1991.

Wyeth, John Allen. *Life of Lieutenant-General Nathan Bedford Forrest*. New York: Harper, 1899.

Young, Stanley P., and Edward A. Goldman. *The Puma: Mysterious American Cat*. New York: Dover Publications, 1964.

The Worlds of Ernest Thompson Seton. Edited by John G. Samson. New York: Alfred A. Knopf, 1976.

Appendix

Non-fatal Cougar Attacks
on Humans

Date	Location	Victim	Sex	Age	Sources	Comments
1800s	Mt. Hood, OR	Unknown	M	Adult	Forked Deer quoted in Fitzhugh, 23; Young and Goldman, 102.	A cougar pounced upon a man sleeping on the ground. He rose and the cougar broke off its attack and ran away.
1800s	MS or LA	Unknown	M	Adult	Audubon & Bachman, Vol. II: 307–309, 312; Fitzhugh, 23.	A raftsman was camped on a riverbank at night when he was attacked while sleeping. He frightened the puma away with a burning stick that he was able to snatch from the fire.
1800s	MS	Unknown	M	Adult	Audubon & Bachman, Vol. II: 307–309, 312; Fitzhugh, 23.	A cotton planter heard his dogs barking outside one evening. He opened the door and they rushed inside. He drove all the dogs back out except one, which was cowering under a table. When he looked under the table, he discovered the "dog" was really a puma. He fought back when it attacked him, and then it fell into the fireplace before dashing back out of the cabin. Once outside, the dogs attacked the puma and the man killed it with a club.
Early 1830s	Near Jasper, AR, close to Hudson Creek	Hudson	M	Adult	*A Reminiscent History of the Ozark Region* 290; Danz, 242–43.	Samuel Hudson and his son had been hewing a tree when the cougar approached. Hudson tossed rocks at the cougar, but did not hit it. When the cougar spotted the man and boy, it stopped and then advanced on them. The cougar crouched and then attacked. Hudson dealt the cougar a blow with his axe, but had to kill the animal with a knife handed to him by his son. Hudson suffered severe lacerations and significant loss of blood.

Date	Location	Name	Sex	Age	Source	Description
1834	Tippah County, northern MS near the TN border	Forrest	F	Adult	Wyeth 8–10; Fergus 34; Danz, 242–43.	Miriam Forrest, mother of Nathan Bedford Forrest (at the time 13), was riding horseback with her sister. Miriam was carrying a basket of hatchling chickens. A cougar, perhaps attracted by the chicks' peeping, chased the pair, then leaped upon Miriam, clawing her neck and shoulder and injuring the horse she was riding. When the horse bucked, the cougar fell off, but further wounded Miriam when it did so. Her screams summoned help. Nathan's dogs treed the cougar, and he shot the animal early the next morning.
June 28, 1852	Headwaters of the Red River in southwestern OK	Marcy	M	Adult	Marcy quoted in Young & Goldman, 32.	A puma was killed as it raced toward Captain Marcy, who was using a deer bleat to decoy a herd of pronghorns.
1854	Nevada	Solon	M	Adult	James Capen Adams quoted in Hittell, 207–18; Danz, 242–243	A cougar attacked Solon, James Capen Adams's partner, from behind. Solon called to Adams for help and Adams shot at it. It fled. The shot apparently missed the animal.
1858	Along Oak Creek east of Sarasota, FL	Unk./Unk.	M/F	Child/12	Fergus, 42–43. See also DeVane, *Early History of Florida*; Danz, 244–45.	Two children were outside a settler's cabin while their father was squaring some logs. A cougar rushed from the woods and grabbed the boy's foot. When the boy's sister pulled on him, the cougar attacked her. Their father, mother and two dogs rushed to the children's aid. The commotion unsettled the cougar, which crawled beneath the cabin floor. The father killed the cougar with an adz.
Before 1864	Ste. Lawrence River in Quebec, Canada	Unknown	M	Adult	*Small Animals of North America* quoted in Barnes, 49; Fitzhugh, 21.	A cougar attacked a man in a boat.

Date	Location	Victim	Sex	Age	Sources	Comments
1870s	McCloud River Canyon, CA	Unknown	M	Adult	Stone quoted in Fitzhugh, 21.	A puma sprang upon a horse while its owner was riding it. The man, a rancher, "barely escaped with his life."
Early 1870s	Near Coalinga, CA	Williams	F	Child	Michael Dickerson in *Western Outdoor News*, April 23, 1993.	This attack took place upon Emma Williams in the early 1870s.
1878	Near Mt. Shasta, CA	Unknown	M	3	Professor W. H. Brewer of Yale to Dr. Merriam, quoted in Goode, 35. See also Danz, 244–45.	A cougar entered a yard and seized a boy by his throat. His mother, rushing to her son's aid, struck the cougar with a broom. A man in the house ran out and shot the cougar.
1880s	Sumas, WA	Jorgenson	M	Adult	Perry, 414–15; Caras, 25; Barnes, 118–19; Jeffcott, 340–41; Danz, 244–45.	A cougar seized Joseph Jorgenson's arm while he was clearing some land. He struggled with the cougar, finally killing it with his spade.
1880s	Northwest Whatcom near Lynden, WA	Unknown	M	Child	Jeffcott, 342–42; Danz, 244–45.	A girl and her younger brother were walking to school when a cougar grabbed the boy by his arm. The cougar broke off the attack when the girl hit the animal with a bottle of milk.
1880s	Northwest Whatcom County, near Ferndale, WA	Drunal	F	Adult	Jeffcott, 342; Danz, 244–45.	Mrs. Jim Drunal was confronted by a large cougar near the Glen Echo mill on the Nooksack River. She opened and closed her umbrella in the animal's face to keep it at bay. The cougar was later poisoned by Hanin Frost.

Date	Location	Name	Sex	Age	Source	Description
1880s	Logging camp near Mt. Vernon, Skagit County, WA	Harmon	M	Adult	Perry, 418–19, Danz, 246–47.	Charles Harmon encountered a cougar while he was searching for some strayed oxen. Although Harmon began yelling, the cougar was not frightened. It followed Harmon back to his camp, at times licking his hands, and it also managed to rip off all of Harmon's clothing before he could make it back to his cabin. The cougar was later shot.
Early 1880s	Near York, B.C.	Campbell	F	Adult	Perry, 425–18; Danz, 246–47; B.C. Ministry of the Environment report.	While traveling on horseback, a cougar startled Mary Campbell's horse and she was thrown. The cougar followed in a threatening manner as she made her way home. It lunged and tore her dress. Her father and his two dogs arrived, though, and killed the cougar.
1883	Mt. Hood, OR	Unknown	M	Adult	Barnes, 118; Fitzhugh, 22.	No other details known.
Spring 1883	Near Pillsbury, MN	Locke	M	Adult	Frank J. Locke quoted in "The Real Cougar," 71, Danz, 246–47.	Locke said that he had had an "encounter with a huge panther. . . ."
July 31, 1883	New Westminster, B.C.	Unknown	M	Adult	Barnes, 118; Fitzhugh, 22.	A puma jumped upon a man hunting grouse. When the man recovered and jumped to his feet, the startled puma ran off.
Spring 1884	Northern ID	Unknown	M	Adult	Seton, 199; Danz, 246–47.	A railroad hand was attacked by two adult cougars who may have been protecting their kittens. The man, who was armed only with a knife, received severe injuries. The cougars were later killed.

Date	Location	Victim	Sex	Age	Sources	Comments
1885	Snohomish, WA	Cathcart	M	Adult	Perry, 419; Barnes, 119; Danz, 246–47.	A cougar sprang at Cathcart, who defended himself with a cane. The cougar was later treed. Cathcart was said to have shot the cat later.
Mid 1880s	Central Idaho, near Mount Idaho, Elk City, ID	Moody	M	Adult	Moody, 635–36; Barnes, 113; Danz, 246–47.	Author Moody's father was followed and attacked by a cougar as he went in search of camp horses. He leaped into a stream and swam to the opposite bank as the cougar prowled the opposite shore searching for him.
Spring 1886	Southwestern MS	Unknown	M	Adult	Dobie, 203–4; Danz, 246–47.	Ben Lilly was in his Mississippi River camp when an associate delivered his mail and told him that he had seen a dead "six-foot pantha" on a train that had recently passed. The cougar had "sprang off the bank out of cane," and caught at a man on the train. Another worker shouted a warning, and dodged the attack. The cougar's claws caught in his clothing. It was beaten by the men wielding shovels, and the train conducter shot it in the head.
Spring 1886	Near Olympia, WA	Farnham/ Farnham	M/M	Unk.	Perry, 413–14; Caras, 25; Danz, 248–49.	The Farnham brothers were returning from school when a cougar seized the smallest boy and dragged him into the undergrowth. Walter, the oldest boy, followed and beat at the cat with a bottle. When the bottle broke, he tried to slash and jab out the cougar's eyes. The third brother went for help. Two woodchoppers returned with him and one shot the cougar, which had retreated up a tree to escape the bottle being brandished by Walter. Both boys suffered scratches and bruising.

Date	Location	Name	Sex	Age	Source	Description
Late 1880s	Salmon NF, central ID	Carpenter	M	Adult	Moody, 635; Barnes, 113; Danz, 246–47.	George Carpenter, a miner, threw a rock at a cougar on the opposite bank of a stream. The cougar leaped the stream and attacked him. When Carpenter supposedly struck a match in the cougar's face, the cougar retreated up a tree. Carpenter suffered minor injuries. He later shot the cougar.
Early 1890s	Missoula, MT	Unk./Unk.	M/M	Adult/Adult	Roosevelt, *Wilderness Hunter.*	Two hunters were walking home carrying their slain deer. A cougar knocked one of them down, grasping at the deer meat, while another cougar approached from the distance. The other hunter shot the first cougar, whereat the second cougar turned and fled into the woods. Neither man was injured.
Late 1800s	Texas	Unknown	F	Child	Nickels.	Two men and a little girl were sitting in a cabin where they'd built a fire in the fireplace. One man opened the door for a moment, while the little girl was seated on the floor. A cougar leaped from the doorway and landed on the little girl. The animal rolled around with her and into the fireplace. Her father jammed his pistol against the cat's head and shot, while yanking the girl away with his other hand.
Late 1800s	Unknown	Lilly	M	Adult	Goode; Fitzhugh, 24.	A "hand-to-claw" fight as related in Goode.
Early 1900s	Tonto, AZ	Holden	M	Adult	Goode (1943); Fitzhugh, 11.	Gene Holden was hospitalized in Flagstaff after being attacked by a puma. The attack ceased when Holden's dogs diverted the puma's attention. Fitzhugh considers this attack unverified.
June 27, 1902	West coast of V.I., B.C.	Daly	M	Adult	Hall.	No other particulars provided.

Date	Location	Victim	Sex	Age	Sources	Comments
1908	Near Silver City, NM	Unknown	F	Adult	Dobie, 57; Danz, 248–49.	Dr. L.S. Peters of Albuquerque treated a woman who had been attacked by a cougar. The animal leaped over her husband in order to attack her inside their cabin.
October 1909	Near Flagstaff, AZ	Fairway/Fairway	F/M	9–7	Hibben, 216–17; Danz, 248–49.	The Fairway children were bitten and clawed by a cougar while on their way to school. The girl lost most of one of her ears. An old emaciated cougar later killed nearby was thought to have been responsible for the attack.
1910	Riverside County, CA	Unknown	M	Unknown	A correspondent to *Outdoor Life* is quoted in *Western Outdoor News*, April 23, 1993.	A cougar attacked a Riverside County Railroad worker, nearly killing him.
1912	East Fork, Bryce Canyon, UT	Neilson	M	Adult	Barnes, 117; Danz, 248–49.	Cub Neilson left his sheep to take care of his horses when a mountain lion sprang upon him. He threw the cat to one side and clubbed it to death with a pine stock.
1914	Near Victoria, V.I., B.C.	Unknown	Unk.	Child	Letter from G.A. West, Feb. 11, 1960, B.C. Ministry of the Environment report.	Two children managed to drive a cougar away after they had been mauled by the animal.
1915	Near Bella Coola, B.C.	Unknown	M	10	J. R. Lowther quoted in Danz, 248–49.	Lowther reported that a boy was standing near his father's home when a cougar attacked him. Lowther also stated that "this was the first instance of a human being attacked in this province."

Date	Location	Name	Sex	Age	Description	Source
1916	Curry County, near Marial, OR	Jones	F	8	Hathaway Jones, who owned a ranch near Marial, was quoted in the *Gold Beach Globe*. Jones had sent his daughter, Myrtle, to retrieve some horses. A large cougar sprang at her and missed, and she screamed for help. Her brother Bill, who had witnessed the near-attack, called for their father. Jones grabbed an axe, while his son raced for a gun. Myrtle showed them the spot where the cougar had attacked. Jones said the cougar "made a spring for my wife," who had also accompanied the party. Jones shot the cougar, but the animal attempted to spring at the woman again before it finally died.	*Oregon Sportsman* 4 (1961), quoted in Danz, 248–49; Young and Goldman, 102.
September 23, 1916	Cowichan Lake, V.I., B.C.	Ashburnham/ Farrar	F/M	11–8	Two children went out to catch their ponies. A cougar first leaped upon the girl. The boy, Tony, jumped on the cougar, which turned its attention to him. Doreen struck at the cougar with her bridle and drove the cougar off. There is some evidence that the cougar was old, blind, and starving. Tony's scalp was ripped severely. Both children later received the Albert Medal for bravery.	*Vancouver Daily Colonist*, June 21, 1950; *London Field*, Dec. 23, 1916; Tinsley, 80; Beier, 404; Hall; Seton, 124; Hornaday, 294; Danz, 250–51.
1920	Duncan, B.C.	Unk./Unk.	F/M	Child/Child	A cougar attacked a brother and a sister. Other details are not known.	Wildlife Branch file, B.C. Ministry of the Environment report.
June 1931	Espinosa Inlet, near Tofino, V.I., B.C.	Wishart	Unk.	Infant	Mrs. David Wishart was about to put her three-month-old infant on the porch for a nap. Her husband looked out and noticed a cougar on the roof of an attached lean-to about to spring on both infant and mother. When Wishart went to get his rifle, the woman saw the cougar and screamed. The cougar fled.	*Vancouver Sun*, June 19, 1931; Danz, 250–51.

Date	Location	Victim	Sex	Age	Sources	Comments
July 1931	Cowlitz Hills, Upper Toutle River, WA	Mattern	M	Adult	*Literary Digest*, 111, (Oct. 24, 1931), and *Philadelphia Ledger Magazine*, (August 1931), quoted in Danz, 250–51.	Mattern was attacked along the railway near a logging camp. The cougar later was shot.
May 4, 1934	Holberg, V.I., B.C.	Unknown	M	56	A. Haimes in letter to W. Mair, Aug. 5, 1952, B.C. Ministry of the Environment report.	The victim was attacked while walking down a road to go cut wood. He was bitten in the arm and the cougar would not release it until he grabbed his fallen axe and struck the cougar. The man spent three days in the hospital.
May, 1934	Holberg, V.I., B.C.	Jensen	M	Adult	Beier, 404; DuFresne, 86; Danz, 250–252; B.C. Ministry of the Environment report.	A cougar attacked a man who was riding a bicycle.
May 1935	Quatsino, V.I., B.C.	Johnson	M	Adult	A. Haimes in letter to W. Mair, Aug. 5, 1952, B.C. Ministry of the Environment report.; Beier, 404; DuFresne, 86, Danz, 250–51.	A cougar attacked Johnson, a logger, while he was working. Upon hearing his cries, two other loggers ran to his aid. Wielding their axes, they were able to free Johnson from the cougar's grasp. It was killed the next day.
October 1942	Between Horsefly Lake and Quesnel, B.C.	Carson	M	Adult	Lesowski, 106–7; Ellis, 67, East, 180–81, Danz, 250–51; B.C. Ministry of the Environment report.	A cougar sprang from the brush toward Carson, but hit a small tree instead. Carson shot the cat as it was attempting to renew its attack. The cougar's udders were full, so she may have been protecting her young.

Date	Location	Victim	Sex	Age	Source	Description
1944	CA	Meiller	M	60	Richard Wright in letter to Monroe H. Goode, quoted in Good, "The Real Cougar."	Sixty-year-old archer, Walter B. Meiller, was severely injured by a cougar. Meiller was able to break free of the cat only due to the efforts of his companion, Jon Longmire. Meiller was confined to a Hollywood hospital for some time recovering from his injuries.
June 1948	York County, N.B.	Saulnier	M	Adult	Froman, 71–2; Clarke, 159; Danz, 250–51.	Saulnier went to a stream for a drink. While he was lying down next to the stream, a cougar leaped upon him and bit into his right shoulder. He was able to free himself and retreat to his logging camp.
August 1950	Naimo, V.I., B.C.	Churchill/ Churchill	M/F	6–5	*Vancouver Sun*, Aug. 4, 1950; Danz, 252–53.	Two children were playing outside when their mother noticed a cougar about to spring on them. She scared the cat away. The cougar was later shot as it still lurked about the Churchill's home.
January 1951	Kelsey Bay, near Campbell River, V.I., B.C.	McLean	M	63	*Vancouver Daily Colonist*, Jan. 27, 1951; *Vancouver Sun*, Jan. 27, 1951; Froman 82–83; DuFresne, 47, 86; Beier, 404; Danz, 252–53; A. Haimes in letter to W. Mair, Aug. 5, 1952, B.C. Ministry of the Environment report.	McLean, a telephone lineman, reported that a cougar leaped through a window to attack him. He stabbed the cat with a butcher knife, escaped his cabin, and left the wounded animal inside. McLean had to row to another line cabin where help could not be summoned until the following morning. The cougar was later killed. McLean suffered grievous injuries and severe loss of blood, but lived.
May 1951	Boston Bar, B.C.	Unknown	M	Adult	G.A. West letter, Feb. 11, 1960, B.C. Ministry of the Environment report, DuFresne, 86, Froman, 83; Danz, 252–53.	The victim stepped out of his cabin door to find a cougar on the porch. The cougar attacked him, knocking him down, and mauling him. The victim's dog came to his aid, and the cougar turned its attention to the dog. The man ran inside his cabin. The cougar departed after killing the dog.

Date	Location	Victim	Sex	Age	Sources	Comments
July 1951	Near Holberg, V.I., B.C.	Unknown	M	Adult	G. A. West letter, Feb. 11, 1960, B.C. Ministry of the Environment report.	A man was mauled by a cougar near Holberg. No other details are known.
July 1951	Northern ID	Peterson	F	2	Froman, 84–85; Danz, 252–53.	A cougar picked up a two-year-old girl, carried her into the woods, but dropped her unharmed when her mother and two brothers chased after it.
December 1951	West bank of Alberni Inlet, V.I., B.C.	Littleton	M	Adult	*Daily Colonist*, Dec. 8, 1951; Danz, 252–53.	William Littleton was working at Grumback Logging when three cougars confronted him. The man set fire to some of his notes and threw them and some rocks at the cougars. When someone responded to his cries for help, two of the cougars left. The three cougars were later killed.
Winter 1951	Alert Bay, V.I., B.C.	Weber	M	Adult	B.C. Ministry of the Environment	An adult male was attacked as he tended his traps. He bent over to inspect a mink trap and a cougar attacked him, biting into his boot. He dragged the cat to his boat where he shot it with a .22 rifle.
Late 1951	35 miles northeast of Wallace, ID	Taylor	M	Adult	Letter from Peterson to the Idaho Wildlife Review (Jan.–Feb. 1952) cited by Fitzhugh, 12.	Carl Taylor was attacked on a trail above a camp near the Hansey Copper & Gold Mines. Taylor killed the puma. Fitzhugh considers this attack unverified.
March 1953	Victoria Lake, V.I., B.C.	Walters/ Richmond	M/M	43/Adult	*Vancouver Sun*, March 2, 1953; Lesowski, 107; Ellis, 67; East, 181–83); Beier, 404; DuFresne, 88; Danz, 254–55; B.C. Ministry of the Environment report.	Walters and Richmond were on a fishing trip when they decided to break for lunch. Walters was gathering wood for a fire when attacked. Richmond responded to Walters's cries for help and killed the cougar with a hatchet. Walters suffered severe injuries. Richmond was only scratched.

Date	Location	Name	Sex	Age	Source	Description
April 1953	Lost Mine Trail, Big Bend NP, TX	Unknown	M	Adult	R. Skiles, BBNP, July 21, 1997; Packard, 3; Beier, 404; Danz 254–55.	A man was walking along the Big Bend Trail when a cougar grabbed him by the pants leg. He shouted and kicked and the cat left. The cat was shot the following day.
June 10, 1953	Near Campbell River, V.I., B.C.	Coon	F	26	*Vancouver Sun*, June 12, 1953; *Vancouver Daily Colonist*, June 12, 1953; DuFresne, 86; Beier, 404; Danz, 254–55; B.C. Ministry of the Environment report.	A cougar had been lurking outside the Coon's home. Despite admonitions by her husband to stay home, Mrs. Coon left their cabin. Some accounts say she followed her husband. The cougar attacked her, crushed her hand, severely clawed her shoulder, and peeled the flesh from her ribs. The cougar was pulled from her by Hilly Lansdowne and later killed by a hunter.
1957	Victoria Lake, B.C.	Unknown	M	Adult	Nicol, *True West* (Jan/Feb 1958).	No other details are known.
July 3, 1957	Near Squamish, V.I., B.C.	Wyssen	M	26 or 29	*Vancouver Sun*, July 3, 1957.	Wyssen, a bulldozer operator, was working at a logging operation north of Squamish when five gaunt cougars attacked him. One of the animals tore off his pants and scratched his legs before he could climb to safety upon his bulldozer. The cougars were all killed. Two weighed no more than thirty pounds each.
July 1958	Lower mainland, B.C.	Unknown	F	Child	Wildlife Branch Files, B.C. Ministry of the Environment report.	Two young girls who were playing on a beach were attacked by two cougars, one male and one female. Considered by the Wildlife Branch to be two separate attacks. (See next entry.)
July 1958	Lower mainland, B.C.	Unknown	F	Child	Wildlife Branch Files, B.C. Ministry of the Environment report.	See above. Both cougars were said to be in good health and condition.

Date	Location	Victim	Sex	Age	Sources	Comments
March 1962	Hinton, AB	Kilbreath	M	6	Beier, 405; Caras, 25–26; AP, March 1962; Danz, 254–55.	Brian Kilbreath was playing not far from his home when he was attacked by a juvenile cougar. A neighbor pulled the cat off him. Kilbreath suffered claw marks to his face and a scratch to his eye. Bruce Wright told Caras that the animal was only half-grown and in very poor condition.
August 1962	Deception Point, V.I., B.C.	Naismith	F	Adult	*Vancouver Sun*, Aug. 2, 1962; Danz, 256–57.	Grace Naismith was attacked by a scrawny cougar. The woman kicked the cat and knocked it away and it retreated to the brush. The woman's dog was mauled, but Mrs. Naismith was not injured. The cougar was later killed.
June 15, 1963	Near Prince George, B.C.	Moore	M	6	*Vancouver Sun*, June 18, 1963; Beier, 405; Danz, 256–57; B.C. Ministry of the Environment report.	Michael, Bobbie, and Diana Moore were walking home from a fishing trip when a cougar attacked Bobbie. Michael picked up a discarded shovel and hit the cat while Diana, age 6, slapped at the cougar with her stringer of fish. Their mother heard them screaming and sent their father to the scene, but the cougar had already fled.
March 5, 1965	Loon Lake, near Clinton, B.C.	Simpkins	M	15	*Vancouver Sun*, Mar. 6 and 9, 1965; Lesowski 107–8; Ellis, 67; East, 183–85; Beier, 405; Danz, 256–57; B.C. Ministry of the Environment report.	John Simpkins was helping Jim Baker build a fence on his ranch when a cougar leaped upon his back. Baker rushed to Simpkins's aid and stabbed the cat with his pocket knife, then pulled the cat from him. He rushed Simpkins to the hospital where he was treated for wounds to the face, head, and arm. The cougar was later killed.

Date	Location	Name	Sex	Age	Source	Description
October 1966	Chilcotin, B.C.	Unknown	M	Adult	Beier, 405; Danz, 256–57; B.C. Ministry of the Environment report.	A cougar mauled a rancher. Beier simply reported that this cougar was underweight.
September 12, 1969	Port Alberni, V.I., B.C.	Zimmerman	M	13	*Times Colonist*, Sept. 14, 1969; Beier, 405; B.C. Ministry of the Environment report.	A boy was attacked by a cougar as he walked to play at his tree fort during the evening. When he tried to back away, the cougar bit his leg. When he waved his jacket, the cougar retreated. Two loggers rushed to his aid and killed the cougar.
June 1970	Lewis, CO	Imel	M	2	Ms. M. Imel, in telephone interview with H. Danz, quoted in Danz, 258–59; Beier, 405.	Travis Imel, 2, was playing in a car in his grandparents' garage. When he got out of the car, he saw an animal that he thought was a large yellow dog. When he reached out to pet the animal, it swatted him several times and bit him in the leg. His grandmother responded to his cries, stared the cougar down, locked the garage doors, and called a neighbor, who was a game warden. The warden tranquilized the cougar, but gave it too large a dose. The cat later died.
June 13 or 15, 1970	Kootenay NP, B.C.	Smith	F	50	*Vancouver Sun*, Dec. 23, 1970,Jan 3, 1971; Ellis, 110; Beier, 405; Danz, 259–59; Hall; B.C. Ministry of the Environment report.	Daphne Smith was attacked while walking a trail separate from her hiking club. She drove off the cat with her backpack, and received only scratches and gashes on one arm. The cougar ran away when other members of her group responded to her cries for help.
December 22, 1970	Harrison Lake, B.C.	Collie	M	29	*Vancouver Sun*, Dec. 23, 1970 and Jan. 3, 1971; Beier, 405; Hall; Danz, 258–59; B.C. Ministry of the Environment report.	Dennis Collie was returning to his bunkhouse at a logging camp when a cougar attacked him. The cougar bit his chin and clawed him. The cougar was then shot.

Date	Location	Victim	Sex	Age	Sources	Comments
July 1971	Eureka County, NV	Bird/Sieh	M/M	Adult/Adult	Dale Elliot in telephone interview with K. Etling, July 2000; Elliot in NV Division of Wildlife memo, July 9, 1971; Beier, 405; Danz, 258–59.	Two geology students were exploring Dry Canyon when one was attacked. The cougar then attacked the other student, who threw rocks at the cat to scare it away. The first student received scratches to the top of his head and his shoulders.
1972	Near Jet City, OR	Unknown	M	Teenager	Amarillo Globe-News, May 6, 2000; AP, May 6, 2000.	A cougar pounced on a teenaged boy while he was walking along a rural road. The boy escaped with minor injuries.
June 1972	Along the Ralph River in Strathcona Park, V.I., B.C.	Unknown	Unk.	Infant	Dan Dwyer, B.C. Fish and Game, July 31, 1997; Beier, 405; Danz, 258–59; B.C. Ministry of the Environment report.	Dwyer reports that a "baby survived a mauling at a Ralph River campsite, cougar was not located." Beier reported that the incident took place in 1972, but Dwyer reported the year was 1970.
June 1972	Strathcona Park, V.I., B.C.	Hurford	M	25	Dan Dwyer, B.C. Fish and Game, July 31, 1997; Beier, 405; Hall; Danz, 258–59; B.C. Ministry of the Environment report.	Dwyer stated that Hurford was in his sleeping bag when he was mauled by a cougar. This attack reportedly took place one week after the Ralph River incident above. Fish and Game also recorded this attack as having taken place in 1970.
July 26, 1972	Campbell Lake, V.I., B.C.	Kelly	M	8	Daily Colonist, July 27, 1972; The Province, July 27, 1972; Vancouver Sun, July 28, 1972; Beier, 405; Danz, 260–61; Hall; B.C. Ministry of the Environment report.	Robert Kelly and his brother, Charles, were returning to their campsite from a swim when a cougar attacked Robert. When their mother heard the boys' shouts, she ran to help. Her screams caused the animal to flee. Robert was critically injured and underwent extensive plastic surgery to his head and scalp. George Taylor, head of the federal game branch, believed this cougar to be the same one that mauled another man six weeks earlier.

Date	Location	Name	Sex	Age	Account	Source
October 1973	Trujillo Creek west of Aguilar, CO	Keller	M	Adult	Carl Keller, a Colorado conservation officer, was startled by a noise while he was hunting deer. He turned to see a cougar staring down at him from a rock. Keller rolled to one side and fired his gun. The shot was later determined to have hit the cat in the side while it was in mid-air. When Keller walked over to inspect the dead cat, another cougar appeared, poised to pounce on him. He killed this cat by shooting it in its face. Keller was judged to have acted in self-defense.	*Denver Post*, Nov. 4, 1973; Danz, 260–61.
January 31, 1974	West of Las Vegas, NM	Chopilote	M	26	Mark Chopilote, a goatherd, was looking at a turkey track when a cougar leaped upon his head and neck. He hurled the animal from him, and fired a rifle to scare it off. The cougar fled. Chopilote suffered scratches to his head, neck, and back.	*New Mexico Game and Fish News*, Feb. 6, 1974.
November 2, 1974	Near Terrero, NM	Mendoza	M	Adult	Mendoza was walking to his bowhunting spot when he became aware of a cougar about to pounce on him from the right side of an old road. The cat drew so near that Mendoza had no choice but to stab the animal with his arrow. He had no time during which he might have nocked it onto his bow string. The cat turned and ran. New Mexico Game and Fish Officer Nordyke later killed the lion, a thin female, but in good condition.	*Rocky Mountain News*, Nov. 7, 1974.
June 1, 1975	Polder Landing on Pitt River, near Coquitlam, B.C.	Jones	M	8	William Atsma, his wife, and her four children were planning a hike. Kevin Jones, 8, and his sister, Marilyn, 13, went ahead of the group. When a cougar attacked Kevin, Marilyn raced to her stepfather for help. Atsma grabbed an oar and went to Kevin's aid, screaming at the cougar with the oar and screaming at it. The cougar left, but was later killed. Kevin suffered serious injuries.	*Vancouver Sun* June 2, 1975; *Vancouver Province*, June 2, 1975; Beier, 405; Hall; Danz, 262–63; B. C. Ministry of the environment report.

Date	Location	Victim	Sex	Age	Sources	Comments
October 10, 1975	Northwest of Ladron Mountain, NM	Atwood	F	Adult	B. C. Hughes, NM Dept. of Game and Fish correspondence.	A lion lunged at Atwood while she was riding horseback, searching for stray horses. The cat tore three holes in her hat and split its brim. The horse spooked and raced through some trees where Atwood's binocular strap caught on a limb and jerked her off the horse. The lion then attacked the horse, but missed. When it leaped at the animal, it scratched Atwood's saddle.
December 1976	Near Rye, CO	Morgan	M	14	*Denver Post*, Dec. 23 and 24, 1976; *Rocky Mountain News*, Dec. 24, 1976; Beier, 405; Saile, 66–67; Danz, 262–63.	Thane Morgan was snowshoeing west of Pueblo, CO, when a cougar attacked him. Morgan was able to reach the knife he'd stashed in his backpack and defend himself. The cat retreated. Thane received over a thousand stitches to repair wounds to his face, scalp, and hand. The cougar was later shot, and was stated to be blind in one eye.
June 1977	Near Enumclaw, WA	O'Neal/ O'Neal	F/F	28/3	*Enumclaw Courier-Herald*, June 30, 1977; Beier, 405; Danz, 262–63.	Cheri O'Neal was sunbathing on a log near the Green Water River while her three-year-old daughter waded nearby. The cougar pounced on O'Neal and dragged her from the log onto the ground. She struggled with the cat, which then turned to daughter Keri. Alerted by their screams, Don O'Neal raced to the scene and the cougar fled. The cougar was later killed. O'Neal's wounds included bites and scratches to her back, thigh, and arm, plus a mutilated left thumb. Keri O'Neal suffered only minor injuries.
November 22, 1978	Big Bend NP, TX	Unknown	Unk.	Child	Beier, 405; Big Bend NP files; Fitzhugh, 7.	No other details known.

Date	Location	Name	Sex	Age	Source	Description
1979	Central ID	Seidenticker	M	Adult	*Merry Crankster Mountain Bike Club of Salem Oregon Newsletter*, May 19, 1998.	Wildlife biologist Seidenticker was moving slowly through some lodgepole pines following the signal from a female lion wearing a radio-telemetry collar. When he heard a hiss from a tree several yards away, he glanced up and saw the cougar lay its ears back and begin to approach. Seidenticker halted the cat by tossing a stick against its face. The biologist later discovered the female's litter of kittens nearby and a recent kill.
February 19, 1979	Boston Bar, B.C.	Fife	F	9	Beier, 405; Danz, 264–64; B.C. Ministry of the Environment report.	A girl did not have time to react before being attacked. She fought back, and the cougar ran away. Beier stated that the cougar's body mass was less than normal for its age.
August 7, 1979	Port Hardy, V.I., B.C.	Walkus	F	4	*Vancouver Sun*, Aug. 10, 1979; Beier, 405; Hall; Danz, 264–65; B.C. Ministry of Environment report.	Eva Walkus was playing on a swing when a cougar attacked. She was injured severely and spent four days in the hospital before returning home. The cougar was later killed.
1981	Oyster River, V.I., B.C.	Unknown	M	Adult	Beier, 405; Danz, 266–67; B.C. Ministry of the Environment internal memorandum.	A cougar pounced upon a man riding horseback, but the man was not injured. The cougar was later killed.
May 27, 1981	Near Canyon Church Camp, Waterton Lakes NP, AB	Orchard	M	12	*Parks Canada*, June 26, 1997; Beier, 405; Danz, 264–65.	Warren Orchard, age 12, was lagging behind his church group as they hiked near their campsite. When he heard something behind him in the brush, he stopped to investigate. A cougar approached him, rolled over on its back, and when Warren yelled, it clawed the boy and then ran off. The scratch to the boy's leg required five stitches.

Date	Location	Victim	Sex	Age	Sources	Comments
July 1981	Near Lone Mountain in Big Bend NP, TX	Atkins	M	Adult	Big Bend, NP files, July 21, 1997; Danz, 266–67; Fitzhugh, 7.	Atkins, a park ranger, was on foot trying to catch horses when a puma charged in and swiped his leg. The cougar abandoned his attack after Atkins hit it with a large rock.
August 1982	Near junction of Bertha Bay and Bertha Lake Trail, Waterton Lakes NP, AB	Bisby	M	9	*Parks Canada*, June 26, 1997; Beier, 405; Danz, 266–67.	Adam Bisby was hiking ahead of his parents when a cougar leaped onto him. The cougar was never located.
1983	Holberg, V.I., B.C.	Unknown	M	16	Beier, 405; Danz, 266–67; B.C. Ministry of the Environment report.	A boy riding a bike on a Canadian Air Force base road was attacked by a cougar. An oncoming vehicle frightened the cougar away. The boy suffered minor injuries.
1983	Esperanza, V.I., B.C.	Unknown	M	Adult	Beier, 405; Danz, 266–67; B.C. Ministry of the Environment internal memo.	"A man on a bridge [was] jumped by cougar but not seriously injured." The cougar was later killed.
April 24, 1983	Port McNeill, V.I., B.C.	Unknown/ Unknown	M/M	10–11	Beier, 405; Danz, 266–67; B.C. Ministry of the Environment internal memo.	Three boys were chased by a cougar through some second growth on a hill above the town. The cougar mauled one boy on the arm, and another on his leg. Officers later killed the cougar.
April 1984	Junction of South Rim and Park Blue Creek trails, Big Bend NP, TX	Roe	F	Adult	R. Skiles, BBNP, July 21, 1997; Packard, 3–4; Beier, 405; Danz, 266–67.	Ranger Susan Roe was walking the South Rim trail when she saw a cougar about to spring. The animal leaped, and hit her with its shoulder, knocking her to the ground. Roe twisted her ankle in the fall.
August 2, 1984	Along the Basin Loop trail, Big Bend NP, TX	Vaught/ Brown	M/M	9– Adult	*Rocky Mountain News*, Sep. 23, 1990; BBNP Incident file #840559;	David Vaught, his mother, and his stepfather, Chris Brown, were walking this trail when a cougar attacked David. While the cougar was

Date	Name	Location	Sex	Age	Description	Source
					still in the process of its attack, Brown hurled himself at the animal and pulled the cougar away from the boy. The cougar continued to threaten the family as they made their way back to the trailhead. David's injuries were many and serious. He needed a number of expensive plastic surgeries to repair the damage to his face, head, and neck. The cougar was killed the next day.	Mueller, 50–51, 108–11; Beier, 405; Danz, 268–69.
May 22, 1985	Cabot	Wilkerson Pass, Park County, CO	M	7	A young boy who was attacked by a cougar suffered numerous bite wounds.	Fitzhugh, 8.
May 28, 1985	Wilson	Pacific Rim NP, V.I., B.C.	M	12	Johnny Wilson was playing close to where his mother and aunt had decided to make camp while hiking the West Coast trail. A cougar attacked him and attempted to drag him away, but his mother and aunt were able to get him to safety. He suffered scalp lacerations and serious puncture wounds and had to be airlifted to a hospital where he was hospitalized for seven days. The cougar was never located.	*Vancouver Sun*, May 29, Aug. 6, 1985, Beier, 405; Hall; Danz, 268–69; B.C. Ministry of the Environment report.
August 3, 1985	Parker	Camp Thunderbird, Sooke, V.I., B.C.	F	10	Alyson Parker was walking with her friends near the YM/YWCA camp when they sighted the cougar. The girls began to run and Alyson tripped and fell. The cougar attacked Alyson. Meanwhile, the children's screams attracted the attention of Lila Lifely, one of the camp counselors. Lifely prevented the cat from dragging the girl from the scene and also provided first aid to the child. The cougar continued to hover near the children until finally frightened away. The cougar was later killed. The girl was admitted to the hospital where she was treated for skull punctures, scalp wounds, and puncture wounds to the neck.	*Vancouver Province*, Aug. 6, 1985, *Vancouver Sun*, Aug. 6 and 7, 1985; Worth, 81; Beier, 405; Hall; Danz, 268–69; B.C. Ministry of the Environment report.

Date	Location	Victim	Sex	Age	Sources	Comments
February 28, 1986	Kings Beach, CA	Butcher	F	26	David Fjelline, CA Department of Fish and Game incident report, March 2, 1986, quoted in Fitzhugh, 12.	Bridgette Butcher was removing wood from a Volkswagon when a puma attacked, tearing her coat. She suffered no injuries and the cougar ran off. Investigator David Fjelline believes this report, while the Department of Fish and Game considers it to be false, per personal communication from Fjelline to Fitzhugh. Attack remains unverified.
March 23, 1986	Caspers Wilderness Park, Orange County, CA	Small	F	5	San Jose Mercury News, March 24, 1986; Los Angeles Times, Feb. 8, 1989, July 25, Aug. 8, 1991, and Sep. 6, 1994, also Orange County Edition, Dec. 17, 1994; Rocky Mountain News, Feb. 2, Sep. 23, 1990; San Diego Union Tribune, Dec. 11, 1994, Jan. 2, 1998; Western Outdoor News, April 23, 1993; Beier, 406; Danz, 268–69.	Laura Small was wading in a stream searching for tadpoles when she was attacked by a cougar that tried to drag her away. A hiker, summoned by her screams, responded and was able to beat the cat off with a stick he'd picked up. Laura was severely injured, including some partial paralysis, nerve damage, and the loss of sight in one eye.
August 23, 1986	Siskiyou NF, near Port Orford, OR	Bess	M	Adult	Range, 34–37; Danz, 268–69.	Ken Bess was bowhunting for elk when a large cougar attacked him. Bess initially used his bow to ward off the cat, but finally had to kill the animal after many minutes of being terrorized and threatened.
September 26, 1986	Near Gallina Peak, NM	Taylor	M	Adult	NM Game and Fish files.	David Taylor was muzzleloader deer hunting when a large mountain lion approached him in a threatening manner. When the lion had closed the distance to fifteen feet, Taylor killed

the animal with a head-on shot. The large female measured eighty-one inches from the tip of her nose to the tip of her tail.

Date	Location	Name	Sex	Age	Description	References
October 1986	Caspers Wilderness Park, Orange County, CA	Mellon	M	6	Timothy Mellon was walking with his family when he bent down to tie his shoelace. As he did so, a cougar leaped upon him and grabbed his head in its mouth. Timothy's father attacked the cougar with a knife and the cougar released the boy. The boy suffered serious injuries.	*Phoenix Gazette*, Oct. 21, 1986; *Audubon*, March 1988; *Los Angeles Times*, Feb. 2, 1989; Aug. 8, 15, and 24, 1991, Feb. 6, 1992, and Sep. 6, 1994; *Rocky Mountain News*, Sep. 23, 1990; *Western Outdoor News*, April 23, 1993; *Orange County Register*, Sep. 29, 1998; Beier, 405; Danz, 268–69.
April 19, 1987	Along the Basin Loop trail, Big Bend NP, TX	Burt	F	31	A family was walking the trail when confronted by a brazen cougar. The father picked up their child and stood his ground, staring at the cat. The mother ran and was attacked. The cougar was later tracked and killed.	BBNP Incident File #870173, *Rocky Mountain News*, Sep. 23, 1990; Bolgiano, 114; Beier, 406; Danz, 270–71.
May 28, 1988	Northeast of Payson, AZ	Fuller	F	6	Sarah Fuller was playing with her sister Amy, 8, outside the family's rented cabin when a cougar rushed toward the girls and attacked Sarah. The girls' stepfather heard the screams and rushed outside. Lisa Egnash, the girls' mother, fetched a .22, which Greg Egnash used to kill the cougar. The girl suffered numerous puncture wounds on her shoulder, arm, and ear.	*Phoenix Gazette*, May 1, 1989; *Outdoor Life* (Jan. 1991); *Arizona Republic*, May 1, 1989, June 1, 1989; Danz, 270–71.
June 25, 1988	Green Valley Campground, Cuyamaca Rancho State Park, C	Unknown	M/F/M	Unk.	Two cougars chased after a couple and their small son in the Green Valley campground of the park.	*San Diego Union Tribune*, Feb. 11, 1996.

Date	Location	Victim	Sex	Age	Sources	Comments
September 1988	Aquarius Plateau, Dixie NF, southern UT	Treadwell	M	Adult	Treadwell, 84–87; Danz, 270–71.	Joseph Treadwell, a bowhunter, was in this Utah forest when he discovered a cougar was stalking him. When the cat crouched nearby, the man shot at it, but the arrow merely glanced off. His next shot penetrated the cat's shoulder.
January 12, 1989	Hot Springs Cove, Tofino, V.I., B.C.	Lucas	M	28	Beier, 406; Hall; Danz, 270–71.	Lucas was gathering firewood when a cougar attacked him. When another resident came to his aid, the cougar fled. The animal was later killed.
April 29, 1989	Canyon Lake, near Paolo Verde boat ramp, AZ	Walsh	M	5	*Phoenix Gazette*, May 1 and 2, 1989; *Arizona Republic*, May 1, 1989; Danz, 27–71.	Joshua Walsh was hiking up a hill with his six-year-old brother when a cougar raced out, grabbed Joshua by the head, and started to drag him off. When Joshua's father hit the animal with a rock, the cougar released the boy. Joshua required more than a hundred stitches to close his head wounds and to reattach his ear. The cougar was not apprehended.
March 3, 1990	Near Boulder Meadows camp #4, Big Bend, NP, TX	Stevens	M	Adult	R. Skiles, BBNP July 21, 1997; Packard, 3–4; Danz, 272–73.	Shawn Stevens was near his campsite when a cougar chased a deer past it. Sometime later, Stevens heard a "chirping" sound, then he saw a cougar. Stevens climbed a tree, and several minutes later two additional cougars entered the campground. Soon afterward, a cougar approached his tree, then climbed up after him so that its head was near the man's feet. He kicked the cougar in the head and screamed. The cougar left the tree, but Stevens remained in the tree until morning.

Date	Location	Name	Sex	Age	Sources	Description
June 2, 1990	Four Mile Canyon, west of Boulder, CO	Walters	F	28	*Los Angeles Times,* March 1, 1992; Turbak, 73–74; *Rocky Mountain News,* June 2, 1990; Sep. 23, 1990; Beier, 406; Danz, 272–73.	Lynda Walters was hiking along a trail when she encountered a cougar. She shouted and tossed rocks toward the animal, to no avail. Walters then saw another cougar moving in her direction. She retreated farther up the slope of the canyon, throwing rocks and twigs at the cats. Walters finally climbed a tree, but a cougar came up after her and severely scratched her leg. She jabbed at the cats to discourage their advances and the animals eventually left the area.
July 1990	East of Bigfork, MT	Quinn	M	Unk.	*Missoulian,* July 13, 1990; *Rocky Mountain News,* Sep. 23, 1990; *Field & Stream,* Jan. 1991; Worth, 70; Turbak, 73–74; Danz, 272–73.	Game warden Mike Quinn was responding to a lion complaint. While he was checking the premises, he got the feeling of being watched. He turned to see a cougar behind him. He attempted to scare it away, but the lion began to stalk him. Quinn shot around it, trying to discourage it, but it charged and lunged. Quinn shot the cougar with his shotgun while it was in midair. The cat's body hit Quinn and knocked him to the ground.
July 23, 1990	Near Apgar picnic area, Glacier NP, MT	O'Hare	M	9	Glacier NP press release, July 23, 1990; *Rocky Mountain News,* July 27 and Sep. 23, 1990; AP Nov. 23, 1991; Worth, 70; Danz; 272–73.	A boy was playing with his friends when he was attacked by a cougar. Several parents ran to the scene and chased it away. The boy suffered wounds to his head, face, and neck.
1991	Anza-Borrego State Park, CA	Boswell	M	Adult	*Western Outdoor News,* April 23, 1993.	Hiker Gary Boswell was chased by a cougar that then backed him up against a large boulder. Boswell was able to escape the cat by beating it with a stick. The man narrowly escaped serious injury.

Date	Location	Victim	Sex	Age	Sources	Comments
1991	San Diego County, CA	Unknown	M	Adult	*Western Outdoor News,* April 23, 1993.	A fisherman who had been wading a creek was attacked while he was returning to his car. The man beat off the cougar with a stick. He received numerous lacerations to his chest and arm.
March 28, 1991	Nellis AFB, Nevada Test Site, southwestern NV	Sacthre	F	20s	NV Division of Wildlife incident report, April 4, 1991, prepared by San Stiver; Division of Wildlife report, April 25, 1991 by Mary B. Sacthre; Danz, 272–73.	Three research biologists were in the field when they approached a cougar's den. The female attacked Sacthre, but was driven off by one of the male biologists. When a tracker responded, the cougar charged him as well. The tracker shot the cat.
June 1991	Near Arboles, CO, close to NM border	Swanemyr	M	Adult	*Rocky Mountain News,* July 20, 1991; Danz, 274–75.	Bob Swanemyr was walking his dog when he was jumped by a cougar, which injured his shoulder. Swanemyr and his dog chased the cougar up a tree. It is not known whether the cougar was later killed.
July 3, 1991	Lillooet, B.C.	Allen/ O'Laney/ Leech	M/ F/F	2–2– 22	*Vancouver Sun,* July 9, 1991; *Seattle Post-Intelligencer,* July 5, 1991; Danz, 274–75; B.C. Ministry of the Environment report.	Five children in the care of day-care provider Larrane Leech were confronted by a cougar while on a picnic. It began licking the face of two-year old Mikey Allen, and when Leech attempted to pull the cat away, it clawed Allen, Leech, and Lisa O'Laney, 2. The injuries to the three were not serious. A neighbor armed with a shotgun later killed the cougar.
Fall 1991	Modoc County, CA	Unknown	M	Adult	CA Department Fish and Game report by warden C.J. Albright quoted in *Western Outdoor News,* April 23, 1993; Fitzhugh,13.	A cougar pursued an unknown deer hunter. When the man fell, the cougar clawed his feet until he was able to shoot the puma. Fitzhugh considers this attack unverified.

Date	Location	Name	Sex	Age	Source	Account
March 1992	Gaviota State Park, Santa Barbara County, CA	Arroyo	M	9	*Western Outdoor News,* April 23, 1991; *Los Angeles Daily News,* April 4, 1992; *Los Angeles Times,* April 3, 1995; *San Diego Union Tribune,* April 15, 1995; *Riverside Press-Enterprise,* March 4, 1996; Danz, 274–75.	Darron Arroyo was attacked by a cougar. Fifty stitches were needed to suture up his wound. The cougar was later killed.
March 29, 1992	Near Sacramento, CA	Eichele	M	Adult	*Los Angeles Daily News,* April 4, 1992; *Sacramento Bee,* April 4, 1992; *San Jose Mercury News,* April 6, 1992; *San Francisco Chronicle,* April 7, 1992; *Western Outdoor News,* April 23, 1993.	Arthur Eichele was bowhunting for turkeys when a cougar leaped upon his head. His head and ear were scratched and his hat was knocked off as he tumbled to the ground. Stitches were needed to close up his wounds.
June 15, 1992	Lake Wenatchee State Park, WA	Vanney	F	5	*Seattle Post-Intelligencer,* July 7, 1992.	Jessica Vanney, 5, was attacked by a cougar while on a trip to the park with her family. The girl suffered cuts, scrapes, and puncture wounds.
June 27, 1992	Along Huckleberry Creek in the White River area, WA	Unknown	M	2	*Seattle Post-Intelligencer,* July 7, 1992.	A cougar attacked a two-year-old boy while he was camping with his family along Huckleberry Creek. The boy suffered scratches.
Summer 1992	Olympic NP, WA	Unknown	M	unk.	*Seattle Post-Intelligencer,* Dec. 7, 1993.	A mountain biker fought with a cougar over the man's bicycle bag. The man suffered scratches and abrasions.
July 2, 1992	West Cracroft Island, near Robsons Bight, V.I., B.C.	Sherman	F	29	*Seattle Post-Intelligencer,* July 23, 1992; Jim Nollman, in *Interspecies Newsletter,* 1993; Danz, 274–75; B.C. Ministry of Environment report.	A cougar was lying in wait for a camper as she hiked along a trail. The cougar attacked, and the woman sustained puncture wounds to her face and thighs. A camper later shot the cougar, but the animal could not be located. That December, a resident of the island supposedly shot a cougar with a wound to its head as it stalked his children.

Date	Location	Victim	Sex	Age	Sources	Comments
August 13, 1992	Glacier NP, MT	Moore	M	12	*Arizona Republic*, AP, Aug. 14, 1992; AP, Aug. 14 and 19, 1992; Glacier NP press release, Aug. 19, 1992; *Los Angeles Times*, Aug. 30, 1992; Danz, 274–75.	Nathaniel Moore and his father, Romano Scaturro, had just climbed up a roadway embankment when a cougar leaped upon the boy. Scaturro responded by kicking and hollering at the cat, and it ran away. The boy suffered facial cuts and puncture wounds to his chest, right arm, and wrist. The cat was later killed.
October 1992	On a logging road north of Columbia Falls, MT	Wensel	M	Adult	*Bowhunter*, (April/May, 1993); Lewis, 194; Danz, 276–77.	Barry Wensel was bowhunting when he was confronted by a cougar. Wensel spoke to the cat, but the cat flattened out and ran at him. Wensel killed the cat with an arrow at thirty-eight feet.
May 16, 1993	Cherryville, B.C.	Unknown	M	16	A. Envet letter to K. Atkinson, May 17, 1993; B.C. Ministry of the Environment report.	A teenaged boy was walking his dog along a creek bank when he was attacked. The cougar jumped on his back and threw him to the ground. The boy threw off the cougar and climbed a tree. The cougar walked away, but was later shot.
May 29, 1993	Cherryville, B.C.	Unknown	M	7	B.C. Ministry of the Environment report, Conservation Officer report #54419, May 29, 1993.	A cougar jumped upon a young boy who had been panning for gold with his father. When the boy cried out, the cougar jumped off and ran for the bush. The boy was not hurt. The owner of the camp walked back to the attack site with a gun and shot the animal when the cougar stalked him.
August 1993	Los Padres NF in Santa Barbara County, CA	Foote	M	6	*Los Angeles Times*, April 3, 1995; Danz, 276–77.	Devon Foote suffered minor injuries when a cougar attacked him. No paw prints were found and so the California Department of Game and Fish reported it as an unverified attack.

Date	Location	Name	Sex	Age	Description	Source
August 15, 1993	Near Wickenburg, AZ	Irwin	F	53	Merlue Irwin had just finished repairing a fence when she saw a cougar run toward her. At a distance of about five feet, the cougar crouched and sprang. Irwin used a cedar fence post to bat the cat in midair. Irwin backed toward her ranch house, but the cat continued to stalk her. When she was inside, she called a friend, who was a tracker. The man's dog treed the cat and it was shot.	*Arizona Republic*, Aug. 21, 1993; *Phoenix Gazette*, Aug. 21, 1993; Danz, 276–77.
September 4, 1993	Cuyamaca Rancho State Park, CA	Brooking/ King	F/M	Adult/ Adult	Horseback riders, Connie Brooking and her father, Dick King, were confronted by a cougar that approached them, its hackles raised. The cougar then chased the pair for more than one-half mile as they galloped their horses back down the trail to safety.	*San Diego Union Tribune*, Sep. 7, 1993.
September 1993	Paso Picacho campground, Cuyamaca State Park, CA	Kowalski	F	10	Lisa Kowalski was playing catch with her father in the campground when the cougar approached. Lisa remained quiet as the cougar drew very near, but it suddenly pounced, biting her on the buttocks. The cougar was later killed.	*Arizona Republic*, Sep. 19, 1993; *Los Angeles Times*, Sep. 19, 1993, April 3, 1995; *San Diego Union Tribune*, Sep. 19, 1993, Dec. 11, 1994; CA Fish and Game news release, Dec. 24, 1994.
January 1994	Cuyamaca Rancho State Park, CA	Unknown	Unk.	Unk.	Three bicyclists were menaced by a cougar while in Cuyamaca Rancho State Park. A lion was later shot nearby after attacking and killing livestock.	*San Diego Union Tribune*, Dec. 11, 1993 and Jan. 12, 1994.

Date	Location	Victim	Sex	Age	Sources	Comments
May 9, 1994	Gold River, V.I., B.C.	Musselman	M	7	*San Diego Union Tribune*, May 10, 1994; *San Francisco Examiner*, May 10, 1994; *San Jose Mercury News*, May 10, 1994; Danz, 276–77; B.C. Ministry of the Environment report, Feb. 26, 1996.	Kyle Musselmann was walking to school with two of his friends when a cougar attacked him. The two friends tried, but were unable, to chase the cougar away. They ran to a nearby home for help. The cougar eventually broke off its attack. It was later killed by a RCMP officer.
May 27, 1994	Along the Pine Creek trailhead, Mt. Jefferson County, NV	Werfel	M	Adult	NV Division of Wildlife memo of June 1, 1994 from Gregg Tanner, *Reno Gazette-Journal*, Jan. 16, 1996; Danz, 276–77.	Werfel was attacked by a cougar on May 27. Werfel was able to drive off the cougar by beating it with a stick.
July 17, 1994	Near Apache Lake, Tonto NF, AZ	Humphreys	M	2	*Phoenix Gazette*, July 20, 1994; *Tucson Citizen*, July 20, 1994; Danz, 276–77.	Jesse Humphreys was sleeping on a mat with his family while camping near Apache Lake. A cougar approached, pawed at the boy, seized the mat in its mouth, and tried to drag him away. When he cried out, his father grabbed him away from the cougar. The cat continued to terrorize the family, which took shelter under their upturned boat. Jesse needed ten stitches to suture his torn ear. The cougar was not tracked down.
August 1994	Near Dos Rios, CA	Winslow/ Winslow/ Strehl/Strehl	F/M/ M/F	48–50– Adult–48	*San Jose Mercury News*, Aug. 17, 1994; *Phoenix Gazette*, Aug. 17, 1994; *San Francisco Examiner*, Aug. 17, 1994; *San Francisco Chronicle*, Aug. 18, 1994; *San Diego Union-Tribune*, Aug. 17, 1994; *Santa Rosa Press Democrat*, Aug. 18, 1994; *Los Angeles Times*, Sept. 6, 1994, April 3, 1995; Danz, 276–77.	Four campers and their dog were attacked by a cougar that was later determined to have been rabid. Tony Winslow's thumb was bitten off. Robin Winslow stabbed the cougar to death with a kitchen knife.

Date	Location	Name	Sex	Age	Source	Description
August 24, 1994	Olympic Peninsula, Olympic NF, WA	Braun	M	5	*The Columbian*, Aug. 24, 1994.	Andrew Braun, 5, was attacked while hiking with his father, Mike, on Olympic Peninsula. The boy sustained two puncture wounds on his chest and a severe gash on his back.
October 7, 1994	Gold River, V.I., B.C.	McKerracher	M	Adult	B.C. Ministry of the Environment report, Feb. 26, 1996; Danz, 278–79.	McKerracher, an off-duty RCMP officer, was riding his horse when a cougar lunged at him from the bushes. McKerracher's right leg was scratched just above his boot. The cougar was never located.
November 1994	East Elk Creek near New Castle, CO	Champagne	M	Adult	*Rocky Mountain News*, Nov. 16, 1994; Danz, 278–79.	Fred Champagne was hunting elk when a cougar attacked him. He shot the first cougar, and a second cougar then approached him. Champagne shot this second animal as well. A judge determined the incident to be self-defense.
December 1994	Ute Indian Reservation, CO	Groves	F	25	CO Division of Wildlife report; Scripps Howard News Services, Dec. 14, 1994; *Rocky Mountain News*, Dec. 14 and 15, 1994; Danz, 278–79.	Suzanne Groves was taking water samples from a stream when the cat, which had been stalking her, attacked. Groves was able to free herself from the cougar by stabbing at its eyes with a pair of forceps she carried with her. A tracker later killed the wounded cat nearby. A necropsy revealed that the animal was in extremely poor condition.
March 1995	Mt. Lowe, San Gabriel Mtns., Angeles NF, CA	Fike	M	27	*Los Angeles Times*, March 24 and 26, 1995, April 3, 1995; *Sacramento Bee*, March 25, 1995; *San Diego Union Tribune*, March 25, 1995, Jan. 7, 1996; *Riverside Press Enterprise*, March 4, 1996; Danz, 278–79.	Bicyclist Scott Fike was clawed and bitten about the head before he was able to drive an attacking cougar off by throwing rocks at it. Trackers later killed the animal. Its condition was said to have been "good."

Date	Location	Victim	Sex	Age	Sources	Comments
May 25, 1995	Creston, B.C.	Unknown	M	Adult	R. Daloise in letter to Matt Austin, June 11, 1997, B.C. Ministry of the Environment report.	A railway worker was mauled on a CPR rail grade near Kootenay Lake. He called for help on a radio and a fellow worker drove the cougar away with a track wrench. He received puncture wounds to the throat and lacerations to his right arm. The cougar was killed.
September 13, 1995	Big Meadows, Tonahuto trail, Rocky Mountain NP, CO	Street	M	47	RMNP incident report # 951759; *Estes Park Trail Gazette*, Oct. 4, 1995; *National Geographic*, Nov., 1996; *Washington Post*, July 13, 1997; Danz, 278–79.	Moses Street, a photographer, was jogging when a cougar suddenly attacked. Street retreated to a tree with a sharpened stick. After prowling about at the tree's base for some five hours, the cougar climbed up after the man. The cougar fled after Street jabbed at it, climbed higher, then jabbed at the cougar again. Rangers discovered Street still in the tree at 2:10 A.M.
January 16, 1996	Cuyamaca Rancho Rancho State Park, CA	Unknown	F	Adult	CA Department of Game and Fish.	A woman on horseback was threatened by a lion. The woman growled, bared her teeth and stared lion down. In response, the next day two wardens and an ADC specialist went to the spot and a lion charged the group. It was shot twice by Lt. Bob Turner of the California Department of Game and Fish.
February 12, 1996	Near Little Espinosa Inlet, Zeballos, V.I., B.C.	Annand	M	36	B.C. Ministry of the Environment report; Danz, 278–79.	A cougar jumped upon Annand's back while he was felling a tree. Protective clothing, the man's defensive reactions, and the sudden appearance of another logger, contributed to the cougar's leaving the scene. The cougar could not be located by a tracker with dogs.

Date	Location	Name	Sex	Age	Description	Source
May 24, 1996	Twenty miles west of Port Angeles near the Whiskey Bend Trailhead in the Elwha Valley of Olympic NP, WA	Anderson	M	28	Phil Anderson, a mountain biker, was attacked along Wolf Creek Trail as he was donning a sweatshirt. Anderson noticed the cat coming and didn't resist, but rolled onto his back. With the cougar above him, Anderson then wrapped his legs around the animal. He clasped the cougar's throat, squeezed, and held it like this for almost three minutes. He could tell the cougar was losing consciousness and yelled for some people in a nearby parking lot to come over to hit the cat in the head. Finally, Anderson shoved the cat away. As the two separated, the cougar's claws and teeth slashed him. He suffered a puncture wound to his hand, as well as scratches and bites to his chest and stomach.	WA Dept. Of Fish and Wildlife report, May 24, 1996; *Spokane Spokesman*, June 30, 1996; *Seattle Times*, May 27, 1996.
June 1996	East Shore Trail, Grand Lake, Rocky Mountain NP, CO	Austin	F	Adult	Linda Austin, a seasonal ranger with the park, was jogging when she noticed a tawny form rapidly approaching. She dodged the charge, but the animal managed to scratch her right elbow and forearm. After ascertaining that it was a cougar, Austin stopped running. She yelled at it and picked up a stick. The cougar retreated into the undergrowth.	*Rocky Mountain News*, July 19, 1997; *Denver Post*, July 19, 1997; RMNP press release by D. Caldwell, July 23, 1997; Danz, 278–79.
June 16, 1996	Cuyamaca Rancho State Park, CA	Unknown	F	Adult	A cougar menaced a woman on horseback. The woman reported the lion to authorities. When trackers responded, the lion charged them and was shot by Lt. Bob Turner of the Department of Game and Fish.	*San Diego Union Tribune*, Jan. 17, 1996.
July 7, 1996	Arrow Lake, near Nakusp, B.C.	Veinguesaner	M	8	Eight-year-old Lance Veinguesaner suffered severe damage to the trachea, vertebrae, and abdomen when he was attacked by a cougar that tried to drag him into the brush.	*Seattle Times*, July 8, 1996; *Animal People*, March, 1997; B.C. Ministry of the Environment report.

Date	Location	Victim	Sex	Age	Sources	Comments
July 7, 1996	Lytton, B.C.	Frank	F	5	*Seattle Times*, July 8, 1996; *Animal People*, March, 1997; B.C. Ministry of the Environment report.	Five-year-old Christine Frank was attacked by a cougar while she was playing on a swing. She had to be air-lifted to a hospital to be treated for her wounds.
August 19, 1996	Near Princeton, B.C.	Parolin	M	6	B.C. Ministry of the Environment report.	See Cindy Parolin under fatal cougar attacks for citations and particulars.
January 6, 1997	Peshastin, WA	Parks	M		WA Dept. of Fish and Wildlife incident report, Jan. 6, 1997.	When Parks went out to feed his dogs in his garage, he found a cougar attacking one of his pets. The cougar then attacked a second dog. Parks leaped atop the cougar and hit it in the head with his fists. The cat tried to escape, but scratched Parks on the forearm. The cougar, which was later euthanized, was reported to be malnourished.
February 18, 1997	Shingletown, Shasta County, CA	Unknown	M	Adult	*Sacramento Bee*, Feb. 21, 1997.	A man reported being attacked behind his home by a cougar as he was walking to a stream to go fishing. The cougar jumped upon the man's back, the pair wrestled in the stream until the man was able to pull out his pistol and fire it. The shot frightened the cat away. The man suffered no injuries in the encounter.
June 26, 1997	Near Nanton, Alberta, Canada	Smith	F	55	Email from Jo Deurbrouck to K. Etling, Feb. 16, 2001; *Wdamage Digest*, Feb. 8 to 10, 2001.	Serena Smith was pushing cattle through some willow brush when she was suddenly thrown to the ground. When she tried to get up again, she realized a cougar had her by her right wrist and began screaming. The cougar dropped her wrist and walked around in front of her and waited, as if unsure how to proceed. Nearby, her husband was driving around the brush on his ATV and came to aid her when he heard her screams. The

cougar eventually retreated. Smith was treated by a doctor for a deep puncture wound of the thigh, three punctures of the right wrist, and deep scratches down the back of each shoulder.

Date	Location	Sex	Age	Name	Description	Sources
July 1997	Mesa Verde NP, CO	M	4	DeGrave	Rafael DeGrave and his family were hiking on a park trail when a ranger informed them that a cougar had been spotted nearby. The DeGraves returned to a parking lot, but the cougar appeared from some underbrush, startling Rafael. He screamed and ran and the cougar gave chase. It seized his head in its jaws and tried to drag him into the brush. The family managed to frighten the cougar, which dropped Rafael and retreated. Rafael suffered wounds to his face, shoulder, and nose, and one ear was severed. Park rangers later shot the cougar.	National Park Service news release, July 14, 1997; *Denver Post*, July 15, 1997, *Rocky Mountain News*, July 16, 1997; CO Division of Wildlife report, July 24, 1997; *San Diego Union Tribune*, Sep. 6, 1997, Danz, 280–81.
July 19, 1997	Summerland Park area, Rocky Mountain NP, CO	M	Adult	Philippi	Seasonal park ranger Chris Philippi was awaiting the coroner after the fatal attack earlier that day upon Mark Miedema. The cougar, upon spotting Philippi, approached to within fifteen feet of the man and crouched in preparation for attack. Philippi shot three times with his revolver at the cougar, wounding the animal. A tracker later treed and killed the cat.	*Rocky Mountain News*, July 19, 1997; *Denver Post*, July 19, 1997; CO Division of Wildlife report, July 24, 1997; Danz, 280–81.
October 1997	Sweetwater Ranch, near Book Maeser, UT	M	64	Massey	Don Massey was herding cattle when he was confronted by a cougar. The cougar clawed his horse, which then bolted, throwing Massey to the ground. The cougar started after the fleeing horse, then turned to go after Massey's Labrador retriever, instead. Massey used a large cedar branch to attack the cougar. He struck it four times, then used a rock to crush its skull. Massey's right thumb was clawed. His dog was seriously hurt.	*Denver Post*, Nov. 7, 1997; Danz, 280–81.

Date	Location	Victim	Sex	Age	Sources	Comments
October 22, 1997	Walker Ranch Trail, west of Boulder, CO	Dunbar	M	25	*Denver Post*, Oct. 23, 1997; *Rocky Mountain News*, Oct. 23 and 24, 1997; Danz, 280–281.	Todd Dunbar was riding his trail bike when a cougar "hunkered down . . . and laid his ears back." Dunbar used his bike as a shield, keeping it between the animal and himself. The cat continually tried to work its way around the bike and Dunbar struck the cat with the bike's wheel. The cougar leaped back and hissed. The cougar followed behind as Dunbar retreated. Dunbar was finally able to mount up and ride away.
December 28, 1997	Caspers Wilderness Park, Orange County, CA	Unknown/ Children	F/ Unk.	Adult	*Orange County Register*, Jan. 1, 1998, Sep. 29, 1998; *Boston Globe Online*, AP, Jan 1, 1998; *San Diego Union Tribune*, Jan. 2, 1998; *Los Angeles Times*, Jan. 2, 1998; *Denver Post*, Jan. 6, 1998; Danz, 282–83.	A cougar approached a group of women and children near the park's day use area. The park had recently reopened for use by minors after having been closed for more than eleven years due to cougar problems. The cougar circled the group in a crouch. The women yelled, but it then began belly-crawling until it was within three feet of the children. A woman threw a hiking boot at the cougar and it finally retreated. The cougar was tracked and shot.
December 31, 1997	Near Ruch, OR	McDonell	M	Adult	*The Everett Herald*, AP, Jan 4. 1998.	Ross McDonell, his wife, two sons, and mother went for a walk and McDonell noticed a cougar rushing toward the group. He told the others to go downhill, then fired a pistol shot over the lion's head. The cat continued to stalk the group, keeping pace with them in the nearby woods. McDonell fired another warning shot from his .45 Glock, then three more. When the cat charged him, McDonell shot it in the neck at close range.

Date	Location	Name	Sex	Age	Sources	Description
1998	Above Kusawa Lakes, the Yukon Territory	Unknown	M	Adult	Klassen; letter from F. Lee Fitzhugh to K. Etling.	A man was out walking with some children and two dogs. He had separated from his group briefly when the cougar attacked. He fought off the cougar with his fists and a walking stick. He finally was able to escape after punching the cougar in its abdomen and knocking the wind out of it. The cougar broke off its attack and escaped into surrounding cover. The man suffered bruising on his face and ribs, as well as scratches and some lacerations.
April 30, 1998	Carpenter Peak Trail Roxborough State Park, Jefferson County, CO	Peterson	M	24	*Denver Post*, May 1, 2, and 6, 1998; *Rocky Mountain News*, May 1 and 2, 1998; Roxborough State Park report, May 5, 1998; CO Division of Wildlife report, May 5, 1998; *Boston Globe*, Aug. 22, 1999; Danz, 282–83.	Andy Peterson was hiking near Carpenter Peak in the early afternoon when he approached a cougar that was lying half-hidden off the trail. The cougar advanced toward him as he tried to back slowly down the trail. As Peterson made his way backward, the cougar attacked, clamping its jaws down on Peterson's head and scratching him. Peterson stuck his thumb in the cougar's eye and stabbed it with a small Swiss Army knife. Wildlife officials tried, but could not locate the animal.
May 25, 1998	Along Pine Canyon Trail in Big Bend NP, TX	Coder	F		BBNP Incident report, May 25, 1998; AP, May 31, 1998; Time.com, Aug. 24, 1998; Reuters New Service/Nando News, June 8, 1998.	Mary Jane Coder had gone hiking with her three children. They had stopped so she could take their photograph, when she noticed a cougar closing in on them. She attempted to get them out of the area. The cougar followed, swatting at her once and inflicting puncture wounds and scratches. It eventually gave up. The cougar was never located.
July 19, 1998	Lyons, CO	Morris	M	Adult	CO Division of Wildlife Report, Aug. 15, 2000.	Morris went outside to check his barking dog. As he passed a tree, a cougar leaped at him.

Date	Location	Victim	Sex	Age	Sources	Comments
July 31, 1998	Marshall Mountains, near Missoula, MT	Swallow	M	6	*San Diego Union Tribune*, Aug. 2 and 16, 1998; *Seattle Spokesman Review*, Aug. 6, 1998; *Los Angeles Times*, Aug. 16, 1998; *Missoulian*, July 5, 1999; Danz, 282–283.	Dante Swallow was hiking with a group of children and counselors when a cougar attacked. Sixteen-year-old Aaron Hall rushed to his aid.
August 1998	Cuyamaca Rancho State Park, CA	Unknown	F/F	Adult/	*San Diego Union Tribune*, Oct. 10, 1998.	An aggressive cougar approached a woman and her friend near Stonewall Peak in Cuyamaca Rancho State Park. After being threatened for approximately fifteen minutes, one woman finally sprayed the cougar with pepper spray. The cougar retreated.
August 1, 1998	Swift Reservoir Campground near Depuyer, MT	Wing	M	6	MT Dept of Fish, Wildlife and Parks incident report, AP at the *Poll-Register*, Aug. 4, 1998; idahonews.com, Aug. 4, 1998; *Missoulian*, Aug. 4, 1998; *Rocky Mountain News*, Aug. 4, 1998.	A cougar stalked Joey Wing, then dragged him into the brush. The child suffered bite and claw wounds to the head and shoulders which required more than 200 stitches to close.
August 4, 1998	Metaline Falls, WA	Schrock	F	8	WA Dept. of Fish and Wildlife report, Aug. 4, 1998; WA Department of Fish and Wildlife news release, Aug. 5, 1998; *Spokane Spokesman Review*, Aug. 5, 6, and 19, 1998, Aug. 25, 1999; *Seattle Times*, Aug. 5, 1998, Feb. 3, 2000.	An eight-year-old girl was trying to catch up with relatives as they walked from their campground to an outdoor restroom when a cougar attacked her. She was critically injured.

Date	Location	Name	Sex	Age	Source	Description
October 10, 1998	Cuyamaca State Park, CA	Turner	M	Adult	*San Diego Union Tribune,* Oct. 10, 1998.	On this day, warden Lt. Bob Turner rode out to the Los Vaqueros horse camp in response to a complaint that a lion had attempted to grab a camper's leg. When Turner entered the nearby woods, he spotted a lion and shot it. The camper yelled that another lion was charging Turner. Turner spun around and shot it, too.
November 12, 1998	Packwood GMU, Lewis County, WA	White	M	38	WA Dept of Wildlife incident report, Nov. 22, 1998.	The victim was elk hunting in Packwood Game Management Unit when a cougar knocked him down, causing a concussion. The effects of the concussion kept White from being able to seek medical help or to find his vehicle for four days. He spent this time in the woods without food or shelter, then spent an additional two days in the hospital for treatment for concussion, cuts, bruises, and hypothermia.
April 17, 1999	Kawkawa Lake, B.C.	Unknown	F	6	*The Province,* April 18, 1999; *Vancouver Sun,* April 19, 1999; *Seattle Times,* April 19, 1999; B.C. Ministry of the Environment report.	A woman on a church outing beat off a cougar with a tree limb after the animal attacked a young girl. The girl suffered serious facial lacerations, puncture wounds to the chest, and severe trauma to one eye. The cougar was later destroyed.
July 20, 1999	Lake Cowichan, V.I., B.C.	Unknown	M	50	B.C. Ministry of the Environment report.	A logger was seated in his truck near noon when he was attacked by a cougar that pawed at his arm and scratched him. The cougar was never found.

Date	Location	Victim	Sex	Age	Sources	Comments
August 24, 1999	WA	Walsh	M		WA Department of Fish and Wildlife incident report, Aug. 24, 1999; WA Department of Fish and Wildlife news release, Aug. 25, 1999; *Seattle Post-Intelligencer*, Aug. 25 and 26, 1999; *Spokane Spokesman Review*, Aug. 25 and 26, 1999; *The Columbian*, Nov. 20, 1999; WA State House of Representative News, Feb. 22, 2000; *Seattle Times*, Feb. 23, 2000.	Jacob Walsh was attacked by a cougar. His wounds required over 200 stitches to close.
September 15, 1999	East of Riggins, along Salmon River in ID	Anderson	M		Spokane.net, AP, Sept. 15, 1999; *Idaho Mountain Express*, Oct. 6–12, 1999.	Eleven-year-old Joel Anderson was playing on a river sandbar with his friend when a mountain lion dashed out of the undergrowth and pounced on him. Daniel McMinn, 11, heard Anderson scream. McMinn ran to get Robert Anderson, young Anderson's father, who sprinted back to the attack scene where he beat the cougar off of his son. The cougar was later killed one hundred yards from the site of the attack.
October 1999	Along the Aspen Vista Ski Trail near Santa Fe Ski Basin in Santa Fe ND, NM	Unknown	M	Adult	NM Department of Game and Fish press release, Oct. 18, 1999.	A man decided to go snow-shoeing. He started moving quickly up the trail to the overlook. He stopped to take in some fluid and noticed a cat charging up the precipice in front of him.

Date	Location	Name	Sex	Age	Source	Description
October 22, 1999	Near Walden, CO	Miller	M	Adult	*Denver Post*, Nov. 2, 1999.	Randy Miller was hunting when he noticed he was being stalked by a mountain lion. Miller made repeated futile attempts to frighten it off. When the cougar would not be dissuaded, Miller shot it.
January 2000	MT	Dodge	M	12	*New York Times*, Jan. 27, 2000.	Jake Dodge, 12, was playing outside his Montana home when his father noticed a cougar stalking him. Dan Dodge ran for his .270 and shot the cat from inside the house, before it could pounce on Jake.
January 24, 2000	Bella Coola, B.C.	Unknown	M	75	B.C. Ministry of the Environment report.	A male responded to a complaint of a cougar killing a dog. When he searched the area behind the house, a cougar was waiting there in a crouched position. The man turned around to get his gun and the cougar attacked, biting his head and neck. The man fell to the ground and yelled for help. Another man responded and killed the cougar. The victim was seriously injured.
April 2000	NM	Sherwood	M	Adult	*The New Mexican*, April 21, 2000.	A cougar attacked turkey hunter Allen Sherwood while he was calling to a gobbler. Sherwood heard something behind him and instinctively put up his elbow as he turned around. The cougar was already charging him. The animal pounced, catching Sherwood across the eyebrow and bridge of his nose with one paw and around his back with its other paw. The pair rolled around for a few moments, but then the cougar leaped up, looking confused. Sherwood stood up, switched off the shotgun's safety, threw up his arms, and yelled. The cougar disappeared.

Date	Location	Victim	Sex	Age	Sources	Comments
May 3, 2000	Siletz, OR	Jones	M	Adult	*Amarillo Globe-News*, May 6, 2000, AP, May 6, 2000; *Missoulian*, May 6, 2000; *San Diego Union Tribune*, May 6, 2000; *Los Angeles Times*, May 7, 2000.	When Jones went into his garage to feed his dogs, he discovered a cougar on top of one of his pets. The cougar abruptly leaped on another of Jones's dogs, prompting the man to grab a shovel and hit the animal in its head several times. The cat scratched Jones on the lower leg. The animal was later shot by authorities.
May 22, 2000	Bartlett Lake, AZ	Unknown	F	5	AZ Game and Fish Department incident report 00–000268; *Arizona Republic*, May 4, 2000.	A small girl who was playing outside her family's tent was attacked and severely mauled by a cougar. The animal dragged the child into nearby brush and left her only when her mother ran screaming toward it. The cougar was later shot and killed while lurking in the very spot where the girl had been taken. The girl was very seriously injured and will need extensive surgeries to repair the damage inflicted by the cat.
February 2001	North Vancouver Island, B.C.	Unknown	M	Adult	Neil Williams in e-mail letter to K. Etling, Feb. 11, 2001.	A man riding a bicycle on north Vancouver Island at night was attacked and knocked from his bicycle by a cougar. A passerby intervened and used the bicycle to beat the cougar off of the victim.

Reported Human Fatalities from Cougar Attacks

Date	Location	Victim	Sex	Age	Sources	Comments
May 1751	Betty's Patch, PA	Tanner	M	58	Young and Goldman, 100; Danz, 226–27; *Daily Local News*, West Chester, PA, Oct. 8, 1956.	A cougar reportedly killed Philip Tanner, a sawmill owner, as he inspected some timber.
Early 1800s	North of Vicksburg, MS	Unk./Unk.	M/M	Adult/ Adult	From Benjamin Vernon Lilly's handwritten manuscript reproduced in Dobie, 186–204. Also in Fergus, 39; Danz, 226–27.	When a squad of workers clearing land noticed a cougar, they warned two brothers who lived nearby. Later, as one of the brothers chopped wood, he heard the other scream. As he rushed to his brother's aid, a cougar leaped on him. The animal killed both men.
Early 1800s	Northeastern LA, near the Bayou Macon River in West Carroll Parish	Unknown	M	Adult	Lilly quoted in Dobie, 186–204; Fergus, 39–40; Danz, 226–27.	Two men separated while deer hunting. One of them eventually returned to their cabin, but the other was found dead the following morning. Tracks "made it plain that a large panther had leaped from a leaning oak tree under which he was passing, knocked him face down, apparently killing him instantly, and then rolled him over and sucked blood from his throat."
Early 1800s	Buttes, west of Cannon Ball, ND	Unknown	M	Teenager	Barnes, 124; Fitzhugh, 20.	An Indian youth, undergoing a ritual of passage, was killed by a puma.
Early 1800s	Southeastern GA or extreme northern FL	Unknown	M	Adult	Theodore Roosevelt quoted in Young and Goldman, 101–2; Danz, 226–27.	A cougar attacked a worker returning home through the swamps. He defended himself with a long knife but was nonetheless killed. The cougar's body was found nearby.
Early 1800s	MS	Unknown	M	Adult	Roosevelt, *Wilderness Hunter*, 345; Danz, 226–27; Barnes, 125.	General Wade Hampton told Roosevelt of a railroad worker who "was waylaid and killed by a cougar later one night as he was walking alone through the swamp."

Date	Location	Name	Sex	Age	Source	Description
Prior to 1827	The Catskill Mountains south of Albany, NY	Unknown	M	Adult	Cuvier and Griffith 438–39; Young and Goldman, 101; Danz, 228–29.	Two houndsmen were hunting when one of them was attacked and killed by a cougar. The other, responding to the report of his friend's gun, discovered the cougar guarding his body where it hung over the limb of a tree. The houndsmen shot the cougar. According to Cuvier, the body of the cougar was preserved in the Museum of New York.
January 1830	Pennsylvania	Unknown	F	Adult	M'Murtrie quoted in Seton, 119–20. See also Cuvier and Griffin, 43; Barnes, 124; Danz, 228–29; True, 602.	Only sketchy details are available on this incident, which was said to be "an unprovoked attack upon an unfortunate woman in Pennsylvania. The ferocious brute seized upon as she passing along the road and killed her in an instant."
1844	Lycoming County, PA	Reinwald	M	Adult	Parsons, 4; Barnes, 124; Danz, 228–29.	A cougar presumably attacked Dr. Reinwald as he was walking through snow to see a patient. His nephew's wife later reported that "the doctor's body was found lying in the snow with the back of his neck bitten through; medical instruments scattered about, large cougar tracks all around."
1867–70	Near Camp Grant, AZ	Unknown	M	Adult	Bourke, 39–40; Young and Goldman; Danz, 228–29.	An injured survivor of an Apache ambush was attacked and killed by a cougar.
1876	Near Indian Creek, Bandera County, TX	Ramsey	M	Adult	Hunter, 110.	Henry Ramsey opened his cabin door and "a large panther sprang into the room and attacked him." Ramsey reportedly died of hydrophobia.
October 1880	Near Dutch Flat, Humbug Canyon, NV	Unknown	M	Adult	Battle Mountain Messenger, Oct. 27, 1880. Information provided by the NV Division of Wildlife. See also Danz, 230–31.	A "California lion" killed an unknown hunter. His body was "almost wholly devoured, only the flesh on the feet remaining."

Date	Location	Victim	Sex	Age	Sources	Comments
March 1882	Near Kalama, WA	Graves	M	5	*Clark County Register*, March 30, 1882; Tinsley, 82; Danz, 230–31.	A cougar attacked five-year-old Gussie Graves while he played near his home. Neighbors responded to Gussie's screams and although they did recover his body from the cougar, they were unable to save him.
September 1885	Near Bruneau, ID	Unknown	M	8	*Idaho Democrat*, Sep. 19, 1885; *White Pine News*, Sep. 19, 1885; *Elko Independent*, Sep. 22, 1885. Information provided by the NV Division of Wildlife. See also Danz, 230–31.	While cutting wood along the Bruneau River, a boy was attacked by a cougar. His father did not have time to run for his rifle before the boy was killed.
Prior to 1888	Near Hickory Grove, MS	Unk./Unk.	M/M	14/11	Lillie quoted in Dobie, 200; Fergus, 40; Danz, 230–31.	Two boys were chopping wood. A cougar attacked the younger boy, who was bending to pick up a stick. The older boy tried to defend his brother, but was also attacked. A young man ran from a nearby barn and managed to hit the cougar with a billet of wood, but it was too late for the brothers, who both died from severe injuries.
Late 1880s	Within the present Capitan Mountain Wilderness Area, about 15 miles from Ft. Stanton, NM	Unknown	F	2–3	Sam H. Nickels quoted in Barnes, 127; Danz, 230–31.	A small girl and her mother were picking acorns near a spring. As the girl bent over, a cougar pounced on her and dragged her away. Searchers later found one of her arms and remnants of her dress, but her body was never recovered.

Date	Location	Name	Sex	Age	Source	Description
Early 1890s	El Dorado County, CA	Unknown	M	4	*Western Outdoor News*, April 23, 1993.	A cougar took a four-year-old boy from an El Dorado County lumber camp. His body was never found.
June 1890	Quartz Valley, CA	Dangle	M	7	Howard, 162–63; Beier, 404; Barnes, 125; Danz, 230–31. See also *Outdoor California* special Mountain Lion Issue, 1995.	Seven-year-old Arthur Dangle was killed as he played near his home. When his father found him, two cougars were on his body. He ran home for his gun. Before he could shoot, his wife drove the cougars off Arthur. Trackers killed both cougars the next day.
Late 1800s	In the Gallinas Mountains, NM	Unknown	M	Adult	Nickels quoted in Barnes, 127; Danz 320–31.	Two men deer hunting decided to separate. One man heard the other shoot, hurried to see what he had taken, and discovered his partner dead. A nearby lion was also dead, killed by the man's rifle shot.
Prior to 1906	Southeast TX	Unknown	Unk.	Child	Lilly quoted in Dobie, 200–02; Fergus, 406; Danz, 232–33.	A family of settlers had moved into a cabin near a thicket. One afternoon as the wife worked in the yard she heard one of her babies crying inside the cabin. She went in, comforted it, then brought the other baby along with her outside and placed it on the ground near her. When she turned away she heard a cry and then saw a cougar running off with the baby in its mouth. The cat was hunted for two weeks, but although eleven cougars were killed, no trace of the missing baby was ever found.

Date	Location	Victim	Sex	Age	Sources	Comments
July 1909	Glen Willis, on Coyote Creeke near Morgan Hill, CA	Kennedy/ Wilson	F/M	Adult/ 10	Howard, 162; Seton, 122–24; Barnes, 125; Hornaday; Danz, 232–33.	Isola Kennedy took Earl Wilson and two other young boys to a creek. The boys were wading when a cougar leaped onto Wilson's back. Kennedy rushed to his aid, and the cat attacked her, too. She managed to hold it at bay long enough for rescuers to arrive. The cat was shot, but believed to have been rabid. Although Wilson's wounds were minor, he died soon after—apparently of tetanus. Kennedy's death, two months later, was attributed to rabies.
1917	Strawberry Valley, San Jacinto Mountains, CA	Boheim	M	Adult	Beier, 404; Barnes, 125; Hornaday.	Boheim, a pig farmer, went out at night to hunt a cougar that had preyed on his pigs. He found the cougar, a female with young. It attacked and killed him.
December 1924	Near Olema and Lake Chelan, Chelan County, Washington	Fehlhaber	M	13	Haley C., 125–27; Hall; Tinsley, 82; Ellis, "The Cougar Does Attack," 114; Duresne, "Hound Man's Dream"; Beier, 404; Young and Goldman, 100; Hilderbrand, 22; Danz, 234–35.	A cougar attacked thirteen-year-old Jimmy Fehlhaber as he was taking a shortcut to a neighbor's house. Search parties found the body, and although they had solid evidence of a cougar attack, reports of this incident vary in their details. Authorities disagree as to whether the cougar was old or young, male or female, well or malnourished.
1940s	West coast of V.I., B.C.	Unknown	M	Child	Wildlife Branch files, B.C. Ministry of the Environment report.	A cougar attacked and killed a small boy. No other details are known.

Date	Location	Name	Sex	Age	References	Description
June 1949	Walter's Bay, near Kyuquot, Vancouver Island, B.C., Canada	Taylor	M	7	*The Province*, June 21, 1949; Tinsley, 82–2; Beier, 404; Danz, 234–35; Ellis, "The Cougar Does Attack," 114; DuFresne, "Hound Man's Dream"; W. Mair in letter to A. Hames, undated, B.C. Ministry of the Environment report. See also *Vancouver Daily Colonist*, Jan. 3, 1971 and the *Vancouver Sun*, Jan. 3, 1971.	Dominic Taylor was picnicking with his family when a cougar attacked him. Members of his family, along with several men, tried to rescue him as the cougar dragged him away. Dominic was injured critically and died six hours later.
January 3, 1971	East of Lytton, B.C.	Wells	M	12	*The Province*, Jan. 3, 1971; *Vancouver Sun*, Jan. 4, 1971; B.C. Ministry of the Environment report; Danz, 234–35.	A cougar attacked and killed 12-year-old John Lawrence Wells, as he played with his two sisters in a culvert on the CP Rail line not far from their home. The girls ran for their father, and he shot the animal as it dragged John away. He was already dead. The cougar was later found dead in the brush. The cougar was said to be below normal weight.
Summer or Fall 1972	Lillooet	Unknown	M	Child	R. Slavens in letter to M. Austin, July 6, 1988; B.C. Ministry of the Environment report.	A cougar killed a young boy in a garbage dump. A sheet of plastic was later found entangled in the bowel of the cougar.

Date	Location	Victim	Sex	Age	Sources	Comments
January 1974	Arroyo Seco, NM	Nolan	M	8	*Albuquerque Journal*, Jan. 22, 1974; *New Mexico Game and Fish News*, Jan. 24, and 28, 1974, Feb. 6, 1974; *The Sentinel*, Feb. 1, 1974; *Rocky Mountain News*, Nov. 7, 1974; Tinsley, 83; Beier, 404; Hibben, 22; Danz, 236–37; internal correspondence NM Department of Game and Fish.	Kenneth Nolan and his half-brother, David Cordry, were playing less than a mile from their home when a cougar attacked Kenneth. David ran to get their father, but Kenneth was already dead, his carotid artery severed. The cat was tracked, shot, and killed.
July 1976	Near Gold River, V.I., B.C.	Samuel	F	7	*Vancouver Sun*, July 15 and 20, 1976; Beier, 404; Tinsley, 83; Danz, 236–37; B.C. Ministry of the Environment report.	Matilda Samuel was picking berries with two teenaged cousins when a cougar leaped from the undergrowth and seized her. Too frightened to attempt a rescue, the teens ran for help. The RCMP later recovered Matilda's body. The cougar was killed. This same cat allegedly chased a motorcyclist in the area earlier in the day, but the man had not reported the incident. The cougar was of normal weight, with fresh deer meat in its stomach at the time of the attack.
May 1988	Near Tofino, V.I., B.C.	Bergman	M	9	*Vancouver Sun*, May 16, 18, and 19, 1988; *Times-Colonist*, May 19, 1988; B.C. Ministry of the Environment internal memos and report; Beier, 404; Worth, 81; Danz, 236–37.	Jesse Sky Bergman, who lived in Tofino with his mother, was visiting his father in the Catface area north of Tofino. While walking on the beach with relatives, he was separated from the group. He was later found dead, a cougar guarding his remains. The cougar was shot. Investigators said that Jessie, who probably mistakenly believed he was too warm, had taken off his light shirt and pants and was weak from hypothermia at the time the cougar encountered him.

Date	Location	Name	Sex	Age	Sources	Description
November 1988	Foothills of the Sierras, Butte County, CA	Gomez Dunton	F	51	Butte County Sheriff's Department, May 17, 1994; *Los Angeles Times*, April 3, 1995; Danz, 236–37.	When Lucy Gomez Dunton was found dead in the Sierra foothills, game wardens suspected that she had been killed by a mountain lion, but could not prove it.
September 1989	Evaro, MT	Gardipe	M	5	*Missoulian*, Sep. 11, 12, and 13, 1989; *Spokesman-Review*, Sep. 14, 1989; *Mountain News*, Jan. 13, 1990, Feb. 2, 1990, Sep. 23, 1990; Associated Press, Sep. 13, 1989; Beier, 404; Lewis, 187; Worth; Danz, 236–37.	A small boy, riding his tricycle in his backyard, was killed by at least two cougars.
January 1991	Near Idaho Springs, CO	Lancaster	M	18	*Clear Creek Courant*, Jan. 16, 1991; *Rocky Mountain News*, Jan. 17, 18, and 22, 1991, Feb. 2 and 3, 1991; Danz, 238–39. See also, CO DOW files and internal correspondence.	Scott Lancaster went jogging when he was ambushed by a cougar and killed. When his body was discovered, the cougar was still standing guard over him.
May 1992	Kyuquot, V.I., B.C.	Williams	M	8	*Vancouver Sun*, May 7, 1992; *Seattle Post-Intelligencer*, July 7, 1992; B.C. Ministry of the Environment internal reports; Danz, 238–39.	Jeremy Williams was sitting on a log at the edge of a schoolyard watching other children play when a cougar attacked and killed him.

Date	Location	Victim	Sex	Age	Sources	Comments
April 1994	Auburn State Recreation Area near Cool, CA	Schoener	F	40	*Los Angeles Times*, April 27, 1994, May 1, 1994 and Sep. 6, 1994; *Phoenix Gazette, April 29, 1994, May 2, 1994; San Diego Union Tribune, April 26, 27, and 29, 1994, May 1 and 3, 1994, Dec. 11 and 26, 1994; San Francisco Examiner, May 3, 1994; Fishing & Hunting News,* May 12–26, 1994; *Sacramento Bee,* June 18, 1995; *Newsweek,* Jan 8, 1996; Danz, 238–39.	A cougar attacked jogger Barbara Schoener from behind. Evidence suggested that she struggled desperately, but the cougar prevailed, killing her. It was tracked down and killed one week later.
December 1994	Cuyamaca Rancho State Park, about 50 miles east of San Diego, CA	Kenna	F	58	*San Diego Union Tribune,* Dec. 11, 19, and 26, 1994, Jan. 28, 1995, Jan. 17, 1996; *Denver Post,* Dec. 13, 1994; *Los Angeles Times,* Dec. 13 and 19, 1994, April 3, 1995; *San Francisco Examiner,* Dec. 13, 1994; Associated Press, Dec. 13, 1994; Danz, 238–39.	Iris Kenna was bird watching in the park when a cougar attacked and killed her. When some hikers happened upon the scene, they discovered the animal was feeding on her body. It was killed some ten hours later.

Date	Location	Name	Sex	Age	Description	Sources
July 1995	Port Alberni, V.I., B.C.	Dayton	M	32	Lloyd William Dayton, 32, had gotten off his mountain bike when he was attacked and killed by a cougar. His body was found about one hundred yards from his bike.	*The Regional News*, July 14, 1995; B.C. Ministry of the Environment report.
August 19, 1996	Near Princeton, B.C.	Parolin	F	36	Six-year-old Steven Parolin fell from his horse when a lunging cougar spooked it. The cougar then attacked the boy. Steven's mother, Cindy, rushed to protect him, managing to fend it off while her other children ran for help. She was mortally wounded in the struggle. A nearby camper, who had been fetched by the children, killed the cougar. Parolin died in his arms.	*Phoenix Gazette*, Aug. 21, 1996; *Rocky Mountain News*, Aug. 23 and 27, 1996; *San Diego Union Tribune*, Aug. 25, 1996; *Alberta Report*, Sep. 2, 1996; *Animal People*, March 1997; B.C. Ministry of the Environment report; Danz, 238–39.
July 1997	Near Summerland Park along the North Inlet Trail on the west side of Rocky Mountain National Park in CO	Miedema	M	10	Mark Miedema had been camping for three days in RMNP with his family. While hiking, he raced ahead of the others to check some acorns he had put out and was attacked by a cougar. Although his mother was a nurse, attempts to resuscitate him were futile. It was later determined that Mark died from asphyxiation, choking on his own vomitus, rather than from direct wounds. The cougar later charged a ranger who was guarding the attack site. The ranger shot and wounded the cougar, which was later killed.	RMNP News Release of July 17, 1997; *Denver Post*, July 18, 19, and 21, 1997, Sep. 4, 1997, May 1, 1998; *Rocky Mountain News*, July 18 and 19, 1997; *Arizona Republic*, July 19, 1997; *Boulder Daily Camera*, July 19 and Aug. 20, 1997; *San Diego Union Tribune*, Aug. 16, 1998; *Los Angeles Times*, Aug.16, 1998; Danz, 240–41; CO DOW Report.

Date	Location	Victim	Sex	Age	Sources	Comments
October 2, 1999	Poudre Canyon, CO	Atadero	M	3	Associated Press, Oct. 7, 1999; *Denver Post*, Oct. 7, 1999; *San Diego Union Tribune*, Oct. 7, 1999; *Fort Worth Star-Tribune*, Oct. 7, 1999.	Jarad Atadero became separated from the others while hiking with his relatives and a church group. When the others discovered Jarad was missing, they searched the area immediately but could not locate him. An angler later remembered seeing the small boy walking up the opposite hill. Mountain lion tracks were discovered in the vicinity, leading authorities to believe that Jarad had been carried off and killed by one of the animals.
January 2, 2001	Along a cross-country ski trail at Lake Minnewanka in Banff National Park, Alberta, Canada	Frost	F	30	*The Calgary Sun*, Jan. 3, 4, 5, 6 and 20, 2001.	While cross-country skiing, Frances Frost was stalked and attacked by a cougar that then quickly killed her. The large male cougar was later shot by officials.

Index